The Lola Papers

The
LOLA
Papers

Marathons, Misadventures, and
How I Became a Serious Runner

AMY L. MARXKORS

BREAKAWAY BOOKS
HALCOTTSVILLE, NEW YORK
2012

ISBN: 978-1-891369-96-4
Library of Congress Control Number: 2012932779

Published by Breakaway Books
P.O. Box 24
Halcottsville, NY 12438
www.breakawaybooks.com

FIRST EDITION

Contents

To my Savior and my God.
Out of the overflow of my heart, may this be a praise offering to You.

Foreword

When I agreed to write this foreword for Amy's book, the book itself was barely an idea. *The Lola Papers* was still just a biweekly journal entry in Fleet Feet St. Louis's newsletter. Initially, I scoffed at the idea of writing the foreword. I mean, while I am awesome, I've never considered myself much of a writer. I agreed to do it anyway, though, mainly because I thought I was agreeing to something I'd most likely never have to do. Don't get me wrong. I knew Amy would one day write a book; I just didn't think I'd be in it. It seems I didn't give myself enough credit . . . which is weird, since I usually give myself a lot of credit.

The creation of *The Lola Papers* was just as much of a journey as the story it tells. I was fortunate enough to be along with Amy throughout most of that journey. I watched her go from a girl who knew very little about running—other than the fact that she enjoyed it—to a serious marathoner. I watched her evolve from a recreational runner alarmed by the concept of split shorts to an arm-sleeve-wearing competitor. I watched her transform a collection of funny, touching, and at times random journal entries into a single, polished story. A story that she had been telling—unknowingly—all along.

Amy likes to give me more credit than I probably deserve. Sure, I served as her coach. But I was there mostly to provide laughs, offer the occasional insight, and, of course, add the good looks. Amy did all the hard work herself. (Except for those cold days when I rode alongside her on the bike while I was injured. She will always owe me for those.) She ran the miles, the long runs, the workouts. She ran the races and learned lessons in both her victories and defeats. All I tried to do was get her out of her own way by convincing her that she really could do the things I knew she could do. And I have to say, I'm honored to have played that role in her journey.

It is Amy's gift of storytelling that makes her writing so unique. She has the ability to share her individual experiences in running in such a manner that anyone—runners and non-runners alike—can relate to them in a very personal, very real way. She makes you feel as though you were right there by her side the whole time. As someone who knows Amy well, I can tell you that her writing is a genuine reflection of her personality. I know you will enjoy getting to know Amy as much as I have.

I couldn't be prouder of you, kid.

—Jake Goldsborough, aka Mr. Speedy Pants

Acknowledgments

This book is a testament to the love, support, and sacrifice of the many wonderful people without whom this story would not exist and to whom I will be forever indebted. It is with humility and gratefulness I give them my heartfelt appreciation.

First and foremost, I thank you, Lord. You have done and continue to do more than I could ever ask or imagine.

To my incredible family: my dad and mom, David and Donna Marxkors, and my sisters and brother, Emily, Alicia, and Joe. You have loved me and put up with me, supported me and strengthened me, you have stayed by my side, you have cried with me and laughed with me and prayed with me and humored my many, many whims and passions, no matter how crazy they were (and are). I praise God every day for you. I love you more than I will ever be able to say.

To Mr. and Mrs. Speedy Pants, Jake and Lauren Goldsborough. Coach, you know I will never be able to thank you enough for all you've done, even with all those invisible checks. (Who can put a price on awesomeness, after all?) Lauren, thank you for being a great friend, for always opening your home to me, for being so supportive every step of the way. And to Lauren's family, the Kuckelmans. Thank you for welcoming a traveling marathoner into your home and treating her like family.

To David and Debby Spetnagel and Fleet Feet St. Louis. You gave Lola a platform and an audience. Thank you for the friendships and community you foster. Thank you for your love for the sport.

To Sally Edwards. Thank you for your passion and enthusiasm and confidence. Thank you for believing in Lola and spearheading her journey to publication. I am honored to know you. I am honored that you would take me under your wing. I am honored to be your friend.

To the dear Pottebaum family: Michelle, Joe, John, Josh, Caleb, Micah, Gracie, and Esther. Thank you for loving me like family. I treasure your friendship, support, generosity, and prayers beyond words. I thank God every day that He joined our lives. I give you all my love.

To the St. Louis Blues of 1996–2000. Thank you for humoring a goofy teenage girl who had big dreams and an even bigger replica Stanley Cup, which she very often wore on her head. Thank you for being so generous with your time and for granting so many interviews.

To David C. Fairchild. I told you I wouldn't forget.

To Starbucks. Thank you for not kicking me out, even though I spent many an hour rendezvousing with my laptop long after my Venti Americano was gone.

And last but not least, to Charles Dickens. Because of you, I am a writer.

Author's Note

The Lola Papers began as a series of journal entries published in a newsletter for a local running store. I wrote about my running experiences as "Lola," a local mystery runner with a propensity for misadventure. After hearing that the race-timing manager of the store was an experienced marathoner and quite the wellspring of running wisdom, I eventually worked up the courage to ask him for some training advice. I thought I would get a tip or two. Instead, I received a training schedule and a full-fledged coach. What followed was a year of training, racing, adventure, and general mayhem. I christened my impromptu coach "Mr. Speedy Pants" and included our escapades in *The Lola Papers*. By the time I began turning *The Lola Papers* into a book, the names Lola and Mr. Speedy Pants were an indelible part of the story.

In order to enhance the flow of the narrative and to maintain contextual continuity, I have altered minor details in the history of events. Primarily, I have concentrated the meeting of Lola and Mr. Speedy Pants, my request for advice, and our subsequent coach–athlete alliance into a single event. I have also changed the names of some races and locations out of respect for the privacy of those involved. However, it all really did happen to Lola as she tumbled, stumbled, and ultimately ran her way to the finish line. This is, after all, her journal. This is her story.

Prologue

Somewhere between miles twenty and twenty-one, the wheels came off.

"The wall" is aptly named. There is no warning. There is no gradual deceleration. It is sudden. It is hard. And when you hit it, there is nothing you can do but try to break through it. In what seemed like a moment, my friend's breathing changed from steady to labored, and her once strong stride slumped with the struggle. I watched her face, now contorted with exertion, and my heart broke. The suffering of the last miles of a marathon is not soon forgotten.

We had only a few miles to go. Her expression was pained, broken with fatigue and doubt. The sweat on her cheeks mirrored the tears brimming in her eyes.

"I . . . I don't think I can do it," she gasped, her tone pleading that we stop.

"Yes, you can. You can do this. You keep going, you hear me? Keep running. No matter how badly it hurts, you can always keep running."

My eyes remained fixed on her, my spirit urging her on, begging her to continue. She was hurting. Badly. We shuffled through a water station and across a sea of paper cups littering the pavement. The cups were empty and crushed and trampled. They were not unlike a broken marathoner.

Okay, Coach, I asked myself with no small measure of uncertainty, *what are you gonna do now? It's clutch time. Step up to the plate.*

And right there, amid the crowds that pressed ever forward in a slow stampede of singlets and bib numbers, every piece of advice Mr. Speedy Pants had ever given me—every encouraging nod and proud pat on the back, every comforting smile and consoling hug, every madcap story and harebrained scheme, every practical tip, every affirmation of confidence, every gentle word of solace—engulfed me in a flood of memory as vivid as the day itself. And I was a beginner, again. I was new to the competitive side of the sport. I didn't know what I was doing. I was goofy. I was afraid. I was excited. I was about to enter the crazy world of marathoning.

And I would never be the same.

WINTER

Chapter One

What did I get myself into? I wondered, staring at the algorithmic numbers that stared right back at me. I had the strange impression the digits were judging me, that they could sense my uncertainty. I held the sheet of paper in my hand—two sheets, really—ink still shiny and wet from the printer, the paper slightly warm. This wasn't what I had expected. I thought I would be getting a few snippets of advice, not a detailed training plan that would dictate my life for the next four months. But there it was, carefully planned and calculated and outlined. Flung across the top of the page in bold black font were the words TRAINING PLAN FOR THE GO! ST. LOUIS MARATHON. The typeface seemed rude and abrupt, as though it were barking orders that weren't even relevant for another—I looked at my calendar—two more days.

Yikes. I thought. *Two days?* I repeated the question that impaled my brain, *What did I get myself into?*

This whole thing started by accident, really. The backdrop was a small, local 5K. The hundred or so runners who milled about the start line stretched their legs and chatted in quips and reluctant gulps of the cold air. I yawned and clapped my gloved hands as I glanced at the sun just starting to peek above the horizon with thick, distant rays. *Time to wake up*, I told myself. I clapped a few more times, slapped my legs, jumped up and down, all in the unsubstantiated belief that doing so would somehow rejuvenate my tired limbs. The sharp wail of a siren cut through the air, signaling that the race would begin in a few minutes. I followed the pack of runners—moving not unlike a herd of cows—as they made their shuffling way to the start corral. I stretched my arms and stifled one last yawn. Suddenly I felt a firm poke in the middle of my back.

"Hey, girl!"

I turned around in surprise.

"Oh, my gosh! Big J!" I exclaimed at seeing the tall, lanky man behind me. "What are you doing here?"

"I"—he straightened his back for emphasis, tilting up his chin—"am getting back in shape."

Big J, whom I affectionately termed "my nomadic SEC friend" due to his religious devotion to Louisiana State University and his proclivity for roaming about the world on an endless succession of whims, finished pinning his bib number on his racing singlet. His bushy brown hair flopped atop his head, sprawling across his face in uncooperative ribbons. It curled and swirled as if in defiance of order and authority, and it occurred to me—as we stood there talking, smooshed by an army of bib numbers and split shorts and shoelaces—that his anarchic hair was not unlike his personality.

"Yep! I'm gonna start running—really running—again," he continued. "This is my third consecutive day!"

I shook my head at his announcement. Big J was more than an accomplished runner; he was a Division I athlete who could hold a faster pace running backward than I could ever hope to hit full stride. Post-college, he was best known for a unique training regimen consisting entirely of a "rigorous taper," a plan undergirded by an aversion to any prospect of overtraining and by the conviction that his legs were in a perpetual state of needing rest.

"Three days, huh? That's pretty impressive."

He nodded with exaggerated significance. "You know it. I even hit the track last week." He laughed. "Ugh. That was . . . not fun. I haven't done a workout in a long time."

"I bet."

"What about you? Are you still playing that crazy Canadian sport?"

By "that crazy Canadian sport" Big J meant ice hockey. He had a strong dislike of anything involving cold temperatures (this I blamed on his Deep South upbringing), and even when he talked about hockey, he treaded awkwardly, as though verbally tiptoeing across the ice. I laughed at his chary treatment of the topic.

"Haha . . . Yeah, I still skate at least once or twice a week. I'm in a league now, so it's been fun playing again. Plus," I added, "it's good cross-training for running."

"In case you ever need to cross-check someone during a race?" he said with a smile.

"Exactly."

The runners pressed toward the start line as the race director bellowed instructions through a bullhorn. We shuffled forward as the crowd tightened and personal space succumbed to a crush of bodies.

"Speaking of racing," Big J said, "do you have any races coming up?"

"Well, I'd like to do a marathon in the spring. Don't know which one, though. I was actually thinking about racing this time around. I've run a couple of marathons, but I've never raced one before. I'd like to really go for it, you know?"

We managed a few more sentences about my training and how I completely lacked a training plan. Big J mentioned a friend who happened to be the race-timing manager for a local running store and, apparently, quite the wellspring of marathon advice.

"He's timing this race," Big J continued. "You should talk to him."

"I don't know . . ."

I wasn't convinced. I had met the man in question once before, but I doubted he remembered who I was. For one thing, he was a very speedy, very experienced marathoner, and I was a season ticket holder in the peanut gallery. For another thing, he had the reputation of being somewhat misanthropic—I believe the phrase *crotchety old man* had been used.

The race director began the countdown.

"Ahh. Good ol' Kronos," Big J said, as if in eulogy. The bullhorn blared. "You should talk to him!" he yelled over his shoulder as he took off down the course, his tall, lanky figure disappearing with the distance.

And on that helpful yet characteristically vague note, I ran the 5K.

I had just over three miles to consider Big J's suggestion. And aside from the momentary distraction of being passed by a man wearing purple knee-high socks, lime-green split shorts, and a matching purple-and-lime-green knit cap, I spent a good portion of the 5K mustering enough courage to approach the sage, race-timing marathon guru.

I really could use a few pointers, I thought as I grabbed a bottle of water from a giant barrel positioned between the finish line and a long table piled high with donuts. Big J must have bolted soon after finishing, for I couldn't find him in the thinning crowd of sweaty runners. No matter. I had decided to heed his advice.

I waited until the final finishers had settled into the plentiful calm of post-race bagels and coffee before I finally made my way back to the flapping banners and waving flags demarcating the old Greek deity's location. I rehearsed what I was going to say, trying to make myself sound as casual as possible yet still deferential. After all, I knew very little about this man. Namely, I knew that he was sometimes referred to as "Kronos, the mythological ancient Greek god of race timing," that he knew everything there is to know about running, that he himself was exceptionally speedy, and that he was to be located somewhere near the finish line.

I soon saw him. He was lean and floppy-haired and wearing a safety-orange sweatshirt and concentrated grimace, both established articles of his race-timing uniform. He looked like a runner, and a fast runner, at that. More telling than his long, svelte frame and deft movements was the experienced air peculiar to runners who have been there and done that, so to speak. His whole demeanor gave the impression that he had covered many miles, and that he had done so in speedy fashion. Very speedy fashion.

Sheets of paper and bundles of wire in hand, he scrambled about the pavement, ricocheting from one end of the corral to the other, like a pinball caroming across the orange cones lining the chute's perimeter. Perhaps it was his reputation as a crotchety old Greek deity. Perhaps it was the preoccupied urgency with which he conducted post-race operations. Perhaps it was the combination of freezing temperatures and my sweaty race clothes. Whatever the case, I shivered. I was intimidated. Scared even. And I was a split second from turning away without saying a word, without asking.

Yet for some reason, flouting the danger of unknown wrath, I spoke, almost against my will. My voice sounded thin and flimsy in the cold air. Mr. Speedy Pants (I had dubbed him thus in my initial survey of his appearance), for his part, stopped what he was doing and spun around, tossing a bundle of wires into a gray bin in the process.

"Yeah-p?" He had a way of pinching his lips together as he said it, effectively pinning a *p* sound at the end of the word.

Taking his response as a cue, I introduced myself. Mentioned that I enjoyed running. That I wanted to improve. Asked if maybe, if he had the time, if he didn't mind, that is, if he would give me a training tip. Maybe two.

"Well, it depends on what you want to do," he said in response to my inquiry, crossing his arms and leaning back on his heels. "I mean, sure, I could give you a general tip or two that might help. But it's not gonna make you that much faster. I can't really help you unless you tell me a little about your training first—your background, your experience, your previous training plans. That sort of thing. Here"—he whipped out a phone—"what's your email? I'll let you know my general philosophy, and you shoot back an email about what kind of running you've done in the past. We can go from there."

My background? Experience? Training plans? Well, there was the shortest email ever written. I had never run competitively—not in high school or college or anywhere else. I ran simply to stay in shape for other sports, ice hockey, in particular. My experience was limited to a handful of 5Ks and two marathons, races I had run just for the heck of it. Concepts such as speedwork and tempo runs were completely foreign to me.

This is going to be a quick transaction, I thought. Mr. Speedy Pants would realize my baneful inexperience and reply with a polite but pithy suggestion. Something along the lines of, "Thank you for your inquiry. Unfortunately, your qualifications don't exist. Please try again later." That's what I thought would happen. I was wrong.

Six days, three emails, and one horrified realization later, I held in my hand my life for the next four months. Numbers mocking me. Phrases like VO_2 *max* and *lactate threshold* taunting me. But there it was. I was committed. No agreement was signed. No oath of allegiance was spoken. So why I felt contractually bound to adhere to the schedule Mr. Speedy Pants designed for me, I don't know. But I did. And it scared the heck out of me.

I don't think I signed up for this, I mumbled to myself, laying the papers on the desk and resuming a perfunctory purging of my inbox. My eyes kept wandering from the screen back to the training schedule. I was strangely intrigued, strangely excited, and—despite my initial trepidation—strangely appreciative of the miles and paces neatly arranged on the proposal before me. It was as though I had accidentally boarded the wrong flight, intending to go somewhere mundane, and instead found myself arriving in an exotic location. Sure it wasn't what I had planned, but it was definitely more exciting.

Maybe this won't be so bad, I thought, giving the schedule one last glance.

Crunch . . . crunch . . . crunch . . .

The numbers on Mr. Speedy Pants's training plan manifested themselves in the soft, gravel thud of each stride, pilgrim steps that left barely perceptible imprints, like lingering shadows, in the pebble drive, steps that led not so much toward a destination as away from the cavalier habits of casual running.

Better get used to this, baby, I thought. *It's gonna be your best friend for the next four months.*

I always start training with a giddy sense of excitement and dread, which is ironic, considering that the commencement of marathon training is, in essence, one of the most anti-climactic beginnings one can experience. The beginning of marathon training is like holding a shotgun start for the compilation of a dictionary. Three weeks into it, you're only on "aardvark," and you find yourself sitting there, pen in hand, thinking, *What the heck did I get myself into?*

This time was no different. There was no blaring siren, no mad sprint toward a foreseeable finish line. There was only the plan Mr. Speedy Pants had made for me. With dedicated enthusiasm, I took the first few steps of training. Three steps later, I realized those steps were merely the first of millions. The first three of millions. The first four of millions. The first five. And six.

Yes, Excitement and Dread are an inseparable couple in my life. Very rarely do I experience one without the other. Perhaps it is the great paradox of the unknown that marries the two emotions, for whenever a new journey is about to begin, there they are, Excitement and Dread, hand in hand, looking up at me with those annoying, lovey-dovey eyes. They are Antony and Cleopatra. Bonnie and Clyde. Sonny and Cher. Simon and Garfunkel (without all the breakups).

Not again, I moaned, as I acknowledged my relentless companions. And like the ill-fated lexicographer defining the nocturnal habits of the aardvark, I found myself wondering uneasily, *What the heck did I get myself into?*

Therein rests the irony of the marathon. It demands faith of its followers. It presents runners with sprawling, convoluted miles and a distant, invisible goal, a goal that is itself the greatest trial of faith. It waits patiently, a silent expanse of asphalt and agony and hours of sustained running. Michelangelo could sculpt a marble statue of the marathon— and still have time to paint a fresco or two before calling it a day. The race is long and demanding. The miles are tranquil and stoic and formidable. But it is the ultimate expression of faith.

Crunch . . . crunch . . . crunch . . .

It was only day one of training. The miles would only get longer, harder, and faster. From here on out, life as I knew it would defer to routine. Wake up. Run. Shower. Work. Eat. Sleep. Repeat. Weekdays. Weekends. Morning. Night. Whether I felt like it or not. Yet, as intimidated as I was by Mr. Speedy Pants's training plan, as unexpectedly as the whole thing had come about, I would continue. And I would be zealous. Devout. Stubborn. Because I believed in it.

Conviction drives the marathon runner. Every early wake-up call. Every cold, dark mile. Every breath of air and every crunch of gravel is the manifestation of a deep, obstinate, incorrigible confidence. The fatiguing monotony of endless daily runs asks, "Do you trust this will work?" The labyrinth of each long run questions, "Do you trust this is worth it?" And every stride, each step, one of millions, answers, "Yes."

Crunch . . . crunch . . . crunch . . .

My steps continued down the gravel road. My breath made tiny white puffs in the air and then vanished as quickly as they appeared. My arms swung back and forth in a whooshing, rhythmic pattern. It was an understated symphony imperceptible to everyone but me. The sounds were soft. Symmetrical. Determined. They were my companions. I knew them from miles past. I greeted them. I welcomed them. For they, like the miles, are always there.

Running may be a sport, but training is a faith. And faith, as they say, requires action.

Chapter Two

One day soon became one week. One week became two weeks. I placed a triumphant checkmark next to the second column of Mr. Speedy Pants's training plan. It had been a solid fourteen days of running.

Big J and I had run several times since bumping into each other at that fateful 5K two weeks ago. My SEC friend was determined to get back into shape, and the secret to his master plan for returning to Division I glory was, logically enough, running. And that only sporadically. (It was the taper theorem.) Considering that his current fitness regimen involved no running whatsoever, his gem of a strategy was bound to occasion no small measure of improvement. My role in Big J's return from unofficial retirement was to provide a default accountability of sorts. He would muster just enough incentive to propose a run. I would accept. He would then be morally bound to follow through with the arrangement. It was accountability at its finest.

Buzz! Buzz! Buzzzz!

I jumped. My cell phone bounced across the coffee table.

"You wanna run Forest Park this afternoon?" a lumbering voice inquired. It was Big J.

"Oh, hey. Sure. What time?"

I had chalked off enough miles over the past few days to feel fatigued, and it was gray and cold outside. The couch was growing more attractive by the minute. I was glad Big J had called. Accountability is a reciprocal commodity.

"How 'bout four o'clock?"

"Sounds good."

A few hours later, I was standing in the parking lot outside the Forest

Park Visitor Center.

"How far are we going?" I asked, balancing on one leg and stretching my quad by pulling my ankle up behind me.

"Let's do a loop. I haven't run over six miles in . . ." He laughed and shrugged. " . . . a long time." His smile morphed into a grimace of repulsion. "Ugh."

I laughed. "Eh, you'll be studly again in no time."

"Hmph." His gaze shifted across the parking lot. "Kronos!" he yelled in a spasm of recognition.

I turned around. It was Mr. Speedy Pants, walking toward us, watch in hand.

"Hey." Mr. Speedy Pants nodded at Big J. "Hey," he said, nodding at me.

"Wanna join us?" Big J ventured.

Mr. Speedy Pants secured the watch on his wrist. "Sure. How far you goin'?"

"Just a loop."

"A loop, huh? Better be careful. You might get yourself back in shape," Mr. Speedy Pants warned.

"You know it." Big J smiled.

We headed out to the paved running trail. Forest Park was quickly becoming one of my favorite places to run. I had never run there until I ran with Big J—the park being in the city and my home being thirty-five minutes to the west—but upon falling in love with its tree-lined paths, serene lakes and fountains, and abundance of architecture and activity, I quickly established it as our home field.

Mr. Speedy Pants asked Big J about his running, which inquiry occasioned a heated discussion regarding various training plans and workouts. Their language was punctuated with enough technical terms and numbers—seemingly tossed about at random—that I was soon unable to understand anything they were saying.

What in the world is a yasso? I wondered. My mind drifted between admiration of the park and the conversation of my two running partners. Mr. Speedy Pants's speech became increasingly impassioned. I turned to listen.

"We were down by eight points with one minute left in the game. *One minute.* We scored eight points in a twenty-four-second span to tie it up. Ended up winning in overtime. Greatest basketball game I've ever watched," Mr. Speedy Pants said.

University of Illinois basketball was Mr. Speedy Pants's favorite topic. Before his detailed play-by-play of the time the Illini came back from a fifteen-point deficit against Arizona in the Elite Eight, he had recapped the previous night's game. The recap had led to a heartfelt account of several classic Illini moments—namely, the Illini losing to North Carolina in the National Championship Game (the worst day of Mr. Speedy Pants's life) and, of course, the comeback against Arizona.

"And I scored some free tickets to the game against Indiana next month," he continued. "Because I'm awesome."

"You going?" Big J asked.

"Yep. Just have to get permission from Mrs. Awesome first," he replied, referring to his better half.

Conversation turned from Illini basketball to Big J's childhood days in Louisiana to a Tom Cruise shrine Mr. Speedy Pants and his "old buddy Tim" had assembled when they shared an apartment. The shrine, which was really quite elaborate considering it had been constructed as a joke, boasted a color photo of Tom Cruise, a candle, and a fake-bloody rag from the set of *Born on the Fourth of July* (the rag was a brilliant eBay find). At random intervals, Big J waved hello to fellow park patrons. (His greetings seemed to favor groups of elderly ladies out for a stroll.)

And in this manner, our trio circled the park.

"Yeah, the kid's gonna do her first track workout in a few weeks," Mr. Speedy Pants said when we returned to the visitor center parking lot.

"Speedwork, eh?" Big J said, a big grin sprawled across his face. "Ah, I love the track. I'm gonna hit the track again this week." He patted his stomach. "I need to." He turned toward to Mr. Speedy Pants. "So, are you coaching her now?"

"Nah. I made a training plan for her. Gave her some tips," Mr. Speedy Pants replied, pulling off his jacket and switching into a dry, warm sweatshirt. He grabbed a water bottle from a duffel bag.

"Gotcha. Well, you ready?" Big J asked. It was his inverted way of telling us he was.

Mr. Speedy Pants and I concurred.

"Hey," Big J called out, just before he shut the door to his truck, "When are we gonna run again?"

Mr. Speedy Pants and I looked at each other. I shrugged.

"What about next Thursday morning?" Mr. Speedy Pants volunteered.

"Sure," I agreed.

"I'm down," Big said.

That was that. We were running again next week. We agreed on a time. We agreed on a place. We said good-bye. And then, we left.

We were a strange trio, Mr. Speedy Pants, Big J, and I. No one could deny that. I smiled as I made my way down the lonely country road, a stark contrast with the previous afternoon's run and all its bizarre highlights. The day's schedule and miles demanded I run from home—early and without the garrulous chatter of my two running buddies.

To put it simply, I live in the boonies. This being the case, I often run in the boonies. Gravel roads. Cows. Cornfields. Trees. Barns. And tractors. Lots and lots of tractors. These are my surroundings when I run. They are my everyday running companions. Only, as I was about to discover, I had never really met them before.

I have a bad habit of falling into my daily routines and letting the monotony render my observational facilities comatose. Wake up. Pull on my shoes. Pull on my shirt. Realize it is inside out. Take off my shirt. Turn it right-side out. Put my shirt back on. Grab my watch. Head out the door. Run. Come home. Done.

Uneventful, to say the least.

On that particular day, however, I was out for a run on my regular route, on the same country roads that I always run, with the same absentminded complacency that characterizes my daily miles, when something caught my attention. It wasn't anything out of the ordinary; in fact, it was something that had been there for every run before the run in question and would undoubtedly be there for many runs to come.

It was a mailbox. More specifically, a name on a mailbox, and the yellowed, uppercase letters announcing the name were now crooked with age. The name, however, remained, and for some reason, it made me stop and look twice.

O. STOUT.

I was surprised I hadn't noticed Mr. Stout's mailbox before. It was an artifact, really, worn and aged but defying the years. The metal flag had long since rusted and fallen off, and the wooden post on which the mailbox was mounted leaned precariously to one side, as if it were threatening to take its own life. Rusted screws, placed distractedly on the relic, jutted from all sides. The screws hinted at repairs made long ago. They did not hint at the success of said repairs. All in all, the mailbox looked as though it were fighting off the end of its existence.

Still pausing in the middle of the road to contemplate the name of O. Stout, I glanced up to see an old white farmhouse. The farmhouse looked even older than the mailbox (logic would demand it be at least its equal), and I assumed it was the residence of the honorable Mr. O. Stout. The house was very tiny. A white porch, which lacked any semblance of perpendicularity, slumped self-consciously beneath peeling paint and splintering support beams. The overhanging roof (which sagged to the left) and the whitewashed plank floor (which sloped to the right) created a modest haven for a solitary wooden rocking chair.

The distinction of Mr. Stout's front porch, however, rested in a tremendous collection of wind chimes, which paraded along all three sides of the porch. Counting the chimes as best I could from the road, I estimated there had to be at least thirty of them. Wooden and metal. Full and sparse. Themed and simple. Mr. Stout did not discriminate among wind chimes, and every ornament clinked and jingled with its own voice.

How could I have missed this before? I wondered.

And then it occurred to me that perhaps there was quite a bit more I was missing in my routine-induced stupor. With a newly piqued sense of observation, I continued on, determined to find out who my daily running companions really were.

I didn't have to go far. Just a few minutes after I lost sight of Mr. Stout's home, I came across the pasture of a neighboring horse farm. There were many horse farms near my house. But this one stood out from the rest, for the horses that pastured there were Clydesdales. More than that, as I had recently discovered, they were retired Budweiser Clydesdales. Several were trotting in the fields, their stately manes flowing behind them, their movements controlled and potent, belying their strength. I stopped to watch them run, imagining them pulling the iconic beer wagon behind them. They were regal in motion. One of them snorted at me. I interpreted his annoyance as an entreaty for me to leave, and I ran on.

I passed dilapidated barns and hidden vegetable gardens secreted away behind fences whose decaying beams could not hide the abundance of vegetation. I passed courageous patches of wildflowers blooming in the woods, defying the trees and creating miniature islands of paradise in the shade. I passed one barn in particular that stood out for no other reason than that it had a gray donkey standing in the open barn door. The grayness of the donkey was accentuated by the sharp red of the barn. The donkey did not flinch as I ran by. It didn't blink an eye or prick an ear or make an indignant snort as any self-respecting donkey should do. It just stared at me. I stared back and felt inferior. Having nothing else to do, the donkey continued staring. I, having nothing else to do, continued running.

Immediately beyond the donkey and his barn door was, of all things, a buffalo farm. And yes, I had noticed the buffalo farm before. (I'm out of it, but not that out of it.) It appeared that the herd had grown over the past year and had become fatigued in the process, for every buffalo was lounging in the field, sleeping or napping or doing whatever it is buffalo do to rest. One of the massive creatures tilted his face to stare at me as I ran by; but even this seemed too much of an effort, and he returned his cumbersome head, beard and all, back to its resting place on the ground.

I passed one last hitherto overlooked artifact before I reached home. It was a diamond-shaped, yellow street sign, carefully positioned by the road. There were no words on the sign. Just a silhouette. A silhouette of a man wearing a straw hat and sitting on a tractor.

Maybe I live even deeper in the boonies than I thought . . .

But I like the boonies. More than that, I am grateful for them. In the country, time moves at a slower pace, and life is peaceful. It is serene. It is home.

Just past the buffalo farm is a small community, a quintessential Mayberry town with tree-lined roads, pristine yards, and all the friendliness and familiarity of a tiny population. I had run hundreds—probably thousands—of miles down the quaint roads. The occasional historic building dots the landscape, including an old general store that has a coffee shop secreted away in the back of the building. In the summer, children on bikes and scooters zigzag down the sidewalks while ladies in wide-brimmed hats water rose gardens and men barbecue on brick patios. Always is the sound of someone mowing grass; always is the sound of distant laughter.

In the winter, however, the scene is much quieter. Picturesque still, but quiet. The rose gardens and wide-brimmed hats in hibernation, lushness gives way to the crisp silhouettes and lines of bare trees and pitched roofs until each object is but a lighter hue of its own shadow.

At the end of town is a small lake, a punctuation mark of sorts that serves as both the end of one scene and the beginning of another, for beyond the lake is an endless expanse of cornfields. The cornfields—which also succumbed to the monotony of the winter palette—presented a bucolic run, even if it was a bit dull.

The countryside thus providing an abundance of run-worthy miles, it wasn't long before Mr. Speedy Pants and Big J made the trek to the boonies for what I termed "the finest in country running."

"So, this is the legendary Mystical Land," Mr. Speedy Pants said as he, Big J, and I splashed our way down a quiet, serpentine country road.

Big J had joined me once before for a run in the country, and in his report to Mr. Speedy Pants had dubbed the picturesque town, with its meticulous landscaping and gray stone houses and tiny general store, "Mystical Land." The name was fitting, and it stayed.

Heavy snowflakes had fallen with a vengeance throughout the night, but the ground being unusually warm, they had melted in meekness upon contact with the earth. The result was a mess of slush and salt that gave the roads the appearance of having been the victim of a snow cone factory explosion. We kicked up giant globs of the icy mixture, and it ran down our legs and into our shoes and socks.

"Yep," I replied, "this is where I grew up running."

Feeling the need to act as a sort of cicerone to my two guests who were new to the haunts of my youth, I decided to highlight sundry points of interest along our route, such as the location of a camping site documented in the journals of Lewis and Clark and a tiny graveyard dating back to the Civil War. I pointed to a building with a long wrap-around porch and two small turrets on either side. It had once served as a train station but now housed several small businesses.

"See that old train station over there? Well, it actually used to be a train station. Isn't that cool?"

I thought it was cool. I would later regret saying so.

"As opposed to a fake train station?" Mr. Speedy Pants laughed.

I rolled my eyes. "A working train station, like, back in the old days."

"Uh-huh."

I realized this was not going to end well. "Well, I mean, it looks like they just built it and made it look old. But it actually was . . . a real train station . . . in the country . . . back in the day . . ." My voice trailed off.

"Phew!" Mr. Speedy Pants exclaimed. "Well, I'm glad that's settled. I was just wondering if that train station over there was a real train station or a fake train station. But"—he looked over at Big J—"it was a real train station." Mr. Speedy Pants rubbed the top of my head, messing up my ponytail. "Ah, you're a great tour guide."

We continued sloshing our way down the road for another mile or so until we reached the lake and followed the dirt path leading away from Mystical Land and into the cornfields. Our conversation, for its part, veered off the main road as much as we did. The Teenage Mutant Ninja Turtles established themselves as the leaders of our cornfield discussion.

"So, kid, which one do you think was the coolest?" Mr. Speedy Pants asked after we had successfully named every character that had appeared in the television series.

"Raphael," I replied without hesitating. (Everybody knows Raphael was the coolest.)

Mr. Speedy Pants was appalled. He began making a case for Do-natello, praising his wisdom and capability. Raphael, he explained, had serious character flaws. Namely, he was a punk.

Big J, ever the peacemaker, voiced his appreciation of Michelangelo.

"Donatello was capable and wise," Mr. Speedy Pants continued, ignoring Big J's sentiment. "Not unlike myself."

"Oh, brother." I laughed, rolling my eyes. "I still like Raphael."

"Raphael was a punk."

"That's dumb."

"You would like Raphael. You're a punk."

"Whatever."

After a mile of impassioned argument, the fascinating topic of the Teenage Mutant Ninja Turtles still had not fully run its course, and it took an intriguing detour regarding Barbie's dating preferences—namely, whether or not she would date one of the turtles. (The path of logic that led to this debate is still a bit hazy to me.) I argued she would not, because Barbie is taller than the Teenage Mutant Ninja Turtles, and Barbie would never date someone shorter than she is. Mr. Speedy Pants disagreed and made a lengthy rebuttal that also involved G.I. Joe.

"You know who has a new training program?" Mr. Speedy Pants soon interjected, ending the Barbie debate and returning once more to the subject of training.

"Who?" Big J asked.

"LL Cool J. I saw his book the other day," Mr. Speedy Pants said. "It's LL Cool J. How could you not get fit?"

"I heard Mario Lopez just came out with a new book," Big J countered. "That *has* to work—it's *Slater*!" He was emphatic about this point. "Haha . . . Slater was the best."

"Ooo . . ." Mr. Speedy Pants tilted his head in contemplation. "Mario Lopez or LL Cool J? That's a tough call."

Deeper into the cornfields we ran. A veritable maze in the summer months, the fields were an expanse of desert in the dead of winter, crops sheared nearly to the ground, the view open and panoramic for miles.

The ground was beset with deep ruts, evidence of the heavy farm equipment that had traversed the path before us. Our ten miles through the fields felt much longer than they actually were.

"You know," Big J said after a moment's reflection, "Mario Lopez and LL Cool J kinda look like Bebop and Rock Steady." (The Teenage Mutant Ninja Turtles was a very persistent topic.)

Mr. Speedy Pants raised his eyebrows in assent. "You know, they kinda do."

I was about to make a comment on Big J's observation when he called out, "Hey, uh, don't look behind you for a second!"

Big J had slowed his pace and dropped back a considerable way from Mr. Speedy Pants and me.

"Why not? What . . . ?" And then I understood. "Oh, my gosh . . . That is so gross." I threw my hands over my eyes to act as blinders as I continued running straight ahead.

Mr. Speedy Pants laughed. "What's gross? Peeing in a field?"

"Yeah . . ."

"What's gross about it? We're out in the middle of nowhere."

"I don't know . . ." I said, grimacing. "It's just . . . not what people do."

"There ain't nothing sacred in running, kid," Mr. Speedy Pants replied, patting me on the head.

"Ugh. I shouldn't have had all that coffee this morning," Big J kindly elaborated as he caught up to our little group once more.

"You," I said, finally removing the blinders and shaking my head, "are gross."

"Gross? What was I supposed to do? Do you see any bathrooms around here?"

"Nope," Mr. Speedy Pants answered. Then he added, "That is, unless you consider the cornfields one giant bathroom. Then you're golden."

"This is true," Big J agreed.

We finished our run and trudged to the general store for some much-needed coffee. I wrapped my semi-frozen fingers around the cup and let the steam warm my face.

"Runners are so weird," I said, surveying my appearance, as well as that of Mr. Speedy Pants and Big J. We were splattered in mud from the waist down. Our calves were crusty with white road salt, and our shoes oozed a brown, grimy liquid. Mr. Speedy Pants and Big J were gross. And I was right there with them.

"Eh, it's all a matter of perspective, really," Mr. Speedy Pants replied. He folded his arms across his chest. "You think we're weird, but I bet a few of the people who drove by while we were running thought you were just as weird. I mean, look at you. You're covered in mud, you're wearing split shorts, even though there is snow on the ground, and"—he smiled—"you're hanging out with us."

I looked down at my mud-splattered legs, blotched with red and white patches, evidence of the cold and the road salt, respectively. I looked at my two running partners. Mr. Speedy Pants did have a point. Perhaps weird is relative. Sure, we had spent ten miles in some rough-hewn cornfields. Sure, we had discussed Barbie's dating preferences in relation to the Teenage Mutant Ninja Turtles. And sure, Big J had made an emergency . . . stop. But whatever. Weirder things had happened in cornfields.

Chapter Three

12 x 400 meters. 5K effort. One minute rest.

Hmm, I thought, looking at the workout Mr. Speedy Pants had given me to run that week. I was one month into marathon training, and the first speedwork session was approaching rapidly. I had never stepped on a track before, much less run an actual track workout. I wasn't overly optimistic at the prospect.

5K effort, I repeated to myself, trying to bolster my confidence. *Sounds simple enough. How hard is 5K effort? Do I have a 5K effort?* I tried to picture myself running a 5K, which shouldn't have been that difficult. I tried to imagine how I felt in the middle of the race. I tried to imagine how I usually feel in the middle of a race. Closing my eyes, I started swinging my arms in a running motion. I pictured myself running hard. I visualized my breathing. *5K effort,* I chanted, *5K effort.* Nothing.

The whole of a workout less than twenty-four hours away hinged on my running 5K effort, and there I was, standing in the middle of the kitchen, swinging my arms in desperation trying to conjure some vague idea, a ballpark estimate, of 5K effort. I was completely clueless to what that should feel like and wholly freaking out that my very first speedwork session was doomed to failure. It really, really shouldn't have been that hard.

Alas, self-doubt overpowered reason, which occurrence was not so much a clean defeat as it was a forfeit, and I decided to question Mr. Speedy Pants on the subject. I hesitated before sending the email. Even though we had run together quite a few times over the past month, I was still intimidated by his experience and found myself self-conscious when discussing matters of training. Finally, I mustered my resolve and sent him what I thought was a calm inquiry.

Hi, it read. *So, I was looking at the schedule, and I saw the quarters are supposed to be run at 5K effort. I was just wondering if you could maybe give me a number or a time for each interval, just in case I don't know what 5K effort feels like . . . ? I'm a little afraid I might go out too fast or run too slow. I mean, I think I'll be fine, and if you don't have time or whatever, it's not that big of a deal. I was just wondering because I'm new at this, and I wanted to make sure I don't mess things up, you know? Anyway, that's it. Thanks. Oh, and how hard is this workout supposed to be? Am I supposed to be really tired or just kind of tired? Thanks.*

I hit SEND and my concerns were soon speeding away through the invisible highway of cyberspace. At the time, I thought my email was nonchalant. Cavalier, even. Mr. Speedy Pants, however, must not have picked up on my breezy insouciance, for within an hour he called in response.

"Tell you what, kid," he said, cutting in on what was bound to be an interminable string of questions and remonstrances. "My old buddy Tim and I were gonna do a track workout tomorrow, but turns out he can't make it. Why don't you meet me at the track, and you can run your workout with me? That way, if you have any mid-run freakouts, you can ask me . . . whatever."

Freakouts? What made Mr. Speedy Pants assume I was going to freak out? There was nothing in my email except imperturbability (at least, I thought so). I consider myself a very levelheaded, self-possessed individual. A few simple questions were representative of nothing more than a fledgling's diligence at running a workout correctly. I felt compelled to inform Mr. Speedy Pants of this.

"What? I wasn't freaking out. I just wanted to make sure I did it right."

"Uh-huh." There was more than a hint of dubiety in his tone. "You were definitely freaking out in your email."

"No way."

"Way. No need to freak out, though."

"I wasn't freaking out at all."

"Well, whatever the case," Mr. Speedy Pants continued, undeterred, "I'll be running at the Webster Groves track tomorrow afternoon. I'll probably get there around three o'clock."

Run a workout with Mr. Speedy Pants? I doubted the wisdom of this idea.

"Oh. Well . . . I've got to warn you. This is my first time on a track. Ever. I'll have no idea what I'm doing out there."

"I know. No big deal. You just run. No different than the roads."

"I don't want to mess up your workout."

"You're not going to mess up my workout. I actually may end up running with you. Help you get your feet wet."

"Umm . . ." I responded intellectually.

What's the matter with me? I thought as the silence lengthened. I was freaking out, that's what was the matter. In the moment Mr. Speedy Pants made his initial proposal, I became acutely aware of my inexperience. Not only would I be running a track workout for the first time in my life, but I would be doing so in the company of a very speedy, very experienced runner. He ran collegiate cross-country. I ran the Jingle Jangle Fruitcake 5K. What if I looked like an idiot? What would Mr. Speedy Pants think of me? What cataclysmic upheaval of the galaxies would occur when our two worlds collided?

"Hello?" Mr. Speedy Pants said.

This was it. This was my invitation to hang with a cool kid. I pictured myself a much younger girl, standing on the playground, my foot swiveling dreamily in the sand, creating a minor crater as I watched the cool kids from a distance. They laughed and talked and were having the grandest time in the history of the universe. Then, suddenly, one of them (the coolest one, of course) turned around and looked straight at me, motioning with his hand for me to join them. "C'mon!" he yelled. "What are you waiting for?"

My faculties of articulation rebounded.

"Okay. Three o'clock. See you then."

"Word."

Against my better judgment, I had committed to running a track workout with Mr. Speedy Pants. I did so without considering the consequences of my response. I am not exactly sure how or why. I hung up the phone in a sort of dazed confusion and harbored the vague yet disturbing suspicion that this was going to turn out very, very badly.

But there it was. Tomorrow. At three o'clock. Once more, I started swinging my arms frenetically. *5K pace. 5K pace.* I jogged about the kitchen and smacked into cabinets and countertop corners. I was excited. I was nervous. I was kind of freaking out. (Okay, I admit it.) But that didn't matter. Because tomorrow, at three o'clock, I was gonna run with a cool kid. At 5K effort.

Clank. Flap . . . snap! Clank. Flap . . . snap!

I grimaced at the flags that popped and clanked in rhythmic chaos as they towered above me. The wind was incensed at something and expressed its displeasure by attacking the flags. The flags, for their part, were very cross at such treatment. They rebelled against the flagpoles, first crumpling in despondency, then exploding to full glory, then collapsing again. It was, all in all, a very anarchic scene.

Conflict, however, was not an entirely unfitting theme for the day, for this was the afternoon of my first track workout, a workout I would be running under the tutelage of Mr. Speedy Pants. My mind felt not unlike the flags that whipped about, an amalgam of excitement, nervousness, anticipation, and hunger (I had eaten a very early lunch). In addition, my ability to run at 5K effort was debatable. I looked at the track. The track looked back at me. It seemed rather elitist. Sure, I had done my fair share of running, but I considered myself a generic athlete, the kind of runner who runs to stay in shape for other sports. Like hockey. I was not a runner-runner. Track workouts, in my mind, were for runner-runners.

Have I ever run on a track? I asked myself, trying to remember any childhood event that mandated a track. My search seemed futile, for even the mile time trials I had run in grade school were done on a paved walking trail around a small lawn (which, upon reflection, seems very unofficial). Then I remembered. Once. When I was nine or ten. My grandparents had taken us to the local high school to play tennis, and after a riveting doubles match, we found ourselves wandering toward the football field and the track surrounding it. My little sister—who was five at the time—ran around the track like a gazelle. My grandparents were exceedingly impressed. Not willing to be outdone, I decided to impress my grandparents as well. However, after sprinting approximately seventy-five meters and hearing no corresponding expressions of admiration, I considered the endeavor of no use, stopped running, and walked back to the car for some chocolate licorice. Such was my auspicious history of running on a track.

My reverie of doubt was interrupted, however, when Mr. Speedy Pants pulled up in his car.

"Hey."

"Hey," I echoed.

He glanced at the snapping flags. "It's gonna be a windy one." He grabbed a duffel bag from the front seat and slammed the door. "You ready?"

"Yep."

The singular, defining feature of the Webster Groves track is a behemoth recreation center towering above the first turn. This precipitate overseer creates two noteworthy effects. First, it imprisons the near side of the track in its ominous—though, in the summer, I suppose, not entirely unwelcome—shadow. And second, it presents fatigued runners on the homestretch the appealing opportunity to run for all they're worth toward a whopper of a luminescent sign glowing boldly against the dark brick building: WEBSTER GROVES RECREATION COMPLEX AND ICE ARENA. For vagrant hockey players who find themselves outside the hallowed walls, lacing up running shoes instead of skates, worried about 5K effort rather than getting body-checked at center ice, wearing skimpy little split shorts instead of the comforting padded bulk of hockey pants, it is nothing short of pure, incandescent motivation.

I gazed at the ice arena and for a split second had the gut-wrenching sensation that I was on the wrong side of the giant sign. Throughout my entire athletic career (I use the term *career* loosely), I had run simply for fun and played hockey competitively. Now, with the situation reversed, I felt out of place. Timid, almost.

Competitive running—and the training it entails—was new to me, for running is unlike any other sport. There is no distraction from the pain—no baseballs to hit or soccer balls to kick. There are no quarterbacks to sack or pucks to shoot. No, there is just you. And distance. And time. And pain. Self-inflicted, nonstop, till-death-do-us-part pain. The only goal of the sport is to increase your ability to withstand the torture. The only scoreboard is an unforgiving clock. The rules are simple: You run as hard as you can until your physical and mental capacities crumble in a spectacular implosion of body and will. And then, you pick up the pieces and do it again.

Mr. Speedy Pants tossed his duffel bag on the metal bleachers lining the far side of the track and pulled out a pair of flashy racing flats. He then changed his shoes with such repose I began to wish I had brought another pair of shoes, too, just so I could relieve my anxiety by changing them.

"So, how long do you usually warm up?" Mr. Speedy Pants asked as we began jogging around the track.

"Umm . . . I never warm up," I replied, looking at him with raised eyebrows, not really understanding what the big deal was. I had the strange feeling that my confession knocked some of the spring out of Mr. Speedy Pants's racing flats.

"You never warm up?" Mr. Speedy Pants repeated.

"Well"—I shook my head—"not really. I just run, I guess."

Mr. Speedy Pants shook his head at my apparent imbecility and launched into a polemic laced with statistics and numbers and other pleasantries expounding the benefits of the warm-up. Meanwhile, the gusty headwinds made it increasingly difficult to carry on intelligible conversation.

"Dude, the guy who won the Olympic marathon—whenever it was—the last Olympic marathon—the guy who won didn't warm up," I countered after Mr. Speedy Pants finished his sermon.

"What?"

"The guy who won the Olympic marathon. He was the only guy out of the whole field who didn't warm up—and he won."

"Oh," Mr. Speedy Pants said, a hint of recognition in his voice, "you mean Bob Dingy?"

"Umm . . . I guess so. Is he the guy who won?"

"Well, he is the guy who won the last Olympic marathon."

Whoosh! A gust of wind slammed into us as we rounded the far turn leading into the final stretch. I lowered my head against the force.

"Huh. Yeah. Bob Dingy then." The name, while unfamiliar, sounded American.

Wow. That's cool, I thought. *An American won the Olympic marathon.* I knew of so few professional runners that I didn't doubt the accuracy of Mr. Speedy Pants's fact.

We finally finished our warm-up (which, to my dismay, capped off at an interminable two miles) and headed back to the bleachers to grab some water. Mr. Speedy Pants began adjusting his stopwatch. I saw this as an ideal opportunity to learn more about the illustrious anti-warm-up Olympic champion.

"So, who the heck is Bob Dingy?" I asked.

"What in the . . . who?" Mr. Speedy Pants seemed flabbergasted. (I would later learn it is no small task flabbergasting Mr. Speedy Pants.)

"Bob Dingy. The guy you said won the Olympic marathon."

Mr. Speedy Pants had not moved. He only held his watch in midair, fingers still primed for action, elbows still up at shoulder height. "You mean Baldini?"

Now I was flabbergasted. "Baldini? *Baldini?* Oh, my gosh." I started to laugh. "I thought you said *Bob Dingy.*"

There are certain moments in every friendship that define the essence of the relationship. This was one of those moments.

"Oh . . . my," said Mr. Speedy Pants, rubbing his forehead with his hand and then scratching his head and then ruffling his hair. He was, it seemed, flummoxed. (Again, as I would later learn, it is not easy to flummox Mr. Speedy Pants.)

"What made you think I said Bob Dingy?" he asked.

"It was windy! It was hard to hear you. It sounded like Bob Dingy."

Mr. Speedy Pants shook his head. "No, I said Baldini, as in the Italian marathoner, Stefano Baldini." He laughed under his breath, hiding a smile as he stepped onto the track. "C'mon, kid. Stop dilly-dallying."

Dilly-dallying over, we began the workout, still laughing about Bob Dingy, the Olympic marathon champion who did not believe in warming up. Mr. Dingy, for his part, served as an effective distraction for my anxiety regarding 5K pace, and we completed two laps before I had time to remember my misgivings.

"How's this pace feel?" Mr. Speedy Pants inquired as we continued looping off each interval.

"Good."

"Does it feel like 5K effort?"

"Umm . . . I guess so." I honestly didn't know.

"You don't know?" Mr. Speedy Pants honestly didn't know how I didn't know.

"Well," I huffed as the interval came to an end and we walked about near the start line, soaking up every moment of our sixty-second rest before we had to start the next quarter, "it kinda just depends on the day."

"So you don't even have a ballpark idea?" He was skeptical.

"Well, I mean, kinda." We lined up on the start line, slapped our watches, and began running again. "I think this feels good," I yelled above the wind and my own breathing.

Lap after lap we clicked off the quarters. Mr. Speedy Pants was alternately encouraging and distracting, buoying my spirits with supportive comments ("Good job, kid. Lookin' good.") and deflecting my attention from the workout to other, more profitable enterprises, such as calculating the percentage of progression through the quarters ("Okay, you just finished your fifth lap of twelve. What percentage of the workout have you completed?"). Whether it was because I was fatigued from the workout or because I am an inordinately poor math student (or both), I don't know. But it took me three full laps to figure out that I had completed approximately 42 percent of the workout. And by the time I figured that out, I was on the ninth lap, rendering my calculations irrelevant anyway. But it made the time pass quickly, and for that I was grateful.

"Okay, kid. Here's what we're gonna do," Mr. Speedy Pants said just before we started the last quarter. "I'm going to race you on this last one."

My stomach tightened. I hate racing.

"I'll give you—" He started mumbling numbers under his breath, sifting through several options before finally selecting the most appropriate one. "—a fifteen-second lead."

"Fifteen seconds?" I exclaimed. "No way. Twenty."

"Twenty?" Mr. Speedy Pants exclaimed in return. "That's too much. It won't even be a contest."

"Twenty."

"Okay. Fine." Mr. Speedy Pants rolled his eyes. "I'll give you a twenty-second lead."

My head swirled. I really hate racing.

He continued, "I always like to hammer the last interval of a quarter workout. But don't be dumb and run the first two hundred in a full sprint. Save something for the end. You gotta be able to kick it into another gear on the homestretch. Ready? Go!"

My heart was beating out of my chest. My throat felt dry. My breathing was strained. I was unabashedly freaking out. I had gone maybe ten meters.

I've always hated the feeling of being chased. When I was a kid, in games of tag, I was the girl who screamed and cowered when the person who was "it" drew near. It is my natural reaction, the human manifestation of a deer in headlights. In fact, if I had been a deer, I would at this moment be carpeting some lonely country highway. And now Mr. Speedy Pants was chasing me. It was horrible.

I don't want to be here, I thought as I hit the backstretch. I looked across the track and saw Mr. Speedy Pants gaining ground.

"Here I come!" he yelled.

Ahhhh! I screamed (in my head, of course) as I rounded the final turn and flung my body down the final one hundred meters. At last, the race was over. Mr. Speedy Pants wasn't far behind. In fact, he was about five seconds behind.

"I told you twenty seconds was too much of a head start," he panted. "Now, if we had done fifteen seconds, things would have been much more interesting . . ."

I didn't answer. My heart was still racing, and the conflicting emotions of post-workout fatigue and post-race relief swelled with every gasp. I had survived.

"Nicely done, kid," Mr. Speedy Pants said, patting me on the back as we caught our breath.

"Thanks."

We embarked on a cool-down run through the streets of Old Webster, passing quaint historic homes and tiny coffee shops. We laughed at our discussion of Bob Dingy, the illustrious Olympic marathon champion.

"Bob Dingy . . ." Mr. Speedy Pants said as we ran. "You're a piece of work, kid."

I smiled. I didn't think I was that big of a piece of work.

"So, you gonna join me and my old buddy Tim next week, same time, same track?"

Whoosh! My freakout returned. Run with Mr. Speedy Pants and his old buddy Tim? Run with not one but *two* cool kids?

"I . . . uh . . . yeah. I mean, as long as you guys don't mind," I said.

"I wouldn't have asked you if I minded," Mr. Speedy Pants said, matter-of-fact as always. Diplomacy was not a required virtue in Mr. Speedy Pants's book.

"Yeah, that'd be cool," I said.

We reached our cars, officially ending the workout.

"Good job, today, kid. Not bad for your first time on the track."

"Thanks!" I looked up at the flags that were still engaged in combat.

Clank! Flap . . . snap! Clank! Flap . . . snap!

"I hear ya," I said. And then I headed home.

Chapter Four

It was, in all honesty, an unassuming inception. But somehow, a couple of Thursday-morning runs with Mr. Speedy Pants and Big J evolved into a strange yet devoted weekly gathering known as the Thursday Morning Breakfast Group or, as we affectionately dubbed it, the TMBG.

The three of us had been running every Thursday morning since our first and fortuitous run together at Forest Park. The pilot episode having gone so well, we continued the series and built the plot around two key events: my weekly long run and a post-run breakfast excursion. We joked about the latter taking precedence over my actual training run and named our group accordingly. The TMBG became a staple in our week. It was faithfully attended. Minor obstacles such as sickness, injury, work schedules, or lack of sleep were unpardonable excuses for missing a TMBG. If a member did have to miss all or part of the morning's adventures, that member was vilified in an official TMBG email as punishment for his or her truancy. We woke up at ridiculously early hours in order to squeeze in both the run and the breakfast before work. We planned intricate routes and incorporated pace-specific training. We researched the finest breakfast establishments in the area. The TMBG was very serious business. That is, as serious as any group could be with Mr. Speedy Pants and Big J as chairmen of the board.

We made it our mission to visit every celebrated hole-in-the-wall diner in the city, and we became fond of two in particular, designating these two spots official TMBG destinations and frequenting them above all others. The two honored establishments were Courtesy Diner and Uncle Bill's 24-Hour Pancake House; and to their hallowed booths we trekked on a fairly regular basis.

The latest edition of the TMBG involved our home away from Forest Park, the bucolic Queeny Park. The running path that surrounds Queeny Park boasts the unique characteristic of being part paved path, part gravel path, and part dirt trail, the last being littered with rocks and roots and the occasional wooden footbridge. The varying terrain melds together seamlessly, and one could quite easily run on gravel for a quarter of a mile and then dirt trail for another quarter of a mile and forget altogether that the path began as a paved surface.

Our breath hung in the air as we ran, each puff frozen in place by the cold, dim light of early morning. The ground was hard and frozen. The subzero windchills were persistent.

"Ha! You've got snow in your ponytail," Big J informed me as we ran. He tugged on my hair for emphasis.

I grabbed my ponytail and pulled it toward my face, twisting my head to see the crystal-crusted ends.

"Oh, yeah . . . I do," I replied. "How weird." Then I began to wonder where exactly the "snow" had come from. "Eww. So, is that sweat snow?"

"Egh. Sweat snow." Big J laughed.

"You're kinda gross, kid," Mr. Speedy Pants added.

The previous thaws and subsequent refreezing had left deep, serpentine gorges in the ground. The stretch of path before us was rough going, to say the least. I screeched as I crashed through ice-covered puddles that weren't quite sturdy enough to hold my body weight.

"Whoa—oop!"

"What in the world are you doing back there, kid?" Mr. Speedy Pants called over his shoulder.

"I . . . can't . . . get my footing . . . agh! Oh . . . man . . ."

In an effort to avoid snapping my anklebone in half, I attempted to dodge one of the gorges and instead plunged my foot into a frozen pool of muddy water. The cold seeped into my shoe as I stepped out of the puddle. I tried to shake off as much ice and mud as I could.

"Agh! It's so cold!" I lamented as I caught up to Mr. Speedy Pants and Big J.

Mr. Speedy Pants and Big J, being the empathetic and concerned running partners that they were, laughed.

"Haha . . . What did you run through the puddle for?" Mr. Speedy Pants asked.

"I didn't run through it on purpose, dude. I was trying to avoid one of those huge divots."

"Uh-huh. I thought you were supposed to be a tough hockey player?"

"Yeah, well, I didn't want to twist my ankle. And there were a ton of frozen mud puddles back there."

He shook his head. "Sometimes you can be such a girl."

Big J added his credentialed observance. "You're actually pretty funny to watch," he said. "When we ran Castlewood, I could tell you hadn't run on trails much. It's pretty entertaining."

Castlewood was a local park with a labyrinth of trails—technical trails with rocks and roots and creeks and other natural obstacles—that wind through the woods and bluffs along the river. I had never run on a technical trail before my run with Big J, and for someone coming from a strict running diet of asphalt and concrete, it was both a liberating and a challenging experience. Big J, for his part, was all about trails. He often talked about moving somewhere—anyplace, really—where he could run nothing but dirt paths cutting across mountains and countryside.

"That was the first time I'd ever run on a real trail!" I defended myself.

"Yeah, that was obvious," Big J said. "That's okay, though. You'll learn."

"The TMBG needs to hit up Castlewood," Mr. Speedy Pants interjected.

"Next week," Big J said by way of agreement. "Oh, man. Trails are the best. That's all I'd run if I could. Pavement kills my legs. Anyway"—he turned to me and poked me in the shoulder—"trails will be good for you. They'll make you strong."

The rest of the run was without incident, except for a few minor screeches on my part. Big J told tales of growing up in Louisiana, most of them beginning with the phrase, "No, really, I was a good kid. But one time . . ." Big J also discussed at length the subject of grits, including the nuances of cheesy grits, cinnamon grits, and spicy jalapeño grits. Mr. Speedy Pants gladly offered anecdotal sarcasm and unsolicited advice throughout Big J's discourse and, as a culinary rebuttal to the grits philosophy of Big J, delved into the world of hash browns, most notably making the strict injunction that they not be soggy. The miles soon traversed, we jumped into our cars and drove the short distance from the park to Uncle Bill's 24-Hour Pancake House for our post-run breakfast.

We started things off with a bottomless pot of hot coffee. Mr. Speedy Pants ordered the two-by-two-by-two-by-two, a Noahic plate of pancakes, eggs, bacon, and toast. Then he ordered a side of hash browns. Big J also requested the two-by-two-by-two-by-two. Then he ordered a side of grits. And I ordered oatmeal. Cream and brown sugar on the side. In keeping with TMBG tradition, Mr. Speedy Pants and Big J made fun of me for ordering oatmeal. I defended my position. And then we ate. Thus went the TMBG.

It's funny how something that seems so incidental at its beginning evolves into something with far more significance. Our crazy little trio had become a highlight in my week, and the prospect of longer runs as training progressed meant more time to talk and laugh and argue and crash through frozen mud puddles. And I had many a long run ahead of me. It was a lovely thought.

To change things up, I decided to run from a local coffeehouse. It was a perfect starting location for a number of reasons, not the least of which was the availability of both bathrooms and coffee, two items that were quickly gaining precedence in my life. Using the former before the run and saving the latter for after, I locked my car, readied my watch, and began.

The coffee shop was located on a particularly busy thoroughfare, across from what I believe to be the largest strip mall in the world. Having dodged an unremitting stream of cars, I made a sharp turn to cross the interstate via a spanking new overpass. It was wide and impressive, adorned with modern lights and statuesque pillars, and was quite delightful to cross. The overpass dumped me on a quiet outer road that wound not along storefronts and chaotic parking lots, but an old earthen levee bordered on one side by soybean fields and on the other by cornfields, each of which seemed a bit more forgotten than the last. The outer road, for its part, seemed upstaged by its interstate brother, so grand and imposing and busy and important. It lay despondently in the shadow of its flashy sibling. Both roads landscaped the same low, monotonous river valley, but simply crossing the overpass seemed to transport me from one world to another. In contrast with its hectic brother, the outer road was almost serene, at least in a neglected, depressed, vapid sort of way.

As one might gather from descriptions such as *soybeans* and *cornfields*, the run was neither exciting nor remarkably pretty. In fact, there was nothing extraordinary about this route except that it was exceedingly average and random. But the existence of the average and random demanded I take notice of said objects. And once I noticed them, I thought about them. I'm not exactly sure why. Goodness knows I've noticed and forgotten more things than I'd like to admit. Perhaps it was boredom. Perhaps it was desperation for something—anything—to pass the time. Perhaps I was losing my mind. Marathon training does that to you.

Whatever the case, the one thing that comes with high mileage is a new perspective, a coerced observation and attentiveness to detail triggered by default. O. Stout's mailbox and wind chimes had become my friends because of it. I had engaged in countless staring contests with an incorrigible donkey because of it. And now I was going to discover the joys of an old utility road because of it.

The first half mile was as thrilling as a treadmill. The landscape changed so slowly as to make any difference in scenery imperceptible. However, the advantage of this phenomenon was the luxury of time—lots of time—to notice, observe, and contemplate my surroundings.

Deep in the cornfields was a dilapidated farmhouse. The roof was caving in on one side, and the windows had long since been separated from their glass panes. I imagined the farmhouse was once vibrant with life and color. Perhaps a family had lived there, and the children had run about the yard, squealing with delight while the mother tended the vegetable garden and the father plowed the field. I imagined that the windows, now barren and hollow, had once boasted flower boxes overflowing with red and orange and purple blooms, and the glass panes had been kept spotless by the mother, who wiped them down religiously, with pride. That was how I saw the farmhouse—not as it existed now, empty, vulnerable, and exposed.

Directly across the road from the barren farmhouse stood a spotless, newly constructed bank. The bank was fashioned entirely out of glass. The glass reflected the sunbeams with such intensity it hurt my eyes to look at the building. It was as though the bank were mocking the old, naked farmhouse. Looming in twenty-first-century glory, the bank gloated in its superiority.

"Look at me, old man," it seemed to say. "You want glass? I've turned away more glass than you've ever seen."

Both buildings were vacant. However, the bank's reason for lack of occupants was its newness, not its age. The two structures stood in stark opposition to each other, incongruous in their proximity. The bank continued to mock the farmhouse. But I had already fallen in love with the family that perhaps once occupied the farmhouse, and, appalled at the bank's conceited behavior, I turned my head and continued running.

At this point, the road began to lean away from the highway. With a gentle nod it rested its length against the cornfields, and a quiet ensued. Only the sound of crunching gravel beneath my feet broke the soft, incessant hum of distant cars. I passed a pool of water best described as an extraordinary puddle. The puddle-pond appeared to be stagnant and not worthy of further consideration. But to my surprise, two ducks fluttered down from the sky and plopped into the water. They quacked and swam and seemed content.

How strangely peaceful! I thought as I ran by the scene.

Suddenly a rude, percolating whir flanked the outer road. I looked up. Two traffic report helicopters were approaching and were on the verge of overtaking me and my duck companions. (The helicopters had followed the interstate, and had thus caught up to us rather quickly.)

"And traffic is backing up *all* the way from Olive Boulevard to the Daniel Boone Bridge," I could hear them say (at least, in my head). "It is gonna be *suh-low* going, folks, and it's only going to get worse as we head into rush hour."

"Quack!" one of the ducks responded.

"You said it," I replied.

The helicopters moved on in aeronautic superiority. But they had missed the puddle-pond, and my duck friends had missed the traffic. Advantage: ducks.

As I and my duck companions emerged from the shadow of the helicopters, it struck me that our experience might have been not unlike that of the moon's during an eclipse. I found this concept intriguing enough to occupy my mind for several minutes, and soon I, like the helicopters, had left the ducks behind me to frolic in the puddle-pond.

Slowly. Slowly. Slowly the landscape changed. To my left (the soybean side), there stood an elaborate Little League ballpark, modern and commercial with its sponsored outfield walls and towering, majestic lighting systems. To my right (the corn side) was a rusty, abandoned driving range, stumpy and dirty and needing a tetanus shot. The driving range seemed to reminisce of the good ol' days, when old men in plaid pants and tall socks came in droves on Sunday afternoons, lugging wooden drivers and iced tea.

"Yep," it called out to the young ballpark, "those were the days. No one sponsored our tee boxes, no sir. Don't let this rust fool you, son. Before you were even a gleam in a developer's eye, I was the big attraction."

"Talk to my agent," the Little League ballpark responded irreverently.

An old pebble path leading to nowhere. A new, shiny black bike path leading to, well, perhaps nowhere, as well. Clusters of wildflowers, flipping and flopping with each tiny breeze. An itinerant McDonald's Happy Meal bag, flipping and flopping down the road. A sudden gust of air as a car whooshed by at an unlawful speed. A returning, eerie quiet. Vestiges of the past mingled with fixtures of the present with seamless ease. I realized that time had run this route before me, and it had littered considerably along the way.

William Wordsworth spoke of the truths imparted from the common things around us. These truths, he said, are the harvest of the quiet eye. That is the gift of running. It gives us a quiet eye, a quiet eye to find truth in the everyday.

Therein lay the revelation of the abandoned outer road. Only when I ran the road did I see it for what it really was. Overshadowed? Yes. In poor condition? Certainly. Dreary? Probably. But without character? Most definitely not.

The past may sometimes be forgotten, but it is not gone. It manifests itself in the details of today's mundane, hiding as a treasure to be found for those who are willing to slow down enough to find it. The old outer road was just a page—a line, really—in the tome of history's memoirs. But for several beautiful, unassuming miles, I was privy to the book.

Chapter Five

Some activities nudge you out of your comfort zone. Others grab you by the seat of the pants and heave you up and over the edge of a cliff. I am always surprised how often life chooses to teach me lessons via the latter option. Granted, experience, which waits below for my prompt and violent arrival, usually proves worth the dive. Sometimes, though, it's just a wee bit scary on the way down.

Thus it was with mixed emotions I plummeted my way to the Webster Groves track. I was running my second-ever track workout, this time with both Mr. Speedy Pants and his old buddy Tim. It was like having the opportunity to flex my vocal prowess for Pavarotti, with the minor complication of having sung only once before. A bit of a thrill? Sure. Intimidating? Absolutely.

I arrived at the track and parked alongside Mr. Speedy Pants and a man whom I assumed to be his old buddy Tim. They were leaning against their cars, chatting and adjusting their wristwatches and taking sips of water and doing whatever it is runners do while waiting in a parking lot.

"Hey," Mr. Speedy Pants said as I got out of my car. He gave the man standing next to him a quick nod. "This is my old buddy Tim." He nodded at me. "This is the kid."

Mr. Speedy Pants's old buddy Tim, like Mr. Speedy Pants, was tall and lean and exceedingly speedy. He tipped his head by way of introduction.

"Hey," I responded. *Just be cool*, I told myself. *Cool.* "Thanks for letting me join you guys."

"Yep. Not a problem," Mr. Speedy Pants said.

Deeming further conversation unnecessary, he and his old buddy

Tim each grabbed a small duffel bag from his respective car and began walking toward the track.

Hmm . . . The return of the duffel bag, I thought. *Must be a cool-kid thing.* And I made a mental note to bring my own next time.

We made our way toward the concrete grandstand lining the far side of the football field and deposited our belongings on the second row of bleachers. As we jogged our warm-up around the track, I learned two important things. First, *jog* is a relative term. Second, a jog for Mr. Speedy Pants and his old buddy Tim was very near my race pace.

"So, the kid doesn't believe in warming up," Mr. Speedy Pants said during a conversational intermission.

"No warm-up, huh?" Mr. Speedy Pants's old buddy Tim replied. It was one of the most ridiculous things he had ever heard.

"Nope. Hey," Mr. Speedy Pants said, intercepting my reply and tossing a mischievous grin in return, "have you ever heard of Bob Dingy, the Olympic marathon champion?"

Mr. Speedy Pants's old buddy Tim had not. Mr. Speedy Pants related the story of the illustrious runner and his gold-medal ways. I was not amused.

"No . . . no. See," I defended myself, "I have only so many steps in me, and I don't want to waste them warming up."

Mr. Speedy Pants and his old buddy Tim exchanged one of those condescending looks that say, "Dear me. How pathetic. This person is an absolute dingbat." Yet, perhaps because I was still the new kid, they refrained from voicing their thoughts.

I followed the lead of Mr. Speedy Pants and his old buddy Tim as they made their way back to the bleachers. Mr. Speedy Pants grabbed a water bottle from his duffel bag.

"So, do you know what you're doing, kid?" he asked.

"Umm . . . 800s?" Of course I knew, but my response sounded more like a guess.

"You know how many?"

"Ten?" (A real guess.)

"Eight."

"Oh, yeah. Eight."

"You know what pace you're gonna run?"

"Uh-huh."

He looked at me skeptically, eyebrow raised. I looked at him, eyebrows raised, though for different reasons.

"No, I really do."

"Okay. Well, just don't do anything dumb like sprint the first four hundred and not have anything left for the second. If you don't do that, you'll be fine."

And on that positive note, our trio started the workout.

Mr. Speedy Pants and his old buddy Tim took off and soon put a considerable distance between themselves and my ungraceful figure. Eight hundred meters, however, was soon traversed. I crossed the start line and slowed to a walk, hands on my hips.

"How'd that feel?" Mr. Speedy Pants asked.

"Good," I gasped—or, to be accurate, lied—terrified he would ask what my time was. Of course, he did ask. I had run too fast. I knew it. Mr. Speedy Pants knew I knew it, too, but—sensing my guilt—he considered my self-inflicted shame punishment enough and brushed aside my pacing gaffe.

"Okay. Slow it up just a bit," he said as he and his old buddy Tim embarked on their second interval. I had a moment to rest before I had to go again. My timing improved on the next lap, though this time I was too slow.

"Don't worry about it," Mr. Speedy Pants reassured me. "It always takes a few laps to settle into the groove. Plus, this is your first time running 800s. Just relax and go on feel."

Interval by interval, we completed the workout. And as I ran, I felt cool. Cool because I was running intervals on a track. Cool because I was running intervals on a track with Mr. Speedy Pants and his old buddy Tim. Cool because they were the cool kids, and I was with them.

"Hey! Hurry up, kid! Stop dilly-dallying!" Mr. Speedy Pants yelled with feigned impatience as I began my final interval. He and his old buddy Tim had finished their workout and were waiting on me once more. I finally finished and made my way to the bleachers. Even though it was early in the evening, the sun was already starting to retreat behind the horizon, and it was taking its comforting warmth with it. The dark sealed in the cold air. I grabbed my water bottle. The cold had permeated the water, and I was forced to take tiny, icy sips.

"So, what did you think?" Mr. Speedy Pants asked.

What did I think? I thought I was completely in over my head, that's what I thought. I thought a few more of those workouts just might kill me. I relayed my feelings to Mr. Speedy Pants with a more positive spin.

"Good!"

"Good."

We grabbed our gear and tossed it in our cars before we made our way down the tree-lined roads of Webster. The jog of a cool-down, I learned, like that of a warm-up, is relative. I had to race to keep up with Mr. Speedy Pants and his old buddy Tim.

"So," Mr. Speedy Pants's old buddy Tim queried as we ran, "are you coaching her now?" He tipped his head in my direction as he spoke.

"Coach? Haha . . ." Mr. Speedy Pants was about to deny any authority regarding my training when he paused, looked in my direction, and said, "You know, kid, I did make a training schedule for you—which you are using. At least"—he poked me in the forehead—"to the best of your ability, anyway."

I shook my head. "Whatever."

"And I did basically coach you through your first track workout. And through this workout—"

He had a point.

"—and you do always come to me for advice when you have your freakout moments."

"I don't freak out!" I remonstrated. I turned to Mr. Speedy Pants's old buddy Tim. "It was a simple email with a few questions. Sheesh."

Mr. Speedy Pants smiled. "Really, if you define what coaching is . . ." He held out his hands. "I'm just sayin'."

"Yeah, yeah. Well, thanks, Coach."

"Ooo! Does that mean I get paid?"

"Sure. I'll send you an invisible check in the mail."

Mr. Speedy Pants pumped his fist in the air. "Score."

The last couple of miles were run in relative calm, I focusing on breathing and Mr. Speedy Pants and his old buddy Tim chatting away about getting lost in a snowstorm in Wisconsin during a long run (or something like that). Finally, we returned to the track's parking lot and prepared to leave.

"Good job on the workout today, kid," Mr. Speedy Pants said as I climbed into my car.

"Thanks."

"Next week?"

"Uh . . . sure!"

"Word."

I had consigned myself to join Mr. Speedy Pants and his old buddy Tim next week. A sense of misgiving mushroomed in the pit of my stomach.

Well, I reassured myself, *it can't be any worse than today. Plus, at least now I have some idea what it feels like to run 800s.*

It feels like jumping off a cliff.

Chapter Six

Snot. (Hold that thought.)

Somewhere, a head craftsman was admiring his latest work of art, a strange and unlikely friendship, forged in the bizarre furnace of distance running. And somewhere, that head craftsman was having a good laugh.

Marathoning, as it relates to friendships and the making thereof, is the sports equivalent of sitting next to a fellow passenger on an international flight. Carry-on secured in the overhead bins and under the seat, you settle into your home for the next eight to ten hours, looking desperately for your luggage on the tarmac below, speculating about the weird brown smudge discoloring the seat pocket in front of you, and secretly fearing that should a sudden change in air pressure occur, yours would be the one oxygen mask that doesn't drop from the panels above.

And yet you realize that despite the disconcerting nature of your reflections, the greatest source of anxiety stems from the anticipation of the arrival of your fellow passengers. More specifically, the passenger who will be sitting immediately next to you.

And then, he arrives. By the time he has stowed his carry-on (which he accomplishes only by beating the oversized bag into submission), you have assessed his character, gauged his future prospects, and evaluated his family genealogy tracing back to the time of Cyrus the Persian. The appraisal is not favorable.

The man finally takes his seat next to you, apologizing profusely for having had to climb across your lap and for jabbing an elbow into your ear. He introduces himself and asks your name. You respond accordingly. He reaches up and adjusts the small air vent to its highest setting, aiming the cold airflow directly into your right eye. In passive retaliation, you reach up and adjust your air vent to its highest setting, aiming the cold airflow directly into his left eye. And then the flight attendant announces that your seat cushion may be used as a flotation device. Awesome.

And yet—somehow—eight to ten hours later you have a new friend. Though at introduction you were reluctant to disclose your first name, you have now discussed everything from that other guy in Wham! to the dream you had last night, which involved a large pirate ship. You shake his hand as you part ways, apologizing profusely for having blown the contact lens out of his left eye.

Yes, the last person on earth with whom you thought you would be friends has become your buddy. It is strange. It is a wonder. But it is so. Because something happens when you are forced to spend a long time with one person in a mind-numbingly dull atmosphere. You bond.

"How you doin', kid? You're kinda quiet," Mr. Speedy Pants asked as we made our way through the infamous cornfields.

"Umm . . . eh . . . okay," I gasped. "I'm actually . . . really tired."

Mr. Speedy Pants glanced down at his watch. "Hmm. We started a bit fast and that first part was pretty hilly—which is why, I imagine, you're starting to drag."

"Yeah."

"Need a drink?"

He grabbed a bottle from the water belt he was wearing and held it out. In addition to coaching me, pacing me, and providing endless entertainment during long runs, Mr. Speedy Pants also served as a water caddy, chivalrously carrying our hydration provisions and reminding me to consume enough mid-run liquids.

I took several sips before returning the bottle. "Thanks, Coach."

Mr. Speedy Pants and I were the sole participants in the week's TMBG run, Big J having to bow out because of a sore throat. (He was duly vilified in a TMBG email.) I needed eighteen miles on the day, and we planned our route accordingly: a nice tour of Mystical Land and then into the cornfields for some pancake-flat miles. Apparently, a few horses had gone before us. Deep, U-shaped gouges in the muddy paths had since frozen over and threatened our well-being as we cut through the fields. A brisk wind swept across the fields, rustling the stubs of corn and sending a few stray pieces of brittle stalks to scuttle atop the mud. Every so often, ponytail sweat or an itinerant snowflake or whatever it was spritzed my face with tiny specks of moisture.

"So . . ." Mr. Speedy Pants said as I wiped my face with the back of my glove, "did I ever tell you about the time I almost died timing a race in Bear Creek?"

No, he hadn't.

"Well, every year on the Fourth of July, we time the Bear Creek 5K. I always drive down the day before the race and stay the night so I have time to mark the course in the morning. But, whatever. Anyway—" Here he paused to farmer's blow his nose. Gross, but true.

He continued his story about the Bear Creek 5K, the highlight of which involved the race-timing bus, no brakes, and an involuntary fifty-mile-an-hour, nonstop tour of the city of Bear Creek.

"Yikes," I said, after he had finished. "That's horrible."

Today was not a good day. I was tired and struggling.

"Eh, everything worked out," Mr. Speedy Pants said. "It was early, and there weren't a bunch of other cars on the road, so it was fine."

He spit and then indulged in another farmer's blow. (Again, gross, but in my short time running with Mr. Speedy Pants and Big J, I had become somewhat desensitized to these uncouth habits.)

"Uh-huh." I wiped my face.

We were quiet for a while, and only the sounds of my labored breathing and Mr. Speedy Pants's regular spitting and periodic freestyle nose blowing broke the crisp silence of the landscape. We had covered approximately fourteen of the eighteen miles, and I was officially pooped out. Feeling remiss in my duties as a lively running partner, I decided to be at least an enthusiastic audience. The stories were a welcome diversion from the fatigue.

"Hey, Coach," I ventured as I found myself unable to keep pace with Mr. Speedy Pants, "how 'bout another story?"

"Another story, huh?" Mr. Speedy Pants repeated, scratching his chin. "Okay. Well, this is really just a continuation of the first one. But the Bear Creek race has tried to take me out twice. The year after the whole no-brakes incident, the race-timing bus blew a tire on the highway. Some debris flew back and pinched the exhaust pipe shut. Big J actually made the trip to help me time the race that year. Anyway, we heard this giant explosion, and then smoke started pouring into the van. Haha . . . We were stuck on the side of the highway for hours."

He proceeded to relate how he had pulled the bus to the side of the interstate only to be berated by a cantankerous state trooper. The Bear Creek incidents launched a series of harrowing tales, many of them involving Mr. Speedy Pants's old buddy Tim. One story in particular—the one in which Mr. Speedy Pants and his old buddy Tim got lost in a snowstorm in Wisconsin—was his favorite. (I knew this because of the frequency with which he told it, each narration beginning with the inquiry, "Did I ever tell you about the time my old buddy Tim and I got lost in a snowstorm in Wisconsin?")

He even expanded his coterie of characters to include his buddy Fagan, who writes for the *Sporting News*. Mr. Speedy Pants was quite emphatic about Fagan's occupation, prefacing every story with the clarifying inquiry, "You remember my buddy Fagan, the one who writes for the *Sporting News*?" Fagan and Mr. Speedy Pants were roommates back in the day, until Fagan (who writes for the *Sporting News*) left for graduate school at the University of Missouri, at which point Mr. Speedy Pants's old buddy Tim replaced him at the residence in question. It was quite the triangle of friendship.

The stories passed the time. Mr. Speedy Pants continued his spitting, nose-blowing ways, and I continued listening and wiping my face. And Mr. Speedy Pants blew his nose. And I wiped my face. And he blew his nose. And I wiped my . . . face. Oh.

I don't know why it took me so long to make the correlation between Mr. Speedy Pants blowing his nose and the occasional spritz hitting my face, but approximately sixteen miles passed before I realized what it was. Snot.

"Oh . . . Oh, my gosh! Eww!" I screeched. "Oh, my gosh! It's snot! You've been blowing your nose on my face this whole run!"

I wiped my face with my glove yet again, but quickly realized that the glove had probably collected its fair share as well. I was appalled. Mr. Speedy Pants thought the whole episode was amusing.

"Haha . . . Sorry, kid," he said, looking back. "Must have been the wind . . ."

I pulled off my glove and felt my face with my bare hand. There was a foreign, crusty speckling.

Eww . . .

I took a deep breath. There was nothing to do but accept the situation, scrape what I could from my cheeks and nose, and keep running.

We finished the run in peace, I taking extra care to keep up with Mr. Speedy Pants or to run far enough behind him to prevent the wind from spackling my face with snot. It was strange, really. I felt surprisingly matter-of-fact about the whole ordeal—that is, after having recovered from my minor freakout. Perhaps the time I had spent running with Mr. Speedy Pants and Big J had chipped away at my sense of decorum and sanitation. Perhaps I was just too tired to care about the peripatetic nasal drippings. Or perhaps something had happened during those miserable eighteen miles that changed the status quo.

I realized I was no longer terrified of Mr. Speedy Pants. From the training schedule he made for me to the encouragement he gave as I ran my first track workout to the stories he told to carry me through a torturous long run, Mr. Speedy Pants had proved to be the opposite of terrifying. And instead of viewing him as a crotchety old Greek deity, I now saw him as a crotchety old Greek deity who also happened to be my friend. And coach. And running buddy.

Something happens when you find yourself in a less-than-favorable situation and choose to make the best of it. Mr. Speedy Pants had seen me at my pooped-out worst, and instead of throwing in the towel and considering the run a bust, he did something that seemed unfathomable at the time. He made it fun.

Yes, in the mind-numbingly dull backdrop of barren cornfields, we bonded. The snot just sealed the deal.

I think I actually overdressed, I thought as I unzipped the front of my pullover.

Just the day before, Mr. Speedy Pants and I had faced an onslaught of biting cold. I had snow in my hair. The ground was frozen. I spent ten minutes scraping the ice off the windshield of my car.

The next thing I knew, the air was warm, fragrant, and almost—dare I say it—spring-like. It was a fanciful change of attitude. After weeks of resistance, nature had finally decided to be accommodating. Even if it was only for a time.

I pulled off the gloves I was wearing. They were lightweight, but it was too warm for gloves at all. I tried to think of other articles of clothing I could discard and still comply with the prevailing standards of propriety. I didn't get very far.

Yep, I definitely overdressed.

I pictured Mr. Speedy Pants shaking his head at me, disapproving of my apparel selection and severely questioning my ability to perform the simplest of tasks.

"What do I always tell you," he would ask, eyebrows raised in expectation of the correct answer.

And I, boasting the undesirable trait of choking under pressure, would comb through six weeks' worth of Mr. Speedy Pants's advice floating through my brain, searching for the right response.

"Umm . . . Don't be dumb?"

"Well, true . . ." Mr. Speedy Pants would say, rolling his eyes, "but more specific. What do I always say about dressing to run?"

He would say dress as if it were twenty degrees warmer than it actually is, that's what he would say. But for some reason, that's not what I did. I showed him.

The warm front had taken me by surprise. I wasn't prepared for the drastic overnight transformation from arctic winds to a warm ocean breeze. Next stop, Palm Springs.

The Midwest's meteorological caprice is nothing new. It's our favorite thing to talk about. We love it, we loathe it, we freak out about it, we deal with it. Yet the sudden climate overhauls never cease to amaze me. The sky dumps a boatload of snow on us one day and then, hours later, repents of its actions. Cold. Hot. Boom. Done. And there we are, wearing Bermuda shorts and snow boots, hanging up our shovels so we can unfold the lawn chairs and sunbathe—relaxed, confused, wondering what just happened but delighted enough not to care.

I wiped a bead of sweat from my forehead and pushed up the sleeves of my shirt. The day was worth my discomfort. My poor legs had forgotten what sunlight looked like, and in their despondency had faded to a disturbing shade of white. I felt as though Frosty the Snowman had sprouted limbs and taken to the streets. My arms also pleaded for sunlight, but alas, they would have to wait. No matter. The sun was lovely. The air was lovely. The fresh, green breeze was lovely. I ran and soaked in every lovely minute. And as I ran, I thought of the past few weeks. Trapped in the dreary cold of yesterday, who would have thought the pleasant warmth of today was possible?

Ah.

A few days before, Mr. Speedy Pants and I had gone on a last-minute run. Amid our aimless chatter, I must have mentioned something—a brief something—to the effect that I admired fast runners, and saw So-and-So who was a fast runner, and wished I could be a fast runner like So-and-So, and highly doubted I could ever be as fast a runner as So-and-So. Blah. Blah. Blah. In my mind, I was being realistic. In Mr. Speedy Pants's mind, I was being dumb.

"Look, kid," he said, "in the big scheme of things, you're just starting out. You've never trained like this before. How do you know you can't be as fast as So-and-So?"

"I don't know. I mean, I'm just not that fast."

"How do you know?"

"She's got natural talent. I don't have that kind of talent. Everything I do in running is forced—like I'm going against my body's natural inclination."

Mr. Speedy Pants rolled his eyes. "Again, you haven't put in the time yet. Look, I'm not saying you're gonna make the Olympics. But you can't write yourself off just because you're not where you want to be right at this moment."

"Yeah, I know. But . . ."

"You have to put in the time. You have to put in the miles. It doesn't matter how fast or how slow you run now. We know you're not as fast as So-and-So now. But you have to learn to separate today's reality from tomorrow's potential."

Wow, I thought, repeating Mr. Speedy Pants's last bit of wisdom, *someone should really put that in a fortune cookie.*

Three days later, overdressed with beads of sweat pouring down my face, I found myself once more quoting Mr. Speedy Pants. *You have to learn to separate today's reality from tomorrow's potential.*

Somewhere between shooting for the stars and sitting on the couch, a line becomes blurred. Sure, we can dream the impossible dream. It's been deemed impossible; we have nothing to lose. If we fail, eh, it was expected. If we succeed, we're heroes. We see the unbeatable foe and the unreachable star and think, *Heck! Why not give it a shot?*

But what about those dreams that are fifty–fifty? Those goals that— if we pursue them for all we're worth—are quite possibly attainable? Those are the dreams that scare us. They scare us because they hold in their hands two options: failure and success. Each is of equal weight. Their penetrating eyes bore into our character and taunt us with superiority and skepticism. "There's a darn good chance you can do this," they say. "Then again, there's a darn good chance you can't. Are you willing to take a chance? Do you have what it takes?" It is not a question. It is a dare.

Enter the blurry line. Fear disguises itself as realism. Pride masquerades as humility. We look down and shuffle our feet and say, "Oh, no, we could never do *that.*" Because assuming a goal rests on an unattainable level is safer than trying and failing. Because by setting our standards high enough or low enough, we don't have to fear disappointment. Pride can withstand the easy. Pride can withstand the impossible. The middle ground is where pride is most threatened, because the middle ground is full of doable things that may or may not be within our realm of ability. Because sometimes it's harder shooting for the thing that is just short of impossible.

The snow continued to yield to the sun's persistence, and by the time I found my way back home, it was as though spring had firmly grasped the earth, squeezing out the last bits of winter in the process. I closed my eyes and lifted my face to the sky. My skin tingled from the warmth.

No, I wasn't as fast as So-and-So. But maybe one day I would be. Maybe not. Only time and trial would tell. In the meantime, I had some middle ground to conquer.

Chapter Seven

"So, kid, my old buddy Tim is officially on the DL," Mr. Speedy Pants said over the phone. "Turns out he's been running on a cracked femur."

"Holy cow." I paused in the process of filling my duffel bag (I had finally joined the club) and readjusted my phone against my face. "That's horrible."

"Yep. I don't know why it took so long for someone to figure out what was going on. It's been bothering him for"—he paused—"probably eight months now."

I was shocked. I knew Mr. Speedy Pants's old buddy Tim had been battling a leg injury for a while, but I had no idea it had been so severe. I couldn't imagine running on a broken leg.

"So, it looks like it's gonna be just you and me on the track from now on," Mr. Speedy Pants continued. "At least for a while, anyway."

I threw a sweatshirt and a hat into the duffel bag and zipped it closed.

"You know, now that I think about it," Mr. Speedy Pants continued, "it may not have been a coincidence that my old buddy Tim just happened to go on the DL after running a track workout with you."

"Uhh . . . ?"

"I mean"—Mr. Speedy Pants sounded somber—"he's been dealing with this thing for almost a year, and suddenly you come out to run with us, and boom! He has to stop running. Maybe . . ." He paused for dramatic effect.

I smiled despite the insult just hurled my way. "Maybe it's me? That is so dumb."

I could hear a laugh in Mr. Speedy Pants's voice. "I don't know, kid. I'm just sayin' . . ."

"Whatever, dude." I made my way to the kitchen and began filling a water bottle for the workout. "I'll see you in a bit."

A bit passed, and soon Mr. Speedy Pants and I were on the track, facing the wind that seemed to accompany us at every workout.

"So, do you remember what you're doing today?" Mr. Speedy Pants asked as we finished warming up and readied ourselves for the looming intervals.

"Yeah . . . 800s and then a two-mile," I responded.

Before each speedwork session, Mr. Speedy Pants would send an email detailing that particular week's workout. For some reason, I could always kind of remember the plan—but not completely. It was not intentional disregard. I simply found myself unable to recall the finer points of the workout, namely, the number of selected intervals and the pace at which I was to run said intervals. I think it was a form of denial.

"Uh-huh . . ." Mr. Speedy Pants replied in a dubious tone, "and how many 800s are you going to run?"

"Yeah . . . I don't remember." There was no point in denying it.

"Why does that not surprise me?"

"I don't know. Six?"

"Five."

"Okay. Five."

"And how long is your rest between the 800s and the two-mile?"

"One minute."

Mr. Speedy Pants rolled his eyes. "Two minutes, kid. But nice try."

"Oh, yeah. Two minutes."

Mr. Speedy Pants patted me on the back. "You're a piece of work."

We stepped up to the start line.

"Ready? Go!"

And at his announcement, we were off.

It was only my third time running a track workout, but I could sense the bulk of my beginner's nerves had worked themselves out in the previous quarters and 800s. Granted, the faithful couple Excitement and Dread still escorted me around the track, but the fear of death by interval training was beginning to subside, and that was nice. As a result of my newfound quasi-equanimity, my 800s were run without incident; that is, except for a small issue regarding a miscreant tarp at the far end of the football field.

A giant blue tarp—much like the heavy tarps used to cover baseball fields during rain delays—lay folded and formidable between the goalpost in the end zone and the final turn on the track. However, the wind (whose character I was by this time beginning to question) had harassed the tarp until the first two layers of canvas fell from their neat perch atop the pile and found their way onto the first two lanes of the track. Here the displaced slabs of tarp flapped and billowed, first bubbling up and then snapping back down.

Lanes one and two thus occupied, Mr. Speedy Pants and I were forced to circumvent the intruder by rounding the final turn of the track in lane three, which situation, while not ideal, was at least manageable. However, envy must have run rampant in the tarp community, for several other layers soon fell headlong onto the track. Now only lane five was available. And our two-mile interval was next in the batting order. Yeah. I don't think so.

"I kept waiting for the wind to blow the tarp off the track," Mr. Speedy Pants said as we caught our breath after the final 800, "but no such luck."

I looked at the tarp and nodded in concession.

Mr. Speedy Pants looked at his watch and then back at the delinquent tarp. "Hmm . . . If I had time to move it off the track, I would. But my rest is up in"—he looked at his watch again—"twenty-two seconds."

Mr. Speedy Pants contemplated the situation a moment more. "I bet I can grab the corner of the tarp right as I hit the curve," he said, pointing to the far end of the track, "and if I hurdle the bulk of it, fold it back over itself, and toss the rest on the field as I come out of the turn . . ." He nodded and smiled, impressed with his potential act of greatness. ". . . I bet I can do it without even breaking stride."

I laughed. "I don't know, Coach," I said, "that's a tall order."

"True. But . . ."

"You're awesome?"

Mr. Speedy Pants smiled triumphantly. "That's right."

He held up his hand for a high five, which I gave, and then started on his final interval. I looked at my watch. I still had eighteen seconds to catch my breath. I took one last swig of water and glanced at my watch. Mr. Speedy Pants was quickly approaching the two-hundred-meter mark, which meant his magnificent tarp-moving feat was only seconds away. I stepped on the start line, slapped my watch, and began. I wanted to make sure I had time to round the first turn—and gain a clear view of the action.

I had just hit the back two hundred when Mr. Speedy Pants swooped toward the menacing tarp. Running full stride, he reached down and grabbed a corner of the tarp. Then came his moment of glory. Pulling the corner behind him, he leaped across the bulk of the tarp's wandering form just as it ballooned up with the wind. Landing clear of the sea of canvas and still firmly grasping the corner of the tarp, he rounded the turn and threw the subdued tarp back on the field, effectively clearing the track. All this he did without breaking stride. Just as he had predicted.

I laughed as he raised his arms in victory and turned his head to look at me.

"Nicely done, Coach!" I yelled from across the football field. And then I rounded the final turn in lane one, which, thanks to Mr. Speedy Pants, was now clear for the passing.

We joked about the incident as we ran our cool-down.

"How about that?" Mr. Speedy Pants said, raising an eyebrow with the question.

"Pretty impressive, Coach."

"Well, I am awesome."

I rolled my eyes. "I know, I know . . ." I said. "Maybe you're a born hurdler, and you just didn't know it."

"Nah, I'm not made for hurdles," Mr. Speedy Pants said. "I could manage one, but then I'd crash headlong into the second. Now," he continued, "if they had a one-hurdle race, we'd be in business."

"Ha! The infamous one-hurdle race," I laughed. "Everyone would be like, 'Did you see how he hurdled that hurdle?' Actually," I said, contemplating the prospect, "that totally sounds like a story." I lowered my voice for the narration. "'This is the story of Howie—'"

"As in Howie 'bout that?" Mr. Speedy Pants interjected.

"Haha . . . Awesome. 'This is the story of Howie Bout-That, the infamous one-hurdle hurdler. No one could hurdle a hurdle like Howie hurdled a hurdle. Until one day, when Howie tragically attempted to tackle a second hurdle . . .'"

Mr. Speedy Pants picked up the pseudo-voice-over. "'. . . and crashed, injuring his pinkie toe in the process. Overcome with disappointment from his devastating defeat, Howie would never hurdle again, and he has since disappeared into obscurity.'"

"Oh, my gosh!" I laughed. "That is such a sad story."

"Howie was overconfident in his ability," Mr. Speedy Pants philosophized. "And look where it got him."

"True, true," I said, shaking my head.

We made our way across an overpass that began with a steep flight of stairs. The first two steps I managed with ease. The third and fourth, however, were more difficult. It was a strange feeling—like running on pavement and then hitting a patch of quicksand. The concrete steps seemed to swallow my quads, and instead of progressing up the stairs I seemed to sink into them. My pace slowed. And slowed. And. Slowed.

"Hey, kid! What are you doing back there?" Mr. Speedy Pants called from atop the stairs.

"I'm—*huff*—coming—" I managed to gasp.

Finally, I lurched my way over the last step.

"Sheesh!" I panted after struggling to catch Mr. Speedy Pants on the overpass. He had waited for me by slowing his pace to something between a jog and a shuffle. "I thought this was supposed to be a cool-down!"

"It is. Dude, we're running slow."

I looked at my watch. Ouch. We were running slow. The workout had not been kind to my legs.

"No worries, though," Mr. Speedy Pants continued.

"Yeah," I huffed.

"So stop your crabbin'."

"Whatever."

And, the tarp having been defeated, the stairs having been conquered, and Howie Bout-That having been eulogized, we completed our run and parted ways.

That was actually pretty impressive, I thought as I leaped over a concrete curb and onto the sidewalk. It couldn't have been easy hurdling—and moving—the tarp without breaking stride. Yet Mr. Speedy Pants had managed to do so without losing pace or slowing down. This was fitting, since I was quickly coming under the impression that Mr. Speedy Pants's primary aim in life was to do as much as humanly possible without breaking stride. This, I supposed, was probably not a bad philosophy to hold.

The TMBG had returned to Forest Park for my long run that week, a no-pressure twenty-miler to be run at a comfortable pace—*comfortable* being a relative term, of course, due to a stubborn cold front that had blustered through the city overnight. A capricious weather system had teased the recent snowfall with alternating warm and cold days, bullying the snow into ugly patches that littered the ground. They pleaded to be put out of their misery.

Also existing in patches was our Thursday-morning trio, which found itself one member short yet again, though this time the shortage was only temporary. Mr. Speedy Pants had been battling an apoplectic Achilles tendon that recently developed a penchant for inflammation. Mr. Speedy Pants would be running only twelve of the twenty miles on the day, leaving Big J and me to run the first eight miles of the journey on our own.

"Hey, look," Big J said, pointing toward a patch of soggy grass separating the sidewalk from the street. "It's a Yaktrax. Just one, though."

Big J and I had taken a small detour from the running path at Forest Park, and we soon found ourselves running down the city streets, streets usually busy with traffic but now quiet in the early-morning hours. I looked to where he was pointing. The item in question was indeed a "Yaktrax"—otherwise known as a runner's snow cleat—identical to the pair I had been forced to use one too many times this winter. And, as Big J had observed, there was only one.

"Hmm . . . How could someone lose one Yaktrax?" I asked. "I mean, those things are strapped to your shoes like nobody's business."

"Maybe it snapped," Big J suggested.

"Yeah, but why would you just leave it there? There is no way you wouldn't feel that thing come off your shoe."

"Maybe he didn't need it."

"Of course he needed it. If you need one Yaktrax, you need two."

"Not if he had only one leg."

Big J then made the argument that somewhere in the city was a one-legged runner who felt the need to rid himself of the burden of a second Yaktrax, or of a two-legged runner who considered traction on both feet something of a luxury. This spurred ridiculous speculation regarding the probable history of the one Yaktrax. The topic carried us back to Forest Park and even back to the visitor center, where I made a brief stop to use the ever-welcome bathroom facilities. When I rejoined Big J, I saw Mr. Speedy Pants had arrived. I was accused of dilly-dallying, and then the three of us started off on the final two loops of the park.

"So, we think that's what happened with the abandoned Yaktrax," Big J said as he finished relating the incident to Mr. Speedy Pants.

"The one-legged Yaktrax guy, huh?" Mr. Speedy Pants said, somewhat incredulous. "I don't know about you two. I let go of the reins for one hour . . ." He paused. "Actually, you know what that reminds me of? Stevie Bout-That, the illustrious one-hurdle hurdler."

I laughed. He was right. "Oh, my gosh. It does! It's totally—wait. Who?" I looked at Mr. Speedy Pants, eyebrows raised.

"Stevie Bout-That, the one-hurdle hurdler. You know—from the track workout the other day?"

Mr. Speedy Pants was about to relate to Big J his feat of awesomeness, but I interrupted. "You mean Howie?" I smiled.

Mr. Speedy Pants stopped his narration, paused for a moment of thought, and then grinned. "Yes. I mean Howie."

"Haha . . . Stevie! Stevie? Stevie Bout-That doesn't make any sense! It ruins the whole point of the name."

"Yeah, yeah. I know, kid. I knew Stevie didn't sound right . . ."

"Uh-huh."

"Watch it," he said, "or you might end up in one of those giant snow piles over there."

I am glad to report that I did not end up in one of those giant snow piles over there, but finished the run and made it to Courtesy Diner without further incident. The subject of Stevie Bout-That briefly resurfaced, along with the hypothesis that Stevie was Howie's brother and was simply continuing the family's history of singular athletic feats.

The smell of fried eggs and bacon accompanied us to our booth as we took our seats at Courtesy Diner. The vestiges of that morning's twenty-miler lingered as well, socializing in the form of red cheeks and stiff legs.

I looked at my two running buddies. Mr. Speedy Pants was consuming a giant stack of hash browns with such efficiency, I found myself marveling as his fork traveled from plate to mouth and back again, carrying an incredible load with each upswing. Big J, for his part, continued to add cream to his coffee until he had built a tower of tiny plastic creamer cups that leaned precariously toward his own plate of grits. I took a deep breath of the steam rising from my coffee and savored the aroma of an old-fashioned breakfast, the company of friends, the satisfaction of a long run completed, and the quiet, blissful contentment of hard-earned fatigue.

"There!" Big J said, sliding a paper napkin toward my bowl of oatmeal. "A pig."

I looked at the napkin. Apparently, Big J and Mr. Speedy Pants had challenged each other to a drawing competition. The contest focused on the ability to depict farm animals.

"Not bad," I said, grabbing the pen from Big J's hand and beginning my own artwork submission. "A pig—made entirely out of circles," I said on completing my drawing. The classic "pig made of circles" trick was one I had learned in the first grade. Little did I know then that it would mark the apex of my artistic career.

Mr. Speedy Pants was next. He wrinkled his face disapprovingly as he spun the napkin around for us to see.

"Uh, yeah," he said, amused by his own drawing, "that didn't exactly turn out like I thought it would."

I laughed as I looked at the napkin. What had "turned out" was a creature that looked something like a cross between a pig and an armadillo.

"Haha . . . What in the world is that?" I said.

Mr. Speedy Pants shook his head and held his hands in the air. "I don't know. It looks like a . . ."

". . . like a pig and an armadillo," I finished.

Mr. Speedy Pants tuned the napkin to look at it one more time. "You're right. It does," he said.

"It's a porkadillo," I laughed.

"Ah! That," Big J exclaimed, "should definitely be the TMBG mascot."

"Agreed," Mr. Speedy Pants said.

The porkadillo was thus deemed the official mascot of the TMBG, the distinction of which was not lost on any of the group's members. The porkadillo also reinforced my conclusion that the sport of running is an incubator, of sorts, for the bizarre. Our most recent training adventures, most notably that particular adventure involving the illustrious one-hurdle hurdler, Howie Bout-That, had served as tangible confirmation that distance running is a carefully constructed environment designed to extract the strangest thoughts from your brain and send them to your mouth, thoughts you would never, in any other situation, consider uttering into the universe. Squeezing your mental reserves like a near-empty tube of toothpaste, marathon training brings forth notions and musings not meant for the light of day. Bob Dingy, Howie and Stevie Bout-That, and even the porkadillo had become real and living characters in our lives. And our acceptance of their existence didn't even faze us.

And why should it have? Mr. Rogers had the Neighborhood of Make-Believe. Alice had her Wonderland. Gulliver had Lilliput. And Mr. Speedy Pants, Big J, and I had Forest Park.

There is something to be said for the fantastic. It represents a peculiar unaffectedness, a certain level of trust that must be obtained and developed before people feel comfortable enough to flout social mores and indulge in uninhibited expression of personality. In ordinary circumstances—those circumstances that make up the everyday—it is a slow maturation process that grows this trust, a fermentation akin to the aging of fine wine. It takes time and patience and sometimes the cold, dark cellar of a shared trial. But in running, the process is accelerated. It is quick. Sudden, almost. Distance is a curious equalizer. Wily but direct, the miles establish a bond that leaves no room for pretentiousness or formality or even etiquette. There is no room for artificiality. There is no room for contrived personality. There is no need. The whimsical milieu of marathon training is a respite from the harsh world of reality.

Out on the roads, fatigued yet exhilarated, sweaty but content, glad in the company of friends who have seen us at our best and our worst, we are lighter for having shed our reservations and self-consciousness. We laugh. We cry. We confess. We hope. We fear. We conquer. We touch on the divine and the ridiculous.

Because, when we are running, there is no one there to tell us not to. Because, when we are running, we find a freer version of ourselves. Because, quite simply, when we are running, we can.

Something had happened in the two months that Mr. Speedy Pants, Big J, and I had been running together. Yes, casual acquaintances had turned into friends. Yes, I had found a coach in Mr. Speedy Pants. Yes, our trio had formed the infamous Thursday Morning Breakfast Group. But something more had taken place, something deeper. In the uninhibited, natural candor of the miles, we had become something rare in a world of affected graces. We had become running buddies.

SPRING

Chapter Eight

My focus was clearer now. I had crested the halfway point of my GO! St. Louis Marathon training program, and upon reaching the summit, experienced a brief moment of clarity before tumbling down the other side of the mountain, modest though the incline may have been.

The apparition that materialized in the mist and made such an impression on my mind was that of myself at the present moment. Objectivity is a rare quality in the survey of ourselves, but I was granted a brief respite from critical evaluation. I saw to my delight that I was improving. This was encouraging. There, before my unsuspecting eyes, was Progress, bashful yet undeniably there. And I was fueled by its existence.

The occasion at which Progress first made an appearance was a sixteen-mile long run on another TMBG favorite route, Grant's Trail. Though the name suggests otherwise, Grant's Trail is actually a paved path that shoots its way behind a string of industrial parks and across several major intersections. Offsetting the industrial flavor of the trail, however, is Grant's Farm, the establishment for which the running path is named. Grant's Farm holds the singular distinctions of having belonged to the eighteenth president of the United States, the honorable Ulysses S. Grant, and of being home to the Budweiser Clydesdales. (It seemed the Budweiser Clydesdales were ever-present overseers of my training.) In addition to the Clydesdales, Grant's Farm also boasts other conventional farm animals, such as goats and cattle, and more extravagant creatures, including zebras and camels. Though only the horses can be seen from the path, it is somewhat exotic to run by the farm and know that just beyond the tree line and wooden fences are elephants.

The allure of the trail, however (at least for runners), is in its being flat and straight. It is like a giant, broken conveyor belt. This conveyor-belt quality was especially attractive to me that day, for my training plan called for an aggressive long run, and I wasn't particularly fond of the idea of hills.

The beginning of the run was unexceptional. We crossed a bridge spanning the interstate, successfully navigated several congested intersections, and passed a series of fourteen numeric markers, the purpose of which was unknown to us, and remains so to this day. The markers in question were a succession of small, low rectangular signs, brown in color and put in place by (according to the signature at the bottom of each sign) the city of Crestwood. Each sign bore only a number—one through fourteen, respectively—and the helpful though repetitive declaration of the city's name, presumably for the aid of absentminded trail users who may have forgotten where they were in the short distance separating one sign from the next. And the distance between the signs is worth noting, if only because the intervals were erratic and without any perceivable organization. Try as we might, Mr. Speedy Pants, Big J, and I could not figure out the system of measurement. Thus, the signs were deemed a mystery, and Mr. Speedy Pants palliated our confusion by yelling at the top of his lungs each number as we ran by, much to the alarm of nearby pedestrians.

"How you feeling, kid?" Mr. Speedy Pants asked after we had pocketed a dozen or so miles.

Mr. Speedy Pants and Big J had the enterprising habit of accelerating with distance. This proved especially profitable for me, for, as Mr. Speedy Pants explained, speeding up as the miles progressed was teaching my body to run fast on tired legs.

"Good," I replied with a tone of surprise.

I knew our pace had increased, yet I felt unexpectedly composed and had not yet begun the death march, the state in which I had become accustomed to finishing my long runs. Something, I surmised, was amiss. I feared a collapse was impending.

However, a few minutes passed and no collapse took place. I was further distracted from discomfiting suspicions by the parley and banter of my two running companions. We had just passed the entrance to Clydesdale Park—an adventure of a detour complete with a fitness trail—when Big J informed us that a stop would be necessary at the next Porta-John. We came upon a small rest area along the trail, a Porta-John was located, and Big J disappeared within.

I am ashamed to admit that Mr. Speedy Pants and I occupied ourselves during the time Big J was in the Porta-John by throwing small rocks at the edifice, much to the agitation of Big J. He emerged from the Porta-John with several colorful phrases and animated gestures. Mr. Speedy Pants laughed. I laughed. And then I apologized. Mr. Speedy Pants did not apologize. And we continued running.

It was at this point that Progress tiptoed to the back door and poked his amiable head across the threshold, though I didn't recognize his good-natured features until after we had finished the run. With two miles to go, I could tell we were running fast (for me, anyway). My breath was becoming shorter, and my legs started to burn not from the duration of the workout but from the quick turnover speed.

"Keep going, girl," Big J said, giving me a push in the back.

Mr. Speedy Pants had pulled a few yards ahead of us, and for the first time I found myself struggling to keep up.

"Push through it," Big J continued. "Don't slow down. C'mon." He jerked his head toward Mr. Speedy Pants as if willing me ahead. "Stay hip-to-hip, and you won't slow down."

Mr. Speedy Pants turned his head to look back at me. "This is when you gotta just grind your teeth and tough it out, kid." He looked at his watch. "Almost done."

I didn't respond. The death march had settled in.

We once more greeted the fourteen mysterious signs (for the signs are all located within a mile and a half of our starting location), and Mr. Speedy Pants yelled the numbers accordingly, though this time, of course, the succession was a countdown. Finally, we crossed the narrow concrete bridge spanning the interstate. The bridge dumped us into the parking lot.

"Good job, kid," Mr. Speedy Pants said, patting me on the back as we caught our breath. "We were rockin' those last few miles."

"Oh, yeah?" I said. I locked my fingers behind my head, face stretched upward as I tried to catch my breath.

"Yep."

Mr. Speedy Pants looked at his watch and read off the mile splits. It was the fastest time I had ever run that distance. In fact, it was my fastest time for any run over ten miles.

"What's your half-marathon PR? This beats it, doesn't it?" Mr. Speedy Pants asked.

It did.

Big J smiled. "Congrats! You PR'ed a half marathon during a sixteen-mile training run." He tilted up his chin and raised his eyebrows. "It's always a good day when you PR."

It had been a good day, and not just by the mile splits on Mr. Speedy Pants's watch. It seemed the majority of my running—daily runs, long runs, track workouts—was done despite fatigue and the distracting suspicion that I was following a training program one level too advanced for me. *A better runner wouldn't be so tired today*, I would think to myself. *A better runner would be able to knock off these intervals with ease.* I would become inferior in my own mind—inferior to the distance, inferior to the pace, inferior to the scores of other runners who, I imagined, improved with every strike of the pavement; who, I imagined, became fitter and stronger with each mile and never found their legs weary. *This can't be how I'm supposed to feel*, I would tell myself. I would begin to wonder if I were eating enough or sleeping enough or running too much or doing anything in excess or with unwise stringency that would sabotage my training program. Discouraged and spent from the sluggish drag of the miles, I would come to the conclusion that I was just not good enough, that instead of improving I was merely breaking down a body not able to withstand the training.

And then Progress arrived. He came quietly, hat in hand, blushing from the attention he knew was about to be cast upon him, humble and meek but nevertheless real and viable. Upon being recognized, he merely tipped his head in deference, uttered a "Good day!" and slipped away as stealthily as he came.

But his fugitive visit was enough. It served its purpose. I saw him and was encouraged, for he was the glorious evidence of miles of exertion and months of discipline. I saw him and knew my goal was not to be abandoned. His existence substantiated my endeavors and reestablished in my mind that which I was beginning to doubt.

I was, indeed, improving.

Victor Hugo spoke of the effects of darkness and light on the human soul. To be cut off from the day, he said, is to know a shrinking of the heart. Mankind needs light, for where the eye sees darkness, the spirit sees dismay.

A glimpse of Progress, then, is vital to perseverance. It reveals to us a sliver of the glory to come, that we may be driven to press onward, fortified by the vision, until we have reached our goal. We see the light, and in a single moment abstract ambition transforms into an unshakable expectancy. What was once merely hoped for is suddenly visible and tangible and real. We become witnesses of the future. We have seen the outcome of our faith. We have seen, in essence, the successful application of hope.

I looked at Big J and laughed in the unexpected pleasure of renewed incentive and the faintest touch of naive admiration, small and innocent though it was.

"Yeah," I smiled, "that is kinda cool."

Two weeks passed, and Grant's Trail was the site of another long run of note. The TMBG discovered itself to be but a coterie of stragglers, and I was the only one able to run the twenty miles. Big J, for sundry reasons, could not participate in the run portion of the TMBG, but he was going to meet up with us for breakfast. Mr. Speedy Pants, for his part, accompanied me for the whole twenty miles, though he did not actually run, due to continuing tensions between himself and his mutinous Achilles tendon. He was forced to engage the services of a bike for the entire out-and-back course.

To add variety to our routine, we decided to begin our run from Mr. Speedy Pants's house and make our way to Grant's Trail via the charming streets of Webster Groves. Charming, despite an endless succession of hills. I began to feel this state of affairs acutely.

"Sheesh. These hills are a tough way to start off a run, aren't they," I said as I lowered my head and plowed my way up yet another monster of an incline.

"Eh, it always takes you a while to get your legs going," Mr. Speedy Pants replied from his perch atop his mountain bike. "Which," he said, his tone reverting to one of condescending wisdom, "is why you, of all people, need to warm up before workouts and races." Mr. Speedy Pants never let pass an opportunity to impart his sagacious advice or to remind me of moments when I had, as he so kindly phrased it, "been dumb."

"Ah . . ." I half laughed and half gasped, "yes, well, good ol' Bob Dingy didn't need to warm up."

"True. But good ol' Bob Dingy is a lot faster than you. You need all the help you can get."

We continued down the broken sidewalk, I running parallel with the bike when I could and dropping back when obstacles—such as utility poles—made running and biking side by side impossible, or at least hazardous. The utility poles are worth noting because of their obtrusive placement in flagrant disregard of sidewalk etiquette. Thus, every sixty or seventy yards, the sidewalk would narrow by nearly half its width to make room for the intrusion, as if holding in its belly to allow a fellow city amenity to pass.

Through Webster we ran. Stately brick homes and quaint white picket fences lined streets with such literary names as Lockwood and Glendale and Rosebury and Edgar. The homes cascaded with the rise and fall of the land, each one greeting us with its own personality as we passed. The familiar welcome of gardens pluming with buttercups and daisies merged easily into the ceremonious reception of rosebushes, regal and refined and conscious of their elite position in the botanical hierarchy. Wooden rocking chairs socialized in pairs, adorning narrow covered porches. Porcelain statues and earthen pots rested contentedly on wide, painted steps. To call the scene quaint would be to commit a great injustice. In the soft budding light of dawn, the streets glistened with a serenity that transcended pure aesthetics.

We soon came to Grant's Trail, and though I had enjoyed the charm of the route that delivered us to the trailhead, I was grateful to climb the last of the hills and engage the luxury of conveyor-belt terrain. And if the miles behind us had been tranquil and picturesque, the miles that lay ahead would be anything but.

The first indication that things were about to take a turn—if not for the worse then at least for the adventurous—came with an intense aroma that swamped the path somewhere between the eighth and ninth mysterious city of Crestwood sign.

"Do you smell that?" I asked, debating whether to cover my nose or take another whiff of air to ascertain the identity of the smell.

Mr. Speedy Pants did smell that.

"It smells like"—I sniffed again—"it smells like permanent markers. Like a Sharpie or something."

"You're right. It does," Mr. Speedy Pants agreed.

Since holding my breath was not a practical option at this point in my run, I had to start breathing again. "No . . . I take it back. It doesn't smell like a Sharpie. It smells like a Marks-A-Lot marker. There is totally a difference."

Mr. Speedy Pants tilted his head as he analyzed the findings of his last breath. "Good call," he said (I think he was impressed with my olfactory skills). "Perhaps there's a Marks-A-Lot factory nearby."

We were running behind the long stretch of industrial park buildings and figured that there very well could be a Marks-A-Lot factory in the area. We also concluded that the factory must have suffered the misfortune of a recent explosion. Having thus explained away the mysterious smell, we continued onward.

Our sense of smell was tried again, however, within the next two miles. As usual, the Clydesdales out to pasture at Grant's Farm carried with them the familiar stench of dirt and manure. On this day, however, there emanated from the general direction of the horses a very peculiar aroma. More specifically, there emanated from the Clydesdales—in addition to the smell of dirt and manure—the distinct aroma of a bean-and-cheese burrito. And not a very fresh one at that. I observed that the horses must have gone out for Mexican food the night before, and I then proceeded to gasp and gag and cover my mouth in an attempt not to vomit. Mr. Speedy Pants acknowledged the strange fetor, though he argued that the smell was not that bad and subsequently ordered me to stop whining. I made a threat involving a large stick and its unfortunate placement in the spokes of his bike wheel, whereupon he acted shocked at my violent ways and counterthreatened to throw me into a nearby creek. Such pleasantries occupied our conversation as we approached our turnaround point, which happened to be located near the entrance to Clydesdale Park and Fitness Trail.

"Hmm . . ." Mr. Speedy Pants said as he attempted to turn his bike around without steering off the narrow path, a feat that demanded a precariously sharp angle. "We should—whoop!—we should check out the fitness trail sometime. Make it an exploration run. I think I've run through there before—it adds about a mile or so. Maybe just over. I can't remember."

"Yeah . . ."

I had become less talkative since we had completed the "out" portion of the course. The trail marker and set of benches designating our turn-around also marked the point at which my stomach began churning. I thought perhaps this situation was prompted by the miasmatic air that had plagued the first portion of the run and hoped the feeling would pass (no pun intended), as such feelings often do. As we continued running, however, I realized my discomfort was only intensifying.

"Ugh," I said, my pace slowing a bit, "I have to go to the bathroom."

"Why didn't you use the Porta-John a mile back," Mr. Speedy Pants asked, adding with a smile, "You know, the one that we threw rocks at?"

"'Cuz I didn't have to go that bad then. But now . . ."

But now? But now I had to go. Bad.

"Agh . . . Kid, what are we gonna do with you?" Mr. Speedy Pants rolled his eyes. "Okay, well, do you want to turn around?"

"Uh . . . no. I think I can make it to the next bathroom. I think. Where is the next bathroom?"

Grant's Trail has the luxury of two separate official trail bathrooms. They are clean, ecofriendly, single-person cabin-bathrooms that are convenient and, because of in-house pump sinks, delightfully sanitary. The problem with the bathrooms, however, is their location within one mile of the beginning of the trail, the planning and selection of which location is perplexing. Thus, the cabin-bathrooms were of no help on this particular occasion.

Mr. Speedy Pants pulled on the brakes to coast alongside me. "There are Porta-Johns by the baseball fields just a little way ahead."

"Okay. Yeah, I think I can make it to the ball fields."

89

By the time we reached the Little League ballpark, my gastrointestinal security was at DEFCON 1. I was in an official state of emergency. The metal fences leering over the dirt infields loomed in sight, and I knew just beyond their shadows was portable relief.

"Oh, man . . ." I groaned.

My pace continued to slow as I lurched forward in agony. *Just a few more steps*, I told myself, *and then . . .*

And then bubkes. There, just ahead of us, not more than one hundred yards away, was the first Porta-John, prostrate and helpless, a victim of a tipper.

"Agh!" I exclaimed in agony.

"Ooo . . . Bummer, kid," Mr. Speedy Pants said. "Don't worry, there's another one up by the next set of fields."

"Ugh . . ." I groaned yet again.

I shuffled my way to the next beacon of hope, lamenting the fate of the first Porta-John. And then we saw it. Parallel to the ground, worse than useless, Victim Number Two. I was running in the wake of a serial tipper.

Mr. Speedy Pants scratched his head and turned toward me with sympathetic uncertainty in his voice. "I'm a little worried about the next Porta-John, kid," he said. "How you holdin' up?"

"Okay . . ."

I was, in fact, panicking. I had to *go-go* to the bathroom, and there wasn't a bathroom facility in sight, nor was there hope of one for another couple of miles. The serial tipper had extinguished all prospect of relief, and I could see no way out of a disastrous situation. What if I couldn't find some kind of toilet in the next few minutes? What if there was nothing I could do? What if I could no longer stave off impending catastrophe? What if . . . if . . .

No! It was too horrific. *There has to be something!* I thought in desperation. *There has to be some way . . .*

What happened next is something of a blur.

We continued running, past the ball fields and the victimized Porta-Johns, past the wooded backdrop of apartment complexes and low spatterings of business parks, which weren't really parks at all, but cubic communities of concrete and smokestacks. We had just crossed over the creek into which Mr. Speedy Pants had threatened to throw me when the familiar yet unsettling stench of a giant bean-and-cheese manure burrito returned, wafting across the pavement. The smell did not reinforce my intestinal fortitude. It did, however, herald our proximity to Grant's Farm.

"What time is it?" I asked Mr. Speedy Pants.

"Six forty-five."

I knew the center wouldn't be open yet. I knew it wouldn't be open for another two hours at least. But I was desperate, and I grasped at even the scraggliest straw of relief.

"What time do you think the information center opens?" I asked.

"Not six forty-five in the morning, I can tell you that," Mr. Speedy Pants answered.

I began wishing one or two singular—though not life-threatening—afflictions upon the tipper who had rendered the Porta-Johns useless. I was fantasizing about spiking the offender's drink with a month's supply of Ex-Lax when I heard a car approaching from the main road running parallel with the trail. I held my breath as the car rolled through the main entrance to Grant's Farm, crossed over the trail just in front of us, and pulled into the parking lot of the information center. I did not need further invitation.

"Oh! Oh! Look!" I exclaimed. "He has to be going in! I bet he'll let me use the bathroom . . ."

I flung my body down the trail and into the parking lot of the information center. I could see the man grab a briefcase from the front seat, lock the car door, and make his way to the main entrance. The man was wearing a suit, and his hurried stride indicated that he was running late (perhaps for a meeting regarding the strange burrito smell emanating from the Clydesdales). By the time I reached the sidewalk leading to the building's entrance, the man was locking the glass doors, separating me from deliverance.

"Wait! Excuse me! Sir! Sirrrr!" I yelled as I ran toward the doors.

The man looked up and stopped, keys in hand, uncertain whether to heed the pleas of a corybantic stranger or call the police. If he had chosen the latter, I wouldn't have blamed him. My appearance was that of a sweaty, deranged Fury of old, and for I all knew the man in the suit may have suspected me of tipping over the Porta-Johns. Thankfully, his concern for mankind overcame his fear of my appearance. After a moment's hesitation, he gave me entrance to the building, pointed me to the bathroom, and retreated, briefcase in hand, down a flight of mahogany stairs, presumably to the meeting for which he was by now quite late.

Several minutes later, I emerged from the information center. Mr. Speedy Pants was waiting a few yards from the entrance, sitting on his bike, feet planted firmly on the sidewalk, arms folded across his chest. I took a deep breath of the cool morning air—the first deep breath I had taken since the turnaround point—and smiled. He just shook his head at me, a wry, amused expression on his face.

"Feel better?"

"Much."

"Good. Then stop dilly-dallying and get goin'. Sheesh. You took forever."

"Whatever. I so did not."

We chalked off the final miles of Grant's Trail, I much fleeter and happier for having flagged down the man in the suit. Really, the convergence of Mr. Speedy Pants, me, and the man in the suit at the information center's parking lot required providential timing. Twenty miles of running and a fortuitous few seconds. What were the odds? Had we been planets or warring nations or volatile organic compounds, a cataclysmic upheaval would have unfolded. As it was, we were merely a man in a suit, a man on a bike, and a girl desperately fending off the collapse of propriety.

We made our way back to the rolling sidewalks of Webster, I saluting the two cabin-bathrooms before we abandoned Grant's Trail. And other than a minor incident involving one of the obtrusive utility poles and an inopportune time to turn my head, the rest of the run was uneventful. Much to the relief (again, no pun intended) of everyone involved.

Chapter Nine

And this also has been one of the darkest places on earth . . .

The day was coming to a close. The dusk had chased and bullied the sun beyond the horizon, stomping down the last resistant rays until the lid of the night sky could be dropped and fastened. No maverick strands of light escaped the coffer or grasped at the night air with desperate flashes of life. The night had ascended with a complete and sudden overthrow of day.

And the sea and sky were welded together without a joint . . .

I said this as I stretched my arms and stared into the nothingness about me. I pictured myself on the low deck of the old cruising yawl from *Heart of Darkness*, silent figures, shadows of men, lounging about me in the stern of the ship, the soundless Thames carrying us farther and farther away from the glitter of London.

Hmm . . . Is it a bad sign that I'm quoting a weathered old seaman? I wondered. It did seem a portentous sign.

My reflections were cut short as headlights pierced the darkness, slicing through the dark with sharp, focused beams. It was Big J. His truck slid into a nearby parking spot, windows and doors rattling with the heavy, muffled *thud! thud! thud!* of his stereo system as it blared a throbbing bass. I smiled. It was probably some southern jam band. Big J was all about jam bands.

This was my second run of the day. I had snagged a solid eight miles earlier that morning, but Big J had called late in the afternoon and proposed a night run in Mystical Land. Aware of my duties as Big J's default bastion of accountability—and, of course, not one to turn down an adventure run—I accepted his invitation and agreed to run another six or seven with him later that evening. The thumping bass continued a few seconds more, and then stopped, leaving an eerie silence, a darkness of sound that matched our surroundings.

"Hey, girl," Big J greeted me, hopping out of his truck. He unzipped his jacket and tossed it in the front seat.

"Hey."

"A little dark, eh?"

"No kidding. I run out here all the time when it's dark, but this is ridiculous."

Big J, a perpetual buoy of optimism, wasn't concerned. "Eh, that's okay. It'll be an adventure. Running is more exciting when you can't see where you're going." He reset his watch and looked up. "Which way?"

And on that rallying cry, we left the parking lot and began our run.

"No purple shorts today?" I asked somewhere between tripping over a curb and twisting my ankle on a loose piece of asphalt. It was rumored that Big J had an impressive collection of purple running apparel, courtesy of his alma mater, LSU. I had yet to see anything but a T-shirt.

Big J laughed. "Ah! I should have worn those. Or my purple tights. My purple tights are awesome."

The deep settled chill of evening established itself across the roads. I could sense Big J running next to me, but I couldn't see him, near as he was. Needless to say, country roads aren't lined with streetlights. Occasionally, an oncoming car would blind us and force us into the grass. We collided frequently. The highlight of our run came when I nearly crashed into the metal base of a yield sign, a circumstance that was not without irony. By a stroke of fortune, however, I evaded disaster by a timely stumble off course. Every great while, a streetlamp rose from the shadows, shedding a murky, yellow glow before receding into the dark. Though brief, these moments of illumination provided at least token confirmation that we were still running on the correct road.

Later that evening, I was struck with the realization that sometimes life is not unlike our run had been. Each of us travels through periods of light and dark, times when our path seems clear and times when we struggle to see just a few feet ahead. We find ourselves in the country, so to speak. Darkness consumes the land, and we question whether there is a path at all. There are no streetlights. There is no moon. And before us looms the unforeseen threat of an unfortunately placed yield sign. Blind to the road before us, we feel abandoned. Confused. Betrayed, even. In those times our hearts stumble as much our bodies do, and our resolve is pained with faltering. We don't understand where the light has gone, and it is all we can do to not give up.

Life is rarely clear-cut. Our vision is often handicapped. The path may be dark. It may be long. We hope our eyes adjust. We know they may not. Sometimes only in the illuminating clarity of hindsight do we see the way we have taken. But we hope. Ever reaching deeper, ever looking ahead, squinting, straining, but ultimately seeing just enough of the road to take one more small step, we continue on.

Perseverance is not contingent on understanding, but on the willingness to press forward. And sometimes simply moving forward is enough. Because, as I had discovered that evening, we're still getting in the miles, even if we can't see them.

"So, you ran eight miles yesterday morning, and then you ran seven miles with Big J last night?" Mr. Speedy Pants asked, a bit perturbed.

"Yes."

"And how fast did you run with Big J?"

"Umm . . . Probably faster than I should have."

"Uh-huh. I thought yesterday was a recovery day?"

I grimaced into the phone. "It was. Supposed to be, anyway," I said, my voice betraying my guilty conscience.

"Kid," Mr. Speedy Pants sighed, "what do I always tell you?"

Mr. Speedy Pants always told me a lot of things.

"Umm . . ."

"Don't be dumb," he answered for me.

"I know . . ."

"And what did you do?"

It was like a parent chastising a little kid.

"I was dumb. But," I added quickly, ready to defend my actions, "Big J wanted to run, and I had already run that morning. Plus, we weren't going to run fast. The pace just kinda picked itself up."

"Uh-huh. Well, it looks like we're going to have to postpone today's speedwork," Mr. Speedy Pants said. He wasn't annoyed, just factual. His tone held the flat apathy of a doctor's diagnosis. "I was gonna have you run twenty quarters, but I want your legs rested and ready to go. The whole point of the workout is running an even pace for each interval. If your legs are shot to begin with, you're not going to reap the physiological benefits of hitting the track in the first place. We'll have to push it back later in the week."

I bit my lip, disappointed that the workout had to be postponed, disappointed in myself for being so cavalier with my training.

"I'm sorry, Coach."

"No need to be sorry. You just need to be smart about resting your legs. It's all about recovery, kid."

Rescheduling the track workout proved to be slightly more complicated than I could have hoped. It was Tuesday. Doing the workout on Wednesday meant no recovery between the twenty quarters and my eighteen-miler on Thursday. Moving the workout to Friday, of course, would put me in the same predicament we were trying to avoid by rescheduling in the first place. Thus, in order to reschedule the twenty quarters, we had to reschedule my long run—and, by default, the festivities of the TMBG.

I was beginning to realize that high mileage is high maintenance. Each run had a particular slot into which it fit, a precise compartment that secured it on either side from contamination by other runs. Two highly combustible runs—a long run and a track workout, for instance—must never come into contact with each other. It was a periodic table of running, an intricate web of space and relationships between long runs and track workouts and two-a-days and recovery miles. Each run had to be carried out according to schedule or the equilibrium would be upset, sparking a domino effect of consequences. Such is life with a poodle of a hobby.

Thankfully, the sport occasionally exercises its forgiving nature (I cannot say the same for poodles), and with a few twists of the Rubik's cube, Mr. Speedy Pants and I rescheduled my long run and slated the twenty quarters for the next afternoon. Of course, the next afternoon, it poured rain. All afternoon.

Whoosh . . . swish. Whoosh . . . swish. Whoosh . . . swish.

My windshield wipers slushed their way back and forth valiantly, attempting to erase the raindrops pelting the car. They were not successful.

This must be punishment for not resting my legs, I thought as I watched the battle taking place on my windshield.

The world outside remained distorted and blurred, visible only in brief strokes of light. The change in schedule mandated a change in location as well, and I found myself staring not at the Webster Groves Ice Arena, but at the "Home of the Mustangs," Marquette High School. Marquette acted as our backup track when the day's activities required a more centralized meeting ground, and Mr. Speedy Pants and I had already trekked there for several workouts.

I unzipped the jacket I was wearing and tossed it on the passenger seat. At least it was warm enough to wear a tank top. Long sleeves in this downpour would have been miserable. I tucked a few remnant strands of hair behind my ears and adjusted my visor, the only protection I would have against the rain. Opening the car door, I stepped into the fusillade and found my body assailed from all sides. Resigning myself to the effects of the rain, I stood outside my car—forlorn, fatalistic—and waited for Mr. Speedy Pants to climb out of the dry warmth of his own vehicle.

This he did shortly, snapping open an umbrella in the process. Mr. Speedy Pants's Achilles tendon demanded he remain on injured reserve for at least a few more days, and with no running on his schedule for the afternoon, he came prepared to brave the weather as a bystander. He tugged on his baseball cap as he began walking toward the track. His shoes splashed across the pavement while the umbrella shivered and pitched with the wind.

"I hope you like running in the rain," he said.

"Love it."

"Good."

We made our way to the start line on the track. There would be no traditional pre-workout ceremonies. No duffel bags on the bleachers. No changing of shoes or leisurely stretching. The weather did not permit such liturgies. I began my warm-up without formality, a simple extension of my walk from the parking lot. I had come to appreciate the warm-up and its benefits. "Twelve to fifteen minutes is the ideal amount of time to get the blood flowing and get your muscles ready for a hard effort," Mr. Speedy Pants would tell me. Experience had proved the truth of this statement. Now, however, battered by the rain, running without the company of Mr. Speedy Pants, I felt the duration of the warm-up acutely. It was a long, dreary two miles.

Mr. Speedy Pants gave me a few final instructions as I readied myself for the workout. It occurred to me, as he spoke, imparting counsel, sheltered by a dome of canvas, surrounded by a ring of water droplets that fringed the edges of his umbrella, that he was not unlike a kind of oracle, a seer of the track. I could imagine myself in the sacred vapor of Delphi, the legend of antiquity, fearfully awaiting the augural frenzy of Pythia.

Such wanderings were quickly reined in, however, not by the ancient prophetess, but by the stolid voice of Mr. Speedy Pants.

"Don't be overly concerned about your time on the first couple of quarters. I'd rather you start on the slow side than go out too fast and not be able to hit your times at the end. After you get the first few laps under your belt, you'll settle into a groove." He smiled and patted my head, "We hope, anyway. With you, we never know."

I had just enough time to make a face before Mr. Speedy Pants snapped his fingers, preventing a retort.

"Ah! I should have grabbed the bullhorn from the race-timing bus. I could have yelled at you while you run." He shook his head. "Oh, well. I'll just have to yell extra loud so you can hear me across the track." He tapped his watch. "All right, kid. Get at 'em. Sixty-second rest."

That afternoon, I learned several important lessons about a twenty-quarter workout. First, it takes a long time to run twenty quarters. Second, when it is pouring rain, it takes an even longer time to run twenty quarters (or so it seems). Third, and this I find the most enigmatic of the lessons, the sixty-second rest between quarters shrinks as the workout continues. I am not sure how this phenomenon occurs, but I was so convinced of its happening—and of its affront to my recovery—that twice I had Mr. Speedy Pants check my watch, just to make sure it was not malfunctioning.

Lap after lap I ran, snagging quick jokes, bits of advice, and random narratives at the end of each quarter, courtesy of Mr. Speedy Pants. It was like running an anecdotal workout, with each interval punctuated by a footnote from the great Oracle of Marquette. I contributed to these annotations at first; however, sometime after the tenth quarter, my conversational skills devolved into a series of responsive grunts.

My feelings as I rounded the back turn of the tenth quarter are vivid still. I had run enough laps at a fast enough pace to be fatigued; yet I was only halfway done with the workout. I still had ten more quarters to go. I experienced an unmistakable sinking sensation. I was in over my head. Gone too far to turn back but not far enough to see the finish line, I knew the distinct demoralization of doubting my ability to finish something I had started.

Something else was being etched in my memory, however, as I ran deeper and deeper into the workout, splashing through puddles, buffeted by the rain, fighting my own psychological warfare as much as I battled the elements around me. An image.

It was a dark silhouette, long and still, covered by a small canopy, the circumference of which was slightly bigger than the silhouette itself. I ran closer and the image came into focus, became clearer, more detailed. It was a man. I could not yet see his face, for a baseball cap pulled low over his eyes cast a darkening shadow, but in one hand he steadied an umbrella while in the other hand, arm extended, he held a stopwatch. He stood in a puddle that covered the bottom of his shoes and splashed his shoelaces and grew with every flip and pop of the raindrops. He was unaware that he was slowly becoming an island; unaware, or perhaps indifferent. His jeans were dark, soaked with water up to his knees. His jacket, too, was drenched, pelted from all directions by the rain that defied gravity and flew in persistent, lateral streams. I ran closer still, and a voice called out. Words of encouragement, inducement to keep going. He must have been cold and uncomfortable, standing there, assailed by the elements, dripping wet, as I slowly—slowly—completed the workout. He made no mention of his discomfort. He simply patted me on the back and told me to keep it up. That I was looking good. That I was halfway done. That I had only three more quarters. Two more. One more. That I did a good job. That he was proud of me.

I walked about the start line, hands on my hips, breathing deeply, muscles fatigued and body depleted. I was nothing short of an utter and complete mess, like a dishrag in running shoes. I ran a very, very brief cool-down.

Post-workout coffee was necessary to counteract the rain that had nearly dissolved my existence. Mr. Speedy Pants ordered the drinks while I headed for the bathroom to change out of my wet clothes. Finally dry, I took the warm coffee mug between my hands and listened as Mr. Speedy Pants recapped the day's workout, inserting the occasional story about his old buddy Tim, his buddy Fagan (who writes for the *Sporting News*), or—when the course of events allowed such an extraordinary convergence—the two of them together. At one point, I inadvertently slammed my knee against the underside of the table, upsetting our coffee cups and sloshing the contents across the table and the floor. As Mr. Speedy Pants rose from his chair to retrieve napkins, I noticed his jeans were still soaked to his knees.

Certain moments in life prompt reflection. It is not a sentimental remembrance, but the detached objectivity of someone viewing another's life from just beyond the realm of interaction. Stepping back from reality, we see ourselves as if in a dream, our bodies merely shadows and our voices silent thoughts not so much heard as understood. In those moments, with the viewpoint of an observer rather than a participant, we see a more complete picture, notice the details, the nuances, perceive how one aspect of the painting relates to and complements the others. And what we thought was just another scene in a never-ending sequence of images turns out to be a great work of art. Nestled amid tattered edges is a canvas, priceless and rare. We pull it from obscurity and hold it up for inspection, admiring a treasure that was nearly lost in the sheer number of pages.

Mr. Speedy Pants continued telling stories and I sat there, fingers wrapped around a hot coffee mug, mind and body enveloped by the delightful, consuming equanimity of hard-earned fatigue. And then, time stopped. And I watched from a distance. The image of a dark silhouette, long and still, returned. It called to me to keep going.

Solitary that I might not be alone. Uncomfortable that I might have comfort. Encouraging that I might be encouraged. As indifferent to time as it was to the weather. An imaged burned indelibly in my mind— of my first big triumph in running, of a new newfound belief that, yes, I can. Of the day I ran twenty quarters in the rain.

Chapter Ten

Also sprinkled throughout my training were several 5K races and time trials. Mr. Speedy Pants had suggested I pick a race or two from the myriad 5Ks littering the area in the weeks preceding my marathon. These, he said, would provide solid speed training and racing experience, both of which would benefit me come race day.

Earlier in the year, Big J had offered his last-minute pacing services for a local 20K. It was a tiny race—there were perhaps only seventy-five participants—and it served as part four in a five-part "Snowflake" road series held in the same location every few weeks throughout the winter months. These Snowflake races were often used by area runners as training runs and tempo work, and I was no exception. I had no expectations going into the Snowflake 20K, partly because at the time I was just beginning my training program, and partly because I had never before raced a 20K. The upside to this scenario, as Big J pointed out, was that as long as I crossed the finish line, I was guaranteed a PR.

"How would you like a pacer for the 20K?" Big J had asked the night before the race.

"That'd be awesome," I said, genuinely glad to have some company for the event. "I'm not really sure what pace I should run, though. This is the first 20K I've ever raced."

A mere ten hours was separating my phone call with Big J from the sound of the starting bullhorn, and still I had no game plan for my run. I was aware of my greenness. I bit my lip, half smiling and half grimacing with the admission.

Big J was undeterred by my lack of planning. It seemed he had predetermined a pace for me. It was an aggressive pace—much more aggressive than I would have chosen for myself—but he was convinced I would be able to hold on for the twelve-plus miles.

"It's a pancake-flat course," he had assured me, further defending his position, "except for a long, steep hill at the end." He laughed. "That hill is a killer. It doesn't start out that steep. It's kind of a gradual incline at first. But it slowly gets worse and worse. It's gotta be a mile long. And"— he paused for dramatic implication—"it's the last mile of the race."

"Uh-huh."

"You'll be fine. All you'll have to do is stay next to me. The rest of the race will already be behind you at that point."

Lo and behold, Big J had been right, and I ended up hanging on by a snowflake, though I did consider throwing myself in front of one of the oncoming cars speeding by the course as I suffered my way up the dreaded mile-long hill.

The Snowflake 20K proved to be a fruitful way to kick off my marathon training, not only because it provided helpful information regarding my current fitness level, but also because it gave my confidence a running start as I tumbled into serious training. The 5Ks I ran during GO! St. Louis training further marked my progress and punctuated the tedium of the miles with minor high points of short, intense racing. The 5Ks also served as a launchpad for consultations with Mr. Speedy Pants regarding my post-St. Louis running goals—namely, a faster 5K time.

The catalyst for our initial 5K discussions was, of all things, a pair of calf compression sleeves. Calf sleeves demand attention. They aid in recovery and the prevention of injury, but they look like brightly colored knee socks. While many runners are familiar with the concept, the general populace tends to view them dubiously. I myself straddled the line separating the two impressions and felt the compression sleeves were appropriate only for runners who were fast and could be easily recognized as such. I was firmly convinced there is nothing worse than an athlete unable to live up to his equipment. For years I had felt the pressure of my hockey skates, skates that were superior to my stick-handling skills. I wasn't about to assume the load of elitist socks.

"Wait." Mr. Speedy Pants shook his head at me, rejecting the mishmash logic I had tossed his way. "So why can't you wear Zensah sleeves?" (Zensah made the calf sleeves of choice for Mr. Speedy Pants.)

"Because I'm not fast enough," I said, not understanding how Mr. Speedy Pants couldn't understand my answer.

He rolled his eyes. "Kid, that's dumb. What do you mean you're not fast enough? Anyone can benefit from calf sleeves."

"Okay," I said, ready to go down with my ship of reasoning, "say you saw a girl running down the street in a pair of Zensahs. Wouldn't you assume that if she's wearing Zensahs she's a fairly serious runner? I mean, really, wouldn't you hope that she was at least semi-fast? Or put it this way," I said, holding out the palm of my hand as though my argument were tangible, "if you saw a girl running down the street in calf sleeves, how fast would you expect her 5K time to be—at the very least?"

Mr. Speedy Pants rolled his eyes. "Oh, my . . ." He rubbed the top of his head, sending his already stubborn hair into riotous fits. "What does it matter what anyone thinks? You're not running for them. You're running for you, for the sport, because you love it. Who cares what others think about what you're wearing? They're probably not thinking about it anyway."

"I know. But I don't want to be all teched out and not be able to carry my own, you know?"

Mr. Speedy Pants sighed. "Okay, so how fast do you want to be before you let yourself wear Zensah sleeves—even though I think your whole line of reasoning is dumb?"

I threw out a number.

"All right, kid. I bet I can get you Zensah-fast before your marathon. How 'bout we make that one of your training goals?"

I wasn't convinced, but being Zensah-fast was a nice thought. I consented to the plan, despite my uncertainty.

"Okay, Coach, sounds good."

"Good. And you need to get it out of your head that you're not fast. You are fast. Tell yourself that." He poked my forehead with his index finger. "And stop being such a headcase."

Thus, nestled within my overall goal of racing a new marathon PR was the secondary aim of becoming Zensah-fast. Mr. Speedy Pants made a few minor adjustments to incorporate more footspeed training into my workouts, and over the course of several weeks I consumed a steady diet of endurance runs garnished with sprints.

Two weeks before the GO! St. Louis Marathon, Mr. Speedy Pants decided the moment of truth had arrived, though he refrained from telling me the small detail of its arrival. Instead, knowing my habit of freaking out, he opted for a backdoor approach to the time trial, simply informing me my next workout would be a surprise—a "Super Secret Workout," he called it.

"Okay, kid," Mr. Speedy Pants informed me as we finished our warm-up, "all you have to do is hang with me. You start when I start and you stop when I stop. Simple as that."

It was early morning, and the sun was just starting to crest the towering bleachers, illuminating the track across the football field but leaving the start line in a lingering shadow. This was fitting since I also remained in the dark regarding the workout I would be running.

"So, what am I doing?"

"Can't tell you," Mr. Speedy Pants said.

"When will you tell me?"

"When you're done."

"Ugh! Will you tell me how long my rests are?" I asked. I believe I was pouting. It was very unbecoming.

"Nope."

Mr. Speedy Pants cleared his watch and took his stance on the start line. "Tuck in right behind me," he said, throwing a quick glance to ensure I was ready. "You can draft a bit and save some energy instead of fighting the wind the whole time. Ready? Here we go!"

I don't believe I ever truly understood the meaning of *interminable* until the Super Secret Workout. For there, on the burnt red track, alternately squinting in the blinding morning rays of sun and relaxing in the relief of the shadows, Mr. Speedy Pants and I ran lap after lap after lap. Speeding past the start line after the first four hundred meters, I figured we were running 800s. As we continued running through the eight hundred mark, I figured 1200s was the distance du jour. Then mile repeats. Then two-mile repeats. Each subsequent lap carried with it the intensified expectation of an ensuing rest. And each time that expectation was disappointed. My resolve was beginning to crumble as my body fatigued and my quads began to burn. I was not having a good day. There seemed to be no end in sight. I was fatigued. I grew tired. I grew discouraged. And I began to fall off the pace Mr. Speedy Pants steadily maintained.

"C'mon, kid," he said when he noticed I was dropping back. "C'mon. Pull up next to me. Don't let yourself drop off."

I tried to surge forward, but nothing happened. My quads refused to fire.

"Are we—*gasp*—almost done?" I gasped.

"Almost. Just keep putting one foot in front of the other."

I saw Mr. Speedy Pants glance at his watch. He then glanced back at me. "Show me what you've got left, kid. Give me everything you've got these last eight hundred meters."

Unfortunately, everything I had left amounted to nothing. I was unable to draw even with Mr. Speedy Pants, and when we finished, there were several seconds between us. I threw my hands to the top of my head and gasped for air. I was done. My body was done. Mr. Speedy Pants looked at his watch and patted me on the back.

"Good job, kid," he said. "Not feeling it today?"

I shook my head and continued gasping.

"Well, did you figure out what the Super Secret Workout was?" he asked.

"A 5K."

"Yep."

"Was this a time trial to see if I'm Zensah-fast?"

"Yep."

"Did I make it?"

Mr. Speedy Pants rubbed the top of my head, rendering my ponytail askew. "Well, you were on pace for the first two miles, but you slowed down a bit after that. I could tell you were struggling. Your breathing was heavier than it normally is. You did good considering it wasn't your day."

Mr. Speedy Pants was breaking the news to me slowly. His tone was calm and reassuring, but I could sense his reluctance to relay the disappointing news.

"How much did I miss it by?"

"Five seconds."

I put my hands on my hips and let out a frustrated sigh. "Well, that stinks," I said.

Mr. Speedy Pants put his arm around my shoulders. "Don't worry about it," he said. "Honestly, I'm positive you can hit your time. Today just wasn't your day. It happens."

"Yeah." I didn't want to seem ungrateful for Mr. Speedy Pants's consolation, but I couldn't deny the panging feeling I had let him down. That I had let myself down.

"I'm sorry, Coach."

"For what? Don't be sorry," he said. "I'm proud of you. Remember what I always tell you? As long as you try as hard as you can, you'll always make me proud."

"I know, but . . ."

"Hey," Mr. Speedy Pants said, interrupting my remonstrance, "I've got something for you."

We grabbed our duffel bags from the bleachers and headed to the parking lot. Mr. Speedy Pants unlocked his car and pulled out a small package.

"It was supposed to be a congratulations present, but, eh . . ." he teased, handing me the gift.

I took the bundle. It was wrapped in paper printed with balloons and streaming banners announcing, HAPPY BIRTHDAY!

"It was all I had," Mr. Speedy Pants explained with a shrug.

Beneath the paper and birthday greetings was a brand-new pair of Zensah sleeves.

"Here," Mr. Speedy Pants said, whipping a card from behind his back. "Again, I assumed you were going to hit your time . . ." He smiled. There was gentleness even in his teasing.

I opened the card and read the note Mr. Speedy Pants had penned in anticipation of my success in the Super Secret Workout.

Kid, it said, *Congratulations on hitting a new 5K PR. I knew you could do it. Now you are officially Zensah-fast. So stop complaining already. Sincerely, Coach.*

Below his name was a strange grouping of additional signatures. I laughed out loud as I read the names: Bob Dingy, Howie Bout-That, Stevie Bout-That, and even the TMBG's Porkadillo. Each character had written a small note of congratulations. Of course, each greeting was written in full personality. (Howie Bout-That made a somewhat bitter reference to his short-lived career.)

"You still PR'ed today, so there is legitimate ground for celebration," Mr. Speedy Pants said as I looked up from the card.

I didn't respond at first. I couldn't. There are times when our emotions compete with one another and disorder our thoughts. The disappointment of missing my goal time—missing it by only a few seconds—was suddenly mitigated by the kindness of Mr. Speedy Pants, by his belief in my ability and his understanding when I fell short. I held the Zensah sleeves in my hand. They were pink. I didn't deserve them. I had missed my time. But Mr. Speedy Pants had not equated deserving with the numbers on a stopwatch; not this time, anyway.

Perhaps I was oversentimentalizing the situation, but I was moved by Mr. Speedy Pants's thoughtfulness. To run is to try, and trying—earnestly, uninhibitedly trying—is personal. Mr. Speedy Pants knew that. Sure, my time wasn't anything special. It wasn't even close to being anything special. But in order to apply myself, I had to invest in myself, invest in my effort. And investment involves risk and fear and the guts to do it anyway. When we try, we make ourselves vulnerable to both failure and success. The Zensah sleeves were more than just a gift. They were representative of someone outside myself who saw the risk of investing, of trying, of running. Someone who knew the risk himself, someone who understood the courage behind the vulnerability. Someone who knew that running is personal.

"Thanks, Coach," I said simply, hoping he knew how much the gift meant.

"No problem, kid," Mr. Speedy Pants replied. He knew.

He sat down in the front seat of his car and began changing his running shoes for a pair of flip-flops.

"Hey, Coach," I said, tugging on the edge of one of the pink sleeves, still neatly folded in the package.

"Yeah-p?"

"What do you say I give it one more shot—next week? I know I can hit my time. May as well go for it."

Mr. Speedy Pants smiled. He tossed his shoes in the back of the car and stood up slowly, walking toward me without saying a word. He stopped approximately two feet from where I was standing and held out his hand expectantly.

"You want me to hold on to those for a few more days?" he asked with a wry smile. "After all, you won't be wearing them until next week anyway."

I grinned and looked down at the Zensah sleeves. I handed them to Mr. Speedy Pants, relinquishing, at least for the moment, my membership to the Zensah-fast club.

"Only for a week, Coach."

"You got it, kid."

One week later, we returned to the track, though this time around it was a different track. Unlike the original Super Secret Workout, which we ran in the morning, the Super Secret Workout II was to take place in the afternoon. Because of the later start time, both the Webster Groves and Marquette tracks were occupied with high school activities. Mr. Speedy Pants and I were forced to call up our third-string track, Crestview Middle School. We had run at Crestview only a handful of times before, but it had served its purpose faithfully.

We tossed our duffel bags on the bleachers and began our warm-up, dodging the occasional errant lacrosse ball that flew across our path. While the track at Crestview was clear for the taking, the football field was teeming with activity. Specifically, it was teeming with a boys' lacrosse team. The team swarmed the field in a flurry of swinging sticks and flying lacrosse balls, the latter items periodically finding their way onto the track.

"You ready, kid?" Mr. Speedy Pants asked as we completed the two miles.

Ready is a relative term. I don't think I've ever experienced readiness to the fullness of its definition. Nevertheless, I doubted my condition could be immediately improved.

"Uh-huh."

"Good."

We made our way to the bleachers and took one last swig of water before the workout.

"All you gotta do is stay with me," he said, patting my back as we headed to the start line. "I'll take the lead, and you tuck in just behind me. It's even less windy today than it was last week, so the wind shouldn't be a factor. Remember—get into a rhythm and relax. Don't tense up. You just gotta hold pace."

I nodded. I readied my watch and looked up expectantly at Mr. Speedy Pants, waiting for the signal.

"All right . . . Go!" he said as we took off.

Following his instructions, I tucked in behind him, hugging the white line separating lane one from the football field. I focused on my breathing, taking slow, deep breaths when I felt myself falling into the labored gasps of a sudden hard effort. We checked off the laps with military precision. Occasionally, he threw a glance over his shoulder to see how I was doing, to encourage me to keep going, or to tell me I was looking strong.

The lacrosse boys, for their part, continued practicing, which, if the number of errant lacrosse balls shooting across the track was any indication, they sorely needed to do. Because I stayed immediately behind Mr. Speedy Pants as we made our way around the track, the lacrosse team fell under the impression that the two of us were racing. Several of the boys began to cheer me on, telling me I could catch him and warning me not to let him get away. I smiled despite the exertion of the 5K time trial.

"One lap to go, kid," Mr. Speedy Pants said as we looped past the bleachers for the final time. "Just bring it home."

My quads felt heavy. My breathing was strained. I was mentally done. I was hurting. But I knew I could keep going. After all, as Mr. Speedy Pants had said, 5Ks are supposed to hurt.

Finally, we crossed our imaginary finish line. I gasped as we slowed our stride.

Mr. Speedy Pants put his arm around my shoulders and smiled. "Twelve seconds to spare," he said. "Look at you, overachiever."

I raised my hands in victory. "Yes!" I laughed. "Zensah-fast!"

"Good job, kid."

(The boys' lacrosse team did not celebrate my triumph, but instead shook their heads in disappointment. Naturally, they assumed I had lost the race to Mr. Speedy Pants.)

"It's about time," Mr. Speedy Pants grinned. "Geez, I thought I was gonna have to return your Zensah sleeves."

We embarked on our cool-down, during which enterprise I discovered my energy suddenly restored. (Such is the effect of success.) My mouth turned up in an involuntary grin. I'm fairly certain I ran the whole of the cool-down with a dorky, self-satisfied expression. It had taken two tries, but I had done it. I had hit my 5K goal time—and had set a seventeen-second PR in the process. The progression of events leading to victory in the Super Secret Workout II hadn't been what I had planned. For one thing, the very existence of the Super Secret Workout II was indicative of failure in the original Super Secret Workout. And racing a 5K time trial only five days out from a marathon, though not unheard of, did entail a few physical and mental risks, not the least of which involved the danger of being nailed by an errant lacrosse ball. Still, the Super Secret Workout II turned out just fine. More than that, it solidified my confidence in the days leading up to the GO! St. Louis Marathon. Plan A thrown by the wayside, we turned to Plan B and discovered a deeper wealth of experience.

Plan B is an underrated plan. Because it comes after Plan A, it is by default viewed as "less than success," as a halfway point between accomplishment and failure. One could say Plan B is the Jan Brady of plans, the Boy Wonder, the Sancho Panza. Plan A gets all the glory (à la

Marcia, Marcia, Marcia), but Plan B stands quietly in the background, sage and observant (though it may occasionally don a wig, just to spice things up). It is surprisingly content in its little corner in the Room of Aspiration. It waits patiently in the shadows, neglected but not sulky, ready to back up its happy-go-lucky brother who, while always a good time, isn't necessarily the best thing for us. Somewhere between the original Super Secret Workout and the Super Secret Workout II, I met Plan B.

For a day or two (or three) after the first time trial, I had been dissatisfied. I felt I had let myself down, that I hadn't done my best. *How could I have suffered through all of Mr. Speedy Pants's workouts only to wimp out on game day?* I thought. It was a classic case of Plan A Syndrome. I was a Gotham City resident waiting to be rescued, and instead of Batman flying from the rafters to come save me, I got Robin, the Boy Wonder. I mean, Robin is fine and all . . . but, dude, where's Batman?

"So you had a rough day," Mr. Speedy Pants had said in response to my lingering disappointment after the first Super Secret Workout. "It happens. You still PR'ed, and you can't be disappointed with a PR, kid."

"Yeah, I know, but . . ."

"Look, goals aren't easy to hit. That's why they're goals. You have to work at them, chip away at them, until you get there. It's like eating an elephant. You gotta do it one bite at a time."

And that was it. Hannibal-esque in its pursuance of victory, crossing the Alps on Mr. Speedy Pants's metaphorical elephant, was Plan B. Sure, things hadn't gone as planned. But in my disappointment and frustration, I had developed a new level of resolve. Instead of just knowing my goal time, I now understood what it would take to reach it. Instead of merely hoping I would succeed, I now had the unshakable confidence I could. We may want Plan A, but Plan B makes us want it more.

Struggles simultaneously expose and build our moral fiber. Trials require and teach perseverance. Perseverance demands and grows character. Character summons and enables us to continue. And continuance is the only way through Plan B.

Nobody dreams of being Robin the Boy Wonder or Jan "the Lesser" Brady. But even superheroes need help every now and then. Who would listen to Batman's ramblings if not for Robin? And what would Don Quixote be without the proverbial witticism of Sancho Panza? That's the beauty of Plan B. Always there. Always waiting in the corner. Always ready to gently instruct but never steal the glory. It pushes us to continue, pushes us to reach for depths of strength we didn't know we had. And upon heeding Plan B's call, we rise from the shadows only to find—somehow—we have surpassed Plan A in the process.

Another process had been in motion, as well, as I scampered my way through Plan A's and Plan B's, through 5Ks and track workouts, through long runs and adventure runs. It was the simple, immutable process of time and the passing of time. At the beginning of marathon training, the race itself was so far away the finish line seemed merely a destination in theory, not in fact. Each training run was but a drop in an ocean of miles. Each rolling wave lulled me to sleep; each rebounding splash distracted me from my ultimate goal. I began to focus on my immediate surroundings and became preoccupied with my current conditions. But then I blinked, and I discovered I had made it across to the other side.

Somehow, when I wasn't looking, the distance was covered and the time was spent. I had survived my training. I was as fit and as prepared as I was going to get. There was no longer any time for improvement. The familiar consolation of separation between the present and race day was no longer. I felt a strange responsibility in knowing I was ready to race, in knowing I had done all I could do. Time had whittled itself away. Months had turned to weeks. Weeks had turned to days. Days had turned to hours. And there was me. And there was the race. And there was nothing standing between us.

Chapter Eleven

It was Friday evening, only thirty-six hours before the GO! St. Louis Marathon. Mr. Speedy Pants joined me for an evening run, and we ran at an easy pace, skimming across the flat roads lining the river valley. Runner's headlamps strapped to our foreheads, reflective armbands flickering in the dark, we blinked and shined our way down the black roads, occasionally blinded by an oncoming car. It was the last real run of my training.

There was something almost surreal in knowing this was the last time I would run with Mr. Speedy Pants before my big race. It seemed so final. I couldn't believe we had traversed as many miles as we had. All the cornfield runs, all the Grant's Trail adventures and Forest Park traditions seemed—as the old cliché goes—like a dream, as if someone else had lived the past few months for me, and suddenly, just before the marathon, our lives had been transposed. I'm sure the shroud of nighttime shadows and faint moonlight surrounding us didn't hurt the Kafka-esque aura of the run.

"So, kid, you're gonna run an easy two miles sometime tomorrow, just to get the blood flowing."

Conversation during the run, of course, had centered on race day and race day preparations.

"Yep."

We made a left turn on Edison, a road that stretches behind the bright lights and busy sidewalks of the storefronts and restaurants lining the valley. I had always assumed the road was named for Thomas Edison. (Honestly, what other Edison is there?) Yet in the pre-race meandering of my mind, it struck me that perhaps the road was not named after the famous inventor at all, but after someone wholly unrelated to

Thomas Alva and the world of inventions. Perhaps this Edison was a beneficent businessman. Perhaps he was a revered county clerk. Or the dog of a revered county clerk. There was no telling, really.

"Now, you know I'm not going to be able to run with you until at least mile twenty, right?"

I snapped back to attention. I did know, but for some reason I had pocketed that small fact and tried to forget its existence. I hadn't thought about Mr. Speedy Pants's absence during the race.

One of Mr. Speedy Pants's many race-timing duties included driving the lead vehicle for various events. And the GO! St. Louis Marathon had engaged his services for just that. On race morning, Mr. Speedy Pants would be manning the flashing, siren-sounding car guiding the lead runner to victory. He would not, as my subconscious had so irresponsibly assumed, be running with me. Thirty-six hours before the race, I finally dispensed with my comforting delusion.

"Yeah, I know."

"But don't worry, kid. We've got it all worked out," Mr. Speedy Pants said, confident and reassuring. He proceeded to detail the plan he had worked out with Big J. He knew me well enough to know I was worried.

"I have to get to the race early to set up the lead vehicle. You and Big J will meet up somewhere on the way downtown and then ride to the race together. Big J is gonna run the first twenty miles with you—or whatever it takes before I find you guys. After that, he said he makes no promises. Good ol' Big J and his taper theorem." Mr. Speedy Pants grinned. His face quickly shifted back to business. "I'm gonna throw my running gear into the lead vehicle. After the first marathoner finishes, I'll change clothes and run the course backward until I find you."

I felt the conflicting emotions of pre-race anxiety and the comforting thought of having company for the entire marathon. I pictured Mr. Speedy Pants hopping out of the lead vehicle, pulling on his running shoes, and flying across the six or so miles it would take before he met up with us, just so he could run the same six miles back to the finish line. He was going to do that for me—and he didn't think anything of it.

"I should be able to catch up to you by mile twenty. Mile twenty-two at the absolute latest," Mr. Speedy Pants continued. "Then it will be smooth sailing to the finish line."

The rest of our discussion consisted of race morning details. Make sure I drink plenty of fluids the day before the race. Did I know when I was going to consume energy gel? Bring a visor. ("You'll waste up to 3 percent of your body's total energy output by squinting," Mr. Speedy Pants informed me.) Don't start out too fast. Be conservative with pace and negative split the second half of the race. Take water at every aid station. Don't forget my race number and timing chip. Sheesh.

We stood outside our cars and stretched for a couple of minutes before calling it a night. I was reluctant to leave. The finality and sentimentality that had plagued me during the first part of our run returned. This was the last time I would see Mr. Speedy Pants before the race. The jittery preparation of race morning, the first twenty miles of the course—those would come and pass before we would run together again.

Mr. Speedy Pants leaned into his car and grabbed a white envelope from the front seat.

"Here. Now, don't open this until tomorrow, got it?"

I took the sealed envelope from his hand. Scrawled across the front was a clue to its contents and a stern warning. YOUR FINAL RACE INSTRUCTIONS, it read. DO NOT OPEN UNTIL SATURDAY.

I smiled. "Yeah, yeah. Geez. Don't you trust me?"

Mr. Speedy Pants folded his arms and leaned against his car. "No. I don't."

"Okay. I promise."

"Good."

He stepped forward to give me a hug.

"All right. This is it. Remember everything I told you. Go get 'em."

I took a slow, deep breath and nodded.

"Yeah."

Mr. Speedy Pants held out his hand for a high five—which I promptly gave, though it was admittedly a bit weak—and climbed into his car. "See you at mile twenty, kid!" he yelled as he ducked his head below the doorframe.

I waved as he drove off. *Yep*, I thought, eyeing the envelope one last time before getting into my car. *See you at mile twenty.*

All right, kid, Mr. Speedy Pants's letter began, *here are your final racing instructions, along with other thoughts, words of wisdom, good luck wishes, etc. There isn't much about race day strategy that you don't already know, so this letter is really just to keep it all fresh in your head . . .*

Mr. Speedy Pants recapped the usual race day logistics and reminded me once more to settle into my pace, not to go out too fast, and not to freak out. He continued with some specific advice regarding the elevation of the course, which had some fairly hilly sections. He assured me, however, I had enough hill training in Mystical Land, Queeny Park, and Forest Park to handle everything the route would throw at me. This was comforting to know.

> *Don't panic if the hills slow you down a bit. Better to stay relaxed and go slightly slower up the hills than to work too hard to keep pace and then redline. Plus, you can look forward to me joining you somewhere between mile twenty and mile twenty-two. As soon as my navigational and clock-operational obligations are over, I'll come back for you. If I'm quick in getting back out on the course, I should be able to meet you with four to six miles to go. I'll bring you home.*

> *So, I think that should cover it. You aren't exactly a rookie—es-*

pecially since your track and field knowledge is so expansive now. (Here I laughed. I could hear his sarcasm even in his letter.) *Anyway, I hope you really are looking forward to your race. I know I am. It's been awesome to see you come so far and take a shot at an incredible time. This is going to be a huge PR for you. Pretty crazy, kid. Just think of the progress you've made—how far you've come since your first track workout when you were so nervous. You had never stepped on a track before and then, in just a few weeks, you were cranking out twenty quarters . . . by yourself . . . in the pouring rain. I was very proud of you that day. Definitely made an hour of standing in the rain and holding that umbrella worth it.*

So, Sunday will be your graduation day. I know you'll rock it out. Not just because I'm an awesome coach—which is obviously part of it—but because you've never disappointed me. Your fitness is there, and the twenty quarters in the rain showed you've got what it takes.

You know, kid, I'm glad you happened to ask me for some "advice"—and that it somehow turned into me coaching you. You've become more than just my star athlete. You've become a great friend. You really are pretty awesome. And I'm glad to know you.

You can always call me with any last-minute questions or concerns. Don't hesitate. I'll try to find you and Big J before the race to wish you good luck. But if I don't—well, good luck, kid. It's been an honor coaching you, and I have full confidence that I'm gonna be very proud on Sunday. Remember what they say: Pressure makes diamonds. (It also makes coal, ironically enough.) So, go get 'em.

Run Well,
Coach

Big J and I threaded our way through the mass of people swelling and shifting toward the start corrals. The runners wedged between the metal gates lining the street bulged and waned with the tension. We were several blocks from our ideal starting position, separated from our destination by a sea of bib numbers and split shorts and singlets and little plastic chips fastened on fidgety shoelaces. Thousands of voices murmured and crackled in a medley of excited pre-race chatter. The occasional call of recognition punctuated the buzzing, while in the background was the MC's voice, droning on about sponsors and participant etiquette and reminders that the race would be starting soon.

I shifted the strap of my duffel bag. My nervousness seemed to rise as the minutes on the clock counted down to the starting gunshot. Two particular factors contributed to my unease. First, several obliging friends had agreed to act as bag drop substitutes, and Big J and I had yet to take advantage of this convenience. Second, and perhaps even more disconcerting, I had to go to the bathroom.

"Ladies and gentlemen! The GO! St. Louis Marathon will begin in twenty-four minutes!" the announcer blared across the PA system.

"Here," Big J said, grabbing the duffel bag hanging despondently from my arm, "I'll drop off the bags and you go find a Porta-John. After I drop off our stuff, I'll make my way to the Porta-Johns and meet you when you come out."

I bit my lip. I wasn't thrilled with the idea of dividing and conquering, mainly because of the dividing part. The crowd was too thick and the race too near to allow the danger of division and the risks it entailed. Then again, battling the urge to go to the bathroom for twenty-six miles carried its own set of risks. I could see the lines of people—some restive, some standing with almost fatalistic resignation—snaking behind the row of green Porta-Johns. There seemed to be no other option but to accept Big J's plan. Time was running short.

"Okay," I relented, "but go fast!"

Big J disappeared in the crowd. I took a deep breath, turned, and pushed my way through the crush of humanity, eyes locked on the dull aqua glow of the Porta-Johns standing at attention in the distance. I selected what I hoped to be the most efficient line, took my place behind the last person, and waited. And waited.

The line wasn't moving. None of the lines was moving. Instead of the frequent hollow thuds of plastic doors slamming shut with an endless succession of occupants entering and leaving, there was only the dull, distant murmur of excited runners already in their respective start corrals, the intermittent sound of someone exiting a Porta-John, and the envious silence of the hundreds who stood in line, impatient, unrelieved, and maddeningly stationary.

I began to panic. I continued to look around, scanning the crowd for Big J, but he was nowhere to be found. *Where is he?* I wondered with heightened alarm.

"Three minutes until the start of the GO! St. Louis Marathon!" the MC yelled with the frenzied fervor of someone one digit away from a winning lottery ticket.

I looked at the dozens of people still in front of me. I would never make it. It was time for an executive decision. Abandoning the Porta-Johns, I again fought my way toward the start corrals, colliding with several people and nearly pitching headfirst into the ground.

"Big J!" I yelled, using one arm to clear a path and the other to cup my hand against my mouth as I called in vain for my nomadic SEC friend. I would have given anything to see him. "Big J! Big J!" I continued to scream as my panic mounted. Several irritated race participants looked in my direction and frowned. I didn't care.

Oh, my gosh. Oh, my gosh. Where is he? Agh! Where are you, Big J? My stomach tightened and wrenched itself into a large, sickening knot. I was seized with fear and claustrophobia. I was in danger of cardiac arrest. The reality of not being able to find Big J hit me with a deep, final oppression.

"Thirty seconds to go, folks! Start your engines!" the PA announcer

continued.

A cheer bubbled up from the crowd as thousands of runners defied social norms and at least two of the participant etiquette rules to press even tighter together in anticipation of the starter's signal. I was too distraught to cry. My eyes swept across the ocean of bobbing heads. Big J was nowhere to be found. I was alone.

"*Ten . . . ! Nine . . . ! Eight . . . !*" The spirited MC led the countdown to the start of the race.

The crowd began moving forward. I made sure my watch was ready to go. I tried to swallow, but was unsuccessful. I jumped up and down and wrung my hands. It was race time.

And then, somewhere between "*Six!*" and "*Five!*" I heard him.

"Hey! Over here!"

I turned my head in the direction of the voice and saw a hand rise above the crowd. My eyes followed the hand down to a tall, lean figure wearing a goofy smile and a purple LSU singlet. It was Big J.

What happened next rivals all the schmaltz Hollywood has ever produced. I had my own *Chariots of Fire* moment, right there in the sardine conditions of the GO! St. Louis Marathon's start corral. The world became silent. The faces around me receded, blurred with the background, inconsequential. I felt my body propelled—almost as if by divine forces—across the pavement and through the invisible throngs toward Big J. I flew through the air and threw my arms around him in a giant, grateful embrace. Big J, for his part, stood there motionless, arms straight at his side, grin still plastered across his face.

"I kept calling your name," he said, as nonchalant as if our reunion had gone exactly as planned and he had no idea why I had been so upset. "What were you doing?"

"*Two . . . ! One! Go!*"

A cheer rose from the crowd as the race began. I didn't have time to answer.

"You ready?" Big J said, patting my back as I tried to regain my composure. "Here we go!"

Before I knew what was happening, I was running, pushed along by a mass of humanity. And there, without ceremony, heart still racing from my recent near catastrophe, gastrointestinal system yet unrelieved, fighting back tears of gratefulness, I began the GO! St. Louis Marathon.

Sometimes we are unaware of our own expectations. Certainly, I had a clear idea of how I would have liked the miles to pass—what the weather would be and how I would feel at mile twenty-two and what the clock would read as I crossed the finish line. I also had several distinct fears regarding what I hoped would not happen. But if someone had asked me before the race how I thought the marathon would go, I don't think I would have been able to answer—not because I didn't have any expectations, but because I simply wouldn't have been able to recognize them.

It is a scary thing when reality and expectation collide, for the sparks illuminate our hidden hopes. It is a battle against an opponent we do not know and cannot see. Only in accomplishing the task before us do we know if we have attained success or let ourselves down. As I crossed the start line of the GO! St. Louis Marathon, I couldn't have said what my expectations were. But I do know I never thought the race would go as perfectly as it did.

After nearly scuttling our mission in the disastrous bathroom episode, Big J and I sailed along the marathon course without further incident. We chatted and laughed and occasionally glanced at our watches to make sure we were on pace. Big J waved and yelled every time we ran by a high school marching band, which was often considering high school marching bands are in high demand at such events. By some miracle, my intestinal system decided it was content to wait until after the race and no longer nagged for attention. At the halfway point, Big J asked if I was ready to negative split the second half of the course. I was. We picked up the pace, and soon, twenty miles had fallen beneath our asphalt-pounding feet.

I only have to make it to Coach, I thought as I grabbed a cup from the water station at mile twenty. *I only have to make it to Coach.*

This was our mantra both before and during the race. Big J had reminded me several times my marathon was simply a twenty-mile run with a 10K pinned to the end. I took a sip and tossed the cup to the side of the road. At any moment Mr. Speedy Pants would be cresting the pavement ahead of us. *Almost there*, I told myself, feeling strong but fearing the infamous "wall" was only a few steps away. *Any time now . . .*

And then, in the distance, running against the stampede, was a lean, floppy-haired man in black Zensah sleeves.

"Kronos!" Big J yelled, waving his hands in the air to catch Mr. Speedy Pants's attention.

I yelled and waved my arms. Mr. Speedy Pants ran straight at us, halted just a few feet from where we were, spun around, and fell in step with Big J and me. I smiled as we ran the first few seconds together in silence. I was having a great race. I knew it. And even though the lingering fear of abruptly hitting the wall loomed over my head, I couldn't stop smiling.

Mr. Speedy Pants looked at his watch. "You disobeyed my instructions!" he scolded me, trying to sound annoyed but failing. "You're two minutes ahead of pace!"

I laughed. "What? Oh, that . . . Well . . ."

"I told you to go out conservative. As soon as I saw you guys, I knew it was too soon." He shook his head disapprovingly.

"I meant to!"

"Uh-huh." Mr. Speedy Pants's smile undermined his feigned disapproval. "Well, you're looking good, kid."

He went on to relate the details of his experience in the lead vehicle, including an incident involving several inattentive spectators and the employment of a bullhorn. I continued to wait for the wall. *I can't feel good the whole time*, I thought. *Marathons hurt. Any moment now I'm gonna come crashing down and wish someone would wipe me off the face of the earth.*

But that moment didn't come.

"See that girl in the pink shoes?" Mr. Speedy Pants asked me at mile twenty-five, pointing about one hundred yards ahead. "Let's chase her down."

We picked up the pace, slowly eating up the ground separating us from Miss Pink Shoes. (We also began to pull away from Big J, whose taper theorem failed him somewhere around mile twenty-four.) Miss Pink Shoes, for her part, kept an even pace, not increasing her speed for a finishing kick. This boded well for Mr. Speedy Pants and me, and I drew strength from seeing the distance between us disappear. By the time we passed her, we had also passed the twenty-six-mile marker and had entered the final stretch to the finish line. Arms raised in victory, laughing with delight at having accomplished the goal for which we had trained so long, we crossed the finish line of the GO! St. Louis Marathon. And in that moment, the past four months of long runs and track workouts, all the hopes and speculation carried throughout training, came to a beautiful completion.

"Well, kid, I guess I won't be mad at you for disobeying my instructions and running too fast," Mr. Speedy Pants said with a smile, giving me a giant hug as we made our way down the crowded finish chute.

I smiled back. "Thanks, Coach."

The ordered chaos just beyond the finish line carried us along as medals were placed around our necks and Mylar blankets draped over our shoulders. Big J had managed to muster enough SEC pluck to make up lost ground in the final quarter mile of the race, and he crossed the finish line just seconds after we did. Our trio shuffled to a row of people clipping the plastic timing chips from the shoestrings of a never-ending stream of finishers. Volunteers offered us water and Gatorade and bananas. Everywhere runners ambled about in lovely, contented, post-marathon exhaustion. For there, in the post-race milieu where people stood in small circles talking about how they felt at such and such a mile; where faces crusty with sweat and eyes squinting in the sun admired bright medals held up for inspection; where a sea of Mylar blankets mirrored the morning sun, once shyly peeking over the horizon, now climbing to midday brilliance; where concepts like schedules and weekly mileage no longer existed, if only for a day; where there was nothing else to do but revel in the satisfaction of having completed the task at hand; there, where the air itself embraced you with warm approval and every passing breeze whispered in a soft, protective tone, "Well done," was the sweet, blissful tranquility of having reached the end of a pursuit and finishing with victory in hand.

The moment—the race—was rare. I knew this, and I savored every second as we lingered about the post-race area, chatting with family and friends who had made the trek downtown to cheer us on. Mr. Speedy Pants greeted Mrs. Speedy Pants with a kiss and a brief report about the race, including the demerit I had received for disobeying his instructions and running too fast. Big J sauntered around, a beverage in each hand, "working the crowd," as he termed it. And I reunited with my family—my dad, mom, sisters, and brother. Hugs and congratulations abounded. My sister held up the giant sign we had made the night before and which she had proudly brandished during the race. In bright red and orange Sharpie it read, GO, BOB DINGY, GO! OLYMPIC CHAMP! NO WARM-UP!

Mr. Speedy Pants's training plan had made me fit; I had been prepared to race. More than prepared. I was a novice runner, a transplanted hockey player hurled into the world of distance running. My potential for improvement had been great, and Mr. Speedy Pants had done much with the raw material he was given. The race couldn't have gone better.

And yet, as we made our way back to our cars—slowly, stiffly—I harbored the strange feeling that this moment, this race, was fleeting, and perhaps once in a lifetime. Future miles would be tougher. This was simply the beginning.

I fingered the medal bouncing around my neck and smiled. It was curious. The weighty medallion with its depiction of several runners traversing the city seemed to speak with two voices—both in harmony, but distinct. The first voice, the more dominant of the two, offered congratulations and announced accomplishment. It was a cordial voice, good-natured and hearty. The other—this one quieter, more thoughtful—spoke softly from the shadows. Instead of looking back at what had been done, it saw only the future and what there was yet to do. It presented new goals, new challenges—and all the struggles they would entail.

I tried to muffle the second voice as our group parted ways. I wanted to enjoy the fullness of success, if only for a few more days. After all, there were plenty of miles ahead, and goodness knows they were only going to get harder.

SUMMER

Chapter Twelve

The adventures of the TMBG did not end with the GO! St. Louis Marathon. Adventure, it seems, comes in many different forms. One man's trash is another man's treasure, after all, and one man's 5K is another man's nightmare. I am, apparently, Another Man.

"Okay, kid, time to get back to business," Mr. Speedy Pants said as he whipped a notebook from a black bag. The yellow lined paper was already littered with numbers and notes, incriminating scribbles from Mr. Speedy Pants's 5K training plans and workouts.

"You surpassed expectations in St. Louis—since you didn't listen to me and ran too fast. You're one of those annoying overachievers."

I smiled.

"But don't let it get to your head," he added, keeping my exultation in check. "We picked a conservative time goal for you. I wanted to make sure the first time you raced a marathon you had a decent experience. No use in having you blow up and hate racing. You're enough of a head-case as it is."

Mr. Speedy Pants had a way of complimenting and insulting people at the same time. In this particular instance, I was content to accept the compliment.

"You hit your goal of becoming Zensah-fast . . . whatever that means," he added, rolling his eyes. "Time to pick a new 5K goal. Keep it realistic."

I shrugged. "What do you think is a realistic 5K goal for me?"

Mr. Speedy Pants leaned back in his chair and lifted his coffee cup to his mouth. "Well, what do you think is a realistic 5K goal for you?" he asked before taking a sip.

"Umm . . . I don't know. I mean, I know what I'd like to run, but I think what I want to run and what I can run are two different numbers."

"Maybe. Maybe not," Mr. Speedy Pants said. "You nailed the Super Secret Workout"—he smiled—"at least, on the second try. And that was on marathon training. You don't really know what you can do on training geared for shorter distances."

"Yeah . . ."

"Perhaps you're not giving yourself enough credit. You're faster than you think, kid."

There is something comforting in the assumption we are a source of untapped potential. Hope, when spiced with a pinch of vanity, is aroused by the slightest prick, innocent and indiscernible though it may be. And perhaps there is no prick quite as effective as the suggestion that greatness may rest within us.

Within two seconds of Mr. Speedy Pants making a casual observation regarding my undetermined 5K ability, I was at the Olympics, dressed in a navy-blue tracksuit, USA printed in bold red letters across my back. With one hand I acknowledged the roaring crowds overflowing the grandstands, and in the other I carried the American flag, waving the Stars and Stripes across the very track on which I would soon be competing for a gold medal.

"Hey, kid. So . . . ?"

Poof! The Olympics disappeared, and I was sitting in a coffee shop once more, staring at the expectant face of Mr. Speedy Pants. It was not the Olympics I was training for, but the Funky Monkey 5K benefiting the city zoo. Almost the Olympics, but not quite.

We continued discussing my 5K goals and came up with a training plan to carry me through the summer and into fall marathon training. Weekly mileage would be lower, but the running—especially the track workouts—would be more intense.

"Instead of longer intervals and pyramids, you're gonna be doing high volume, high intensity, short intervals," Mr. Speedy Pants said as he jotted down workout ideas, counting and re-counting the weeks separating us from the 5K and the 5K from the fall marathon season.

I looked over the sets of numbers as they progressed down the sheet of paper. The mileage was doable. That wasn't the problem. It was the pace at which the miles were to be run. Fast. Uncomfortably fast. I was about to voice my concern—which would have sounded uncannily like a complaint—when Mr. Speedy Pants hammered the final nail into my 5K coffin.

"And . . . I think it would be good for you to race a 3K. The track club holds a 3K every summer at the Brentwood track. It'll get you used to racing at an aggressive pace, and you need the experience."

"A 3K? On a track?"

"That's the general idea."

I imagined a local 5K crowd and then transplanted the participants to a high school track. The image was unsettling.

"So, how does everyone fit on the track?"

"Well, kid," Mr. Speedy Pants said, shaking his head, "everyone doesn't go at the same time. They hold the race in heats according to age group and gender."

"Oh. That makes more sense."

"Yep. It'll probably be a waterfall start, too, which will spread things out even more."

"What's a waterfall start?"

"It's your classic track start. The runners are staggered across the track from the inside lane to the outside. So, if you're on the outside lane, you'll be positioned in front of everyone else. The person on the inside starts the farthest back."

"Oh." That sounded far too serious. "But I've never raced on a track."

"So?"

"So . . ." I bit my lip. I tried to do the math in my head. *How long is a 3K?* I wondered. I came up with a number just shy of two miles. *Ugh. That's a sprint. On a track.* I pictured myself trying to run on the inside lane, crushed by a pack of experienced runners, getting jabbed by a dozen elbows and trying my best not to trip in a tangle of legs. The image cementing itself in my mind was a cross between a horse race and a roller derby. I saw myself being trampled to death by girls with names like Sally Spillblood and Bertha Destruction. It wasn't pretty.

"Racing on a track is so aggressive."

"Aggressive? Well, yeah, but . . . wait, you're a hockey player. What do you mean racing on a track is aggressive? Shouldn't that be a good thing?"

Again the roller derby image came to mind. I decided there are different kinds of aggression, some of which are good and some not so much.

"So you think I should do it, then?" I asked with uncertainty, my voice pleading that he did not.

"Look, kid, I'm not gonna make you do anything you don't wanna do. All I'm saying is I think it will benefit you. You need the experience. Plus, it'll be fun. Racing is fun."

Although the truth of Mr. Speedy Pants's last statement was debatable, I agreed to risk my life in the track club's upcoming 3K.

"I'll email you this week's mileage and workouts later tonight," Mr. Speedy Pants said as we left the coffee shop. "I'll have the rest of the schedule done in a few days. Of course, it's all tentative. We'll change it up as we go depending on how you're feeling and progressing."

We parted ways—Mr. Speedy Pants to his race-timing duties and I to finally get cleaned up from the morning's run. My post-St. Louis training respite was over. I had a tempo run the next day. Training for the Funky Monkey 5K—and the roller derby 3K—had begun.

"So you finally got yourself some racing flats?" Mr. Speedy Pants said as I reached into my duffel bag and pulled out a new pair of shoes, bright orange and obviously new. Two black jagged lines, like bolts of lightning, slashed across the middle of the shoes, giving the appearance (at least, I thought) of speed.

I handed one of the shoes to Mr. Speedy Pants for inspection. Mr. Speedy Pants was fending off another Achilles tendonitis flare-up, and while he would be running the cool-down with me after the workout, he had to take a rain check on the speedwork. I grabbed a towel and wiped the sweat from my legs. It was late afternoon, and the day's heat lingered in the air.

Perhaps it's my hockey background, but I'm a cold-weather runner. I like brisk temperatures and cold air, dull gray skies and a crisp breeze. Training for the St. Louis marathon had been winter training. But now I was training for a 5K. And we were deep into summer. Midwest summers are paralyzing. One-hundred-degree temperatures. One hundred percent humidity. Scorching sun. Oppressive air. It is enough to reduce a distance runner to a sorry puddle on the pavement, with only a pair of running shoes and some split shorts to float upon her remains (very much in the fashion of the Wicked Witch of the West). It was hot. And even my two-mile warm-up was a challenge.

"Very nice, kid. Today will be a perfect time to try them out. I always like breaking in my flats on a track." He handed the shoe back to me. "You know what you're doing?"

"Eh, kinda."

Mr. Speedy Pants outlined the progression of the workout as we walked onto the track. I was surprised by how light the racing flats felt. I felt official. I felt fast. I felt, like, totally cool.

"So, while you're running your 200s, I'll cut across the football field and meet you on the other side of the track. That way we can chat during your rests."

"Cool."

"Four sets of 200s, then six sets of quarters, then four sets of 200s. Got it?"

"Yep."

"Good. Now stop dilly-dallying and get at it."

I smiled and cleared my watch. "Yeah, yeah . . ."

My big racing flat debut turned out to be anti-climactic. I had somehow managed to buy the racing flats a half size too big. To this day, I don't know why. I have worn the same size running shoe since I was twelve. But for some reason, during the purchase of my racing flats, I decided it would be delightful to go up in shoe size. Thus, I bought a pair of shoes too large for my feet. And as I ran my 200s, I began to regret my indiscretion. I could feel the extra room between my toes and the front of the shoes. It was driving me nuts. It consumed my thoughts and made the 200s feel longer than they should have felt—which is ironic considering the nature of the problem. After the third 200, I communicated the issue to Mr. Speedy Pants.

"How in the world did you buy the wrong size?" he asked, rolling his eyes and shaking his head.

"I don't know! They didn't feel this big in the store."

"What size do you normally wear?"

"Seven."

"And what size is that?"

"Seven and a half."

"Do you ever wear a seven and a half?" he asked.

"No."

"Have you ever worn a seven and a half?"

"No."

"So, why would you think that you suddenly wear a seven and a half?"

"I don't know. I think I thought the shoes ran short or something. But obviously . . ." I bent down to feel just how much extra room I had, "they don't."

"Uh-huh. Well, no use having your shoes annoy you the whole workout. Finish up the 200s and then switch back to your trainers before you start your quarters."

This I did, though I felt a sense of loss in removing the lightning bolts from my feet. My regular trainers were fine. But they didn't have lightning bolts.

The 400s conducted themselves well. Mr. Speedy Pants told stories during my rests, confining his monologues to forty-five-second slices, which added both encouragement and amusement to the intervals. I also had the unexpected support of a high school boys' track team. More specifically, a troupe of high jumpers. Several boisterous members of the troupe cheered me on and even entreated me to join their practice. Their bravery spearheaded an onslaught of support, which culminated in an invitation to the prom.

"Nicely done, kid," Mr. Speedy Pants said after I finished my last interval. He patted me on the back as I tried to catch my breath.

"Thanks, Coach."

After a brief transition at our cars—I grabbed some water while Mr. Speedy Pants grabbed his running gear—we headed out for my cooldown miles.

Over the course of several months, Tuesday afternoons had become the official time slot for our track workouts. This being the case, we had observed certain patterns of events in and around Webster Groves that had become nothing short of sacred ritual by the time Funky Monkey training began. In addition to our customary bathroom stop during the last lap of our warm-up and my weekly inability to remember the finer details of the selected workout, there were two singular phenomena that ingrained themselves as permanent fixtures in our Tuesday routine.

The first was the abundance of landscaping activity throughout the neighborhoods of Webster. Such prolific yard work on such a grand scale prompted us to christen Tuesday "National Landscapers Day." The second phenomenon was running cool-down routes that were entirely uphill. Every week we defied the adage "What goes up must come down" by perpetually running up.

"Yee—oww . . ." Mr. Speedy Pants exclaimed as he lumbered his way through the first few steps of the cool-down. "My Achilles isn't happy about working again."

"A little stiff?"

"Just a bit," he mumbled.

We trudged up a steep incline, our steps keeping rhythm with the drone of industrial lawn care. The usual casserole of topics surfaced—the NFL, indie bands, tales of yore involving Mr. Speedy Pants's old buddy Tim and his buddy Fagan (who writes for the *Sporting News*). One especially fascinating story involved Fagan (who writes for the *Sporting News*), a buffet, three fortune cookies, and an apple. Of course, University of Illinois basketball was also discussed in detail, the topic being a particular favorite of Mr. Speedy Pants's. Once Illinois basketball bubbled its way into the conversation, I knew I wouldn't have to talk for a good three or four miles.

"Hey, Coach," I said after Mr. Speedy Pants had paid his respects to the Illini loss to North Carolina, "I wanted to thank you for being there for me during all my workouts and long runs—especially when you had to ride the bike or just stand there."

"In the rain," Mr. Speedy Pants added.

I smiled. "Yeah. In the rain."

"Eh, it's nothing, kid. That's why you pay me the big bucks. You know. All those invisible checks."

"Haha . . . Yeah, well, I'll be sure to throw in an invisible bonus the next time around." I paused. "But seriously, Coach, thanks."

"No problem. You are my protégée, after all. I feel a sense of responsibility when it comes to your training. Plus, you'd be lost without my wisdom, guidance, instruction, and awesomeness."

"Oh, brother." I shook my head. "It's amazing you don't tip over with an ego as big as yours is."

"Incredible, isn't it?"

"Hmm . . . You know what I think?" I wondered aloud, contemplating the strange mystery of befriending Mr. Speedy Pants.

"With you, there is really no telling."

I ignored his sarcasm. "You can be such a . . ."

"Jerk?"

"Haha . . . Yeah. You are so cocky—"

He tipped his head to confirm the truth of this statement.

"—but you're likable. Strangely enough. Everyone likes you."

Mr. Speedy Pants sighed, resigned to his unsolicited popularity. "I know. I don't know why."

I laughed. "Yeah, yeah. Well, despite my better judgment, I like you. Can't help it. You're cocky, but likable."

"Cocky but likable," Mr. Speedy Pants repeated. He nodded. "I can live with that. Hmm . . ." he said, pursing his lips in contemplation. "Now, how would I describe you . . . ?"

I rolled my eyes. There was no way this was going to be good.

"You," he said after a moment, "are dorky, but endearing."

"Umm . . . Thanks?"

He smashed the hair on top of my head. "Ah, we make a good team. To put it in hockey terminology—you know, so you can understand—we're like Wayne Gretzky and Jari Kurri of the old Edmonton Oilers. You would be Jari Kurri," he continued, "and I, of course, would be Gretzky."

"Because you're The Great One?" I said, laughing at the assuredness with which Mr. Speedy Pants designated our roles.

"Well"—he held out his hands—"can you argue? Plus, Kurri was a star in his own right. But their glory days were when they played together."

"They were the best."

"I know. I wouldn't have picked anything less for Team . . ." he paused. "Hmm . . . What should the name of our team be?"

"Uh . . ."

"Team Rodrigo," Mr. Speedy Pants declared before I had a chance to voice any suggestions.

"Team Rodrigo?" I asked.

"Yep. It sums up the whole coach–protégée dynamic."

"Oh, really? And how is that?"

"Well, remember the 'Brown-Eyed Girl' discussion?"

"Yes."

"And remember how you thought the first line was, 'Hey there, Rodrigo!' instead of 'Hey, where did we go?'"

I rolled my eyes. "Uh-huh."

"And remember how you were wrong?"

"Yes."

"And I corrected you?"

"Is there a point to this?"

"I'm always right. You'd be lost without my wisdom and guidance."

"Uh-huh."

"And I'm awesome."

I shook my head. "Cocky, but likable."

"Dorky, but endearing."

One mile later, Team Rodrigo finished its cool-down and returned to the parking lot.

"How'd the Achilles hold up, Wayne?" I asked as I took off my running shoes and slipped into a pair of flip-flops.

"Eh, it's there. But, really—" Mr. Speedy Pants stopped as he pulled a dry shirt over his head. "—when am I not hurt?"

"Rarely," I consented.

"Hey, kid," he said, waving an admonishing finger at me as I climbed into my car, "don't forget to change out those racing flats for a size that actually fits you."

"Okay. I won't forget."

"Uh-huh," Mr. Speedy Pants said.

"Uh-huh," I said back.

Before I drove away I reached into my duffel bag and pulled out the oversized racing flats, placing them in a prominent position on the passenger seat. I was positive I wouldn't forget to exchange them before the next track workout. But still.

Chapter Thirteen

It's funny how certain things pique your memory. You go about your merry way, unsuspecting, and then suddenly something random—a smell, a sound, a feeling—brings to mind the past with startling vividness. The recollection is intense, concentrated, a collision of time so forceful that a strange but fleeting emotional reality is formed. And for that one moment, what once was, is. You see it. You hear it. You smell it. You taste it. You want it to last. But it cannot. Powerless you felt it come upon you; powerless you watch it slip away. It fades into the distant shadows of the past, and is gone.

Training for the Funky Monkey 5K involved lower mileage than marathon training, but the miles were more intense. Instead of two-mile repeats at 10K pace, I was running 200s at I-never-run-this-pace pace. Press runs that were supposed to be, as Mr. Speedy Pants euphemized, "uncomfortable but not quite all-out racing" systematically chipped away at both my resolve and my stamina—perhaps more than they should have. The enchanted forests of Castlewood, then, with all their muddy trails and precipitous climbs and complete disregard for pace, became a frequent haunt during my recovery runs and on any other days during which I recoiled from the steaming asceticism of asphalt roads.

The sky was imposing as I laced up my shoes and prepared to head out on the trails. My quads were fatigued and sluggish from the previous day's workout, and I took my time stretching in the parking lot. Finally, I walked across the parking lot to the trailhead and began running.

Dark, looming clouds hung over the tree line and the air was thick with the smell of rain as I made my way down the trail, the ground a soft cushion silencing my steps. The leaves fluttered in gentle fits as the breeze swirled and eddied its way around the branches. A heavy mist enveloped the woods. The birds seemed discontent, ruffling their feathers as they swooped from perch to perch. And the smell of summer—restless and earthy and verdant—was heavenly.

Deeper into the woods I ran, captivated by the lushness. I glanced at a patch of wildflowers growing along the trail in brave little clusters. The petals trembled with each raindrop, and the tiny stems bent with the extra weight. It took but a moment to notice and pass the brave little bunch, leaving them to quiver and bloom on their own.

But in that moment, I saw her face.

I saw her face as she sat in the grass, cross-legged, just like she used to. She was tying together the stems of wildflowers, making a dainty necklace to match the garland already gracing the top of her head. The summer breeze played with her long blond hair, flipping stray wisps across her face, while the blueness of her eyes mimicked the clearest day with their sparkling, ethereal hue. She was laughing—always laughing—laughing for no other reason than just because she felt like it, just because laughter came easily to her. She sat there, weaving treasures of wildflowers. And she was happy.

I was startled by the memory—startled by how suddenly, how unexpectedly it came. Nearer the river I ran, the trail winding and looping through low meadows. It was the flowers, I knew. But I had seen many flowers since that time not so many years ago.

I saw two little girls flitting about in a tiny pink bedroom. We were preparing for a dance recital. We had braided each other's hair the night before and were now attempting to pin sparkling diamond barrettes in the bouncy curls. Dressed in crystal-studded leotards and matching tulle tutus, we felt entirely beautiful, entirely glamorous, and altogether grown up. We imagined we were the most graceful of ballerinas. And I danced. And she danced. And we were happy.

By now the mist had turned to a timid rain, intensifying the rich colors around me. The soil grew darker, and the saturated greens of the foliage contrasted sharply with the chocolate earth. The trees were stark, black silhouettes that rose stubbornly against the steady rain like battled-hardened soldiers, and the pungent smell of earth was heavy and over-powering. But I didn't notice.

We were sitting in the backseat of my mom's station wagon. We were on our way to soccer practice, and we sang goofy songs, keeping rhythm by clacking our shin guards together. She was one of the best players on our team; I was not. But she would always pass the ball to me anyway, and I adored her for it. We sat in the backseat and sang and asked if we could have a sleepover after the game and waved to the amused drivers behind us. Our team wasn't very good. We rarely won a game. But it didn't matter to us then. We were happy.

The path grew muddy, and my shoes slapped the ground, sending sprays of dirt and water in every direction. It was getting harder to breathe, for my throat felt tight, painfully tight, and it hurt to swallow. My eyes burned with the tears that wanted to come. My breath came in short, disruptive gasps. If only I couldn't see her so clearly.

We were graduating high school now. My! We had so much ahead of us! We sat on the wooden porch swing at her house, eating a giant bag of pretzels, talking for hours about our dreams and plans and futures. Every squeak and groan of the rickety swing prompted a new question. What would college be like? Whom would we marry? Where would we live? Of course our families would be close, and our kids would grow up together, just as we had. Back and forth the swing traveled. It creaked and groaned in protest.

"Don't worry," she would laugh, "some things will stay the same, no matter how old we get."

She gazed at the sky. She was holding a pretzel in one hand—comically, almost—as she turned to look at me.

"Take this swing, for instance. You know what's good about this swing? Fifty years from now, it'll still be here. Yep," she said, "I'm pretty sure this will be here *forever*."

"Yeah," I agreed, chomping on a pretzel of my own, naive to the youthful shortsightedness restricting the future to a small, narrow realm of experience, "some things just never change."

And then, she disappeared. And I was standing alone. And there were flowers, many flowers, more flowers than I had ever seen. They were for her. And there was a crowd of people. And there was the swing. It was empty and silent and still.

I stopped running now. I couldn't run. I couldn't breathe. The rain was heavy by this time, and the trail had long since been deserted by the sensible people of the world. There was no one around. And I missed her. So I stopped—in the middle of the trail, in the rain, in the mud—and with my chest heaving from the exertion of the run and the great sobs swelling within me, I wept.

I wept hard—violently almost—and my tears splashed into the puddles that littered the trail. I was sad, happy, angry, confused. I felt the joy of having known her. I felt the painful, stabbing grief of losing her so suddenly. I felt glad to remember her. I felt the simple contentment of two little girls sitting on a porch swing for hours on end, swinging back and forth, back and forth.

I don't know how long I stood there. Probably only a few minutes. It felt much longer. But I could breathe again, and I filled my weary lungs with great gulps of the saturated air. I shivered in the cold, apathetic rain that fell from the sky. And I began to run back home. Past the soldiering trees. Past the fitful birds. Past the brave patch of wildflowers that fought valiantly against the rain.

She was not unlike the wildflowers. Peaceful, delicate, free-spirited, lovely. She graced the world with her presence and lined the path with beauty. But only for a season. Her blue eyes sparkling, her blond hair tossed about by the wind, her smile was almost a laugh, easy and fluid and bright. And she lived. And she sang. And she was happy.

Chapter Fourteen

Why I was so reluctant to race 5Ks, I don't know.

Well, maybe I do know. The 5K was made to be run hard from start to finish. There is no "easy" in the 5K racing instruction manual. There are no directions to just "settle in and relax." No, the 5K is all about blood and guts and glory. You go out fast, you stay fast, and you finish fast. The 5K, in the words of Mr. Speedy Pants, is supposed to hurt. Well, that doesn't sound like much fun at all.

I think it wise to question any event requiring you pay a fee to run yourself into the ground. Sure, the bagels at the end of the race are a perk. But I doubt the cost of registration is based solely on bakery expenses. I mean, really, have you ever tried eating thirty dollars' worth of bagels in a single sitting? I am convinced the 5K is simply humanity's most inconvenient method of obtaining a T-shirt. Nordstrom never makes me run sprints to finalize a sale. And I like Nordstrom.

"Wait," Mr. Speedy Pants said as he looked up from his laptop and the mounds of paper littering a makeshift workstation inside the race-timing bus, "so you made a conscious decision to slow down? In the middle of a 5K?"

I winced. It sounded so much worse when Mr. Speedy Pants described it. I stared at the crisp white sheets of race results percolating from the printer and dropping into tight, clean stacks. I looked at the laptop perched atop bundles of wires and crumpled paper. I looked at a half-eaten donut and a cup of 7-Eleven coffee nestled within the center of a roll of duct tape. I did not, however, look at Mr. Speedy Pants.

"So," Mr. Speedy Pants continued, leaning back against the seat and crossing his arms, "why would you slow down?"

"Because . . . I got *tired* . . ."

Yes. That was my reason. In retrospect, I realize my defense may not have been as solid as I'd originally thought.

Mr. Speedy Pants rolled his eyes. "Kid, you're running hard. You're supposed to get tired. The trick is to keep going. You can always push yourself more." He leaned forward and poked my forehead with his index finger. "It's all in your head."

Ah, my head. Mr. Speedy Pants had a point. My head hates running fast just as much as my body does. Probably more.

"I know. I know. But 5Ks are hard the whole time. As soon as the gun goes off, I feel like I'm gonna die. And I get tired. And then I panic."

I had just finished racing the You Run, Eye Run 5K, the first in a series of practice races Mr. Speedy Pants had worked into my schedule en route to the Funky Monkey 5K. Not only was the You Run, Eye Run 5K the commencement of an island-hopping race strategy, but it also marked three milestone events in my running career. It was the first time I ever warmed up for a race (I did hold a brief moment of silence in honor of Bob Dingy), the first time I ever raced in racing flats (newly exchanged size sevens, lightning bolts and all), and the first time since falling under the tutelage of Mr. Speedy Pants that I raced without the personal pacing services of Mr. Speedy Pants or Big J. In other words, the You Run, Eye Run 5K was my first race as a grown-up. Almost.

After a brief warm-up, a last-minute bathroom crisis, and a momentary standoff between my watch and the satellite powers that be, I wiggled my way through the hordes of runners crowding the start line and readied myself for my first solo racing venture.

"Runners! On your mark . . . Go!" the announcer yelled over the PA system.

I started my watch and took a deep breath, momentarily carried along by the whoosh of eager participants, each of whom was driven by the short-lived but fervent belief that a new American 5K record was about to be set by the entire front corral of the You Run, Eye Run 5K.

I had no idea what pace I was running. I had difficulty determining 5K effort while doing 400s on a quiet track in Webster Groves; discerning 5K effort in an actual 5K—surrounded by hundreds of runners and mentally overstimulated by pre-race nerves—was impossible. My body mutinied against the shocking transition from a standstill to a sprint. The first half mile of my race was graced with gasps of hyperventilation, sluggish legs, and the uncomfortable sensation that my chest was about to explode. I recited Mr. Speedy Pants's instructions as I ran.

Don't start out too fast. Gradually pick up the pace after the first mile. Try to fall in with someone running your pace. Kick at the end. It may be a half mile. It may be a quarter mile. Just don't kick too early and run out of gas before you cross the finish line. Grind your teeth and finish strong.

I was almost two miles into the race. A 5K is a sprint compared with a marathon, but it's a marathon compared with a sprint. My watch beeped as I began the third mile. I looked at my time. *Yikes*, I thought. *I've never run this pace before.* The first mile had gone according to schedule, but mile two had been fast. Too fast. *I don't think I can hold this pace*, I worried. I began to panic. Up to that point, I hadn't felt that tired. Up to that point, I had been surprisingly heedless of pace. But as soon as I looked at my watch, as soon as I realized I had just chalked up the fastest mile in my sorry little racing career, I freaked out. The theory of numbers overwhelmed reality, and I convinced myself a disaster was forthcoming. I convinced myself I was tired, that I was going to grow more tired, that I wouldn't be able to finish. And so I made a deliberate, conscious choice. And I slowed down. Not because I had to. Not because my body wouldn't allow me to continue at that pace. But because I was afraid I was running beyond my ability. Because I was afraid how bad the last part of the race was going to hurt. Because, simply, I was afraid.

I still ran a strong race. I even managed a three-second PR. But I could have done better. And I knew it.

"You slowed down? On purpose?" It was Big J. He had volunteered to help Mr. Speedy Pants with setting up and tearing down the start and finish lines of the race. Now that the last runners had made their way through the finish chute, he poked his head inside the bus and caught the last part of our conversation.

"Man," he said, shaking his head, "you don't slow down in a 5K. A marathon, maybe. But not a 5K. If you could run a 5K so that you died as you crossed the finish line, it'd be the perfect race. 5Ks aren't fun. They're torture." He smiled. "That's why they're fun."

I grimaced. "I did run hard."

"Hard, yeah. But not hard enough," Big J said.

"What?"

"You waved and smiled at me at mile two," he offered as explanation. "If you can smile and wave at someone during a 5K, you're not running hard enough."

"Hey," Mr. Speedy Pants interjected, looking at Big J, "don't you have some timing equipment to tear down?"

"Oh. Ha . . . Yeah," Big J said as he hopped down from the bus. He smiled and waved, mocking my salutation at mile two.

"Look, kid," Mr. Speedy Pants said, turning to me and gathering the stacks of results sheets piled up on his desk. "Do you want to be fast?"

I shifted my body weight, tightening my ponytail once more before planting my hands on my hips. "Yes."

"Well, then you need to accept the fact that running fast hurts. Once you stop fighting the pain and learn to accept it, you'll be free to run even faster."

Ugh. Accept the pain. Being free sounded nice. Being fast sounded even better. The pain? Not so much.

"I know. But . . ."

"But what?"

"But . . . I want to be fast . . . without . . . having to try that hard."

149

Silence.

I have yet to find words adequate to express the look Mr. Speedy Pants gave me at that moment. Part disbelief. Part horror. Part condescension. Part pity, perhaps? Mr. Speedy Pants couldn't find the right words, either, for he just sat there, staring at me. That is, once he removed his hands from his face, which he had covered in the initial shock of my statement.

But there it was. I had said it. With those words I had committed an act of sacrilege in the running universe, and I felt the shame of history on my wimpy little racing flats.

Yet I also felt a strange sense of relief in the admission. In some bizarre, roundabout way, there was liberation in finally confessing my dread of running hard. It was as though up to that point, I held some expectation that real runners are supposed to love running hard. That they are supposed to torture their bodies with pace. And love it. That they are supposed to live for running themselves miserable. And because I wasn't particularly fond of self-inflicted agony, I felt inferior. I felt like a fake. In my mind, signing a 5K registration form was equal to signing a binding contract to beat myself over the head with a baseball bat for twenty minutes. Not good in theory or reality.

But, having acknowledged my fear, having finally disclosed the existence of a nagging, persistent dread, I felt more equipped to face it. I didn't like the pain of running hard. So what? I liked running. I loved running. And, yeah, I did want to be faster. And if becoming faster required a little discomfort, well, so be it. It didn't mean I had to like it. It only meant I didn't like it, but I did it anyway.

Mr. Speedy Pants was always reminding me that racing requires experience. The mind must be trained as well as the body. The mental must overcome the physical. It can be a tough concept. It must be practiced. For some people, running hard comes naturally. For others, running hard must be learned. I fell into the latter category.

"Kid," Mr. Speedy Pants said, finally breaking the conversational impasse, "what are we gonna do with you?"

I smiled. I didn't have an answer. But I did have a registration form for another 5K. And that, at least for the time being, was good enough.

The sport of running has the strange habit of illustrating life lessons when you least expect it. It's uncanny, really. Discipline, perseverance, pain, personal accomplishment—all can be illustrated by this race or that training run or, as the case may be, buying the wrong size of racing flats.

The You Run, Eye Run 5K had been no exception. Beyond the obvious opportunity for growth granted by a race of firsts, the race also provided a revelatory glimpse into the fragility of my mental disposition. There was a current flowing through my entire You Run, Eye Run 5K experience, a small stream that trickled into pre-race nerves and spilled into mid-race doubt and surged into a torrent of panic. Self-confidence had been swept away and, surrounded by the waters, I had surrendered to fear. Fear of failing. Fear of pain. Racing a 5K at that pace was something new. I didn't know what to expect. Unable to see the end result, I found myself afraid of the journey. I found myself afraid of what I would encounter along the way. I found myself afraid to pursue the unknown. And I slowed down.

Not long after the You Run, Eye Run 5K, I went out for a comfortable, easy six miles. The day was very hot and very humid. A friend had told me about a trail just off the main road in Mystical Land, a meandering, lollipop loop. I *thought* my friend had told me the actual trail part of the loop was just over two miles long. I planned my route accordingly.

The feeling I had as I left the main road to venture forth on an unknown trail was that of quiet elation. The natural motion of running. The subtle relief of the trees softening the summer sun. The feel of the indulgent dirt in opposition to the pavement. The excited uncertainty that so often couples itself with adventure. The woods grew more and more remote until it seemed as though I were running away from civilization itself, my lone figure cutting away from reality. There was nothing but the occasional breeze, the crunch of leaves, and the sound of my own breathing. I fell into a runner's utopia and became oblivious to time. Which is why it took me so long to realize I had enjoyed more time on the trail than should be allotted for a two-mile loop. And by the time I realized I had enjoyed more time on the trail than should be allotted for a two-mile loop, I had actually enjoyed more time on the trail than should be allotted for a three-mile loop. And that's when the enjoyment stopped.

I continued down the path, looking for a sign that I would soon emerge from the remote jungles beyond Mystical Land, yet the path seemed to lead only farther into the wilderness. The bucolic setting—which had seconds before felt serene—morphed into an ominous road to nowhere. I passed an abandoned deer stand in a large oak tree and, in the midst of my sudden confusion, had the vague idea I was about to be shot. I nearly expected to see a POINT OF NO RETURN sign. Each step led me farther and farther from civilization. I became aware of the heat. And of thirst. And of fatigue.

After a few more minutes of flustered running, I rounded a bend, hoping to see the path turn back toward the road—or at least toward the direction I suspected would lead to the road. However, the path led to an old rotting gate nearly hidden by the dense green foliage. There was a sign nailed to the gate: DUCK POND. Beyond the gate—at least as far as I could see—was more trail, leading deeper into the woods. At this point, I was just over four miles from where I had left the road. I decided enough was enough, and I turned back. Thus, on that lovely, one-hundred-degree summer afternoon, my comfortable six-mile run turned into a panicked twelve-miler.

"So, I still don't know where, exactly, the trail dumps you back out on the road," I complained to Mr. Speedy Pants the next day. I had told him of my little adventure, not going out of my way to downplay the dangerous aura effected by the deer stand.

"First of all, kid, I thought you said the path was four miles long, not two. Second, why do you always panic? I'm sure your friend wouldn't send you on a death run into the wilderness."

"I totally said two miles. At least, I'm pretty sure I did," I said. I actually didn't know anymore, but I defended myself anyway.

Later that day, I climbed into my car to search for the Path of No Return. I remembered my friend had said something about the path leading to an unmarked gravel road before spilling back into the heart of Mystical Land. After two or three unsuccessful drive-bys, I finally found the gravel road and turned accordingly. As the tiny rocks clinked against the undercarriage of my car, I scanned the woods for signs of the path. The dense green foliage shrouded the woods in a blanket of vegetation, a blanket so thick I nearly missed an old rotting gate hidden beneath the leaves. An. Old. Rotting. Gate.

Throwing my car into park, I hopped out and made my way through the weeds and vines. Rounding the gate and viewing it from the other side, I noticed a weathered sign hanging on for dear life. The sign simply read, DUCK POND. Just beyond the gate, the path split. From the woods, you couldn't see the second path leading back to the road, even though the road was only a few hundred yards away.

"Well, what do you know . . . ?" I queried the woods and its inhabitants. I thought of how lost I had felt in those woods, how I had thought I was miles away from where I needed to be, how I had even thought I was running in the wrong direction. If only I had known then how close I was to reaching my destination. If only I had known, I wouldn't have turned back.

I was almost there! I thought.

I am the ultimate Monday-morning quarterback. I have very wise afterthoughts. But in the moment? Not so much. Life's lessons usually aren't apparent to me until after the event has passed. The illuminating wisdom of hindsight provides a cleaner, more objective prospect, and what I don't see in the midst of the struggle usually becomes clear upon looking back. Like the path just past the DUCK POND sign.

It's funny how our confidence rises and falls with our familiarity with the path before us. The You Run, Eye Run 5K had demonstrated my fear of the unknown. (I slowed down.) The Duck Pond run had taken that truth even farther. (I turned back.) In both cases I had given up when I was only steps from the finish line. In both cases I let doubt and uncertainty overwhelm my desire to keep going. In both cases I let fear rob me of joy.

I have discovered I am pretty good at persevering through trials when I can see the light at the end of the tunnel. I may crab a bit, but I tough it out. The problem comes when the light at the end of the tunnel is blocked by a bend in the road. Suddenly in the dark, I find myself succumbing to fear. Not able to see the path, I give in to fatigue and lose confidence in my abilities—often when victory is just around the corner.

I climbed back into my car and tried to turn around on the narrow gravel road. It wasn't easy.

How ironic, I thought as I made several unsuccessful attempts to maneuver my vehicle back to the paved streets. *If only it had been this hard to turn around yesterday.*

You Run, Eye Run 5K Lesson Number One: When you find yourself in the unknown, when you can't see the path ahead, when everything around you is screaming to turn back, when fear overcomes your desire to continue—just keep moving forward.

You Run, Eye Run 5K Lesson Number Two: If you can smile and wave at someone during a 5K, you're not running hard enough. (I consider Lesson Number Two a bonus.)

Chapter Fifteen

"Oh, man . . ." I tugged on the handle of my front door. "Nooo . . . C'mon . . ." I jogged to the back of the house and tried the patio door. And the basement door. And all the windows on the lower level of the house. No luck. "I can't believe this," I grumbled as I headed back to my car.

I was supposed to meet Mr. Speedy Pants at the track for a workout in thirty minutes. I had rushed home from work, figuring I had approximately three minutes to change into my running gear, grab a bottle of water, and still make it to the track on time. What I didn't realize, however, was that after running the day before, I had failed to reattach my car key to the carabiner. The carabiner held the rest of my keys, such as my house key. Which was now in my house. Locked up. With my running gear.

"Hey," I said into the phone after I had assessed the situation and devised a plan to still run the workout, "I totally locked myself out of my house. I can still do the workout, but I'll probably be at least thirty minutes late. Does that work or do we have to cancel?"

"Bummer, kid," Mr. Speedy Pants said. "Well, that should work. We'll have to skip the cool-down though. I have to be done by six. I have a date with Mrs. Awesome."

"That's cool." My car threw clouds of dust in the air as I drove down the gravel drive. "Sorry, Coach."

"No need to be sorry. It happens. See you in a bit."

The brilliant plan I concocted consisted of making a quick stop at the local running store on my way to the track and picking up a few necessary items—namely, running shorts and a pair of socks. Other than that, the situation wasn't as dire as I had initially thought. I had an extra pair of shoes in my car. My GPS watch was in my purse. I could beg water from Mr. Speedy Pants. And I could do without a visor for one work-out.

One hour and forty-two dollars later, I arrived at the track.

Mr. Speedy Pants was standing outside his car when I finally pulled into the parking lot of the Webster Groves Recreation Complex and Ice Arena. He tapped his watch and shook his head at me as I climbed out of my car.

"Ugh. Well, that kinda stunk." I grimaced, "Sorry, Coach."

"Un-ac-ceptable," he said.

I smiled. "Oh, and I don't have any water. Do you mind sharing?"

He rolled his eyes and groaned. "Unbelievable. I don't even know why I coach you."

"For the invisible checks, remember?"

"Ah! That's right. Okay, then. Let's go."

Although the workout had started on shaky ground, the Webster Groves track did its best to counteract the unfavorable karma of the afternoon. Over the course of a few hours, a carnival had apparently blossomed from the pavement of the parking lot. Several brightly colored tractor-trailers advertised such delights as the "Tilt-A-Whirl" and the "Wheel of Fun." One of the trailers advertised funnel cakes, popcorn, and something about a two-headed snake. (I imagine the last item was unrelated to the first two.) A small Ferris wheel glittered and shined in the afternoon sunlight. It was the smallest Ferris wheel I had ever seen, and it was named, ironically, "The Giant." A solitary worker attempted to change one of the red lightbulbs adorning The Giant's circular frame.

"Ooo . . . A carnival!" Mr. Speedy Pants said as we lapped off warm-up loops around the track. "The 'Happee Day Carnival,' no less," he said, reading the large letters splashed across one of the trailers. "That is stellar."

The Happee Day Carnival created a jovial amusement aside from the usual habitué of the track. It also provided a sharp contrast with the rest of my workout, which was not in any way "happee." It was a pyramid workout, and it was ugly.

"Okay, kid, remember what you're doing," Mr. Speedy Pants said. It was not a question. "You're gonna go 2000, 1600, 800, 400. Then you'll build back up again—400, 800, 1600, 2000. Your rest between the two 400s will be slightly longer than the other rests."

"Okay."

"And what are you not going to do?"

"Go out too fast."

"Good." Mr. Speedy Pants looked at his watch and stepped up to the start line. "Although that won't really be an issue, since I'm running the workout with you."

"And because you're awesome?"

"Well, that's a given." Mr. Speedy Pants smiled.

So began the Workout of Death.

Running is a fickle sport. One week you hammer a long run. The next, you slog your way through the miles. You feel like you were born on the roads. You feel like you've never run a single step in your life. You love it, you hate it, you do it anyway. And sometimes, you have to stop.

The 2000 had been rough—way rougher than it should have been. I was tired. And behind pace. The 1600 was even uglier.

"We're a little slow, kid," Mr. Speedy Pants said after the first lap of the 1600. "Think you can pick it up a bit?"

Mr. Speedy Pants was being kind. I was not a little slow. I was a lot slow.

"Uh . . . I don't know." I was hurting, and Mr. Speedy Pants knew it. "I'm having a really hard time breathing," I gasped as we continued to run. "I feel like I can't catch my breath."

"Okay, well, let's at least see if you can get close to your time. If not, we may have to call it a day."

Two laps later, I couldn't, and we did.

"Not feeling it today, huh?" Mr. Speedy Pants asked as we pulled up, officially bagging the workout.

I sighed. It felt horrible to quit. I hadn't felt like this since the failed Super Secret Workout. "Yeah, I guess not."

"Don't worry about it. It happens. You just have to know when it's time to grind your teeth and gut it out and when it's time to throw in the towel. Today just wasn't your day. You weren't going to gain anything from slogging through the intervals and missing your times."

"Yeah."

Mr. Speedy Pants patted me on the back and smiled. "Hey, this is kinda like the Super Secret Workout—the first one, anyway."

I rolled my eyes. "Yeah. Sheesh."

Mr. Speedy Pants sat down on the bleachers and reached for his duffel bag. "Looks like we'll have time for a cool-down after all—get an extra mile or two."

"Actually," I said, my voice somewhat apologetic, "why don't you finish up your workout, or at least run some quarters. You already had to wait almost an hour for me to show up. No need to totally hose the afternoon."

Mr. Speedy Pants stood up. "Good point." He looked at the track. "Okay, I'll just do a few quarters."

"Go for it, Coach."

I climbed up on the low concrete wall separating the bleachers from the track, wrapping a towel around my neck and grabbing a few sips of water from Mr. Speedy Pants's water bottle.

Oops, I thought. *Better save some for him.*

It was good to see Mr. Speedy Pants running again. His Achilles tendon injury had sidelined him for too long. As he lapped off each quarter, I realized I had never before really watched him run. He was always running with me, or biking alongside me, or standing on the side of the track cheering me on. In the rain. But as he flew across the track, I saw Mr. Speedy Pants, the runner, for the first time. His gait was smooth and graceful, effortless yet powerful, each stride a perfect duplicate of the last. The ground beneath him, his forward motion, and even his own body seemed to be calculated to perfect symmetry. He was a runner, a runner-runner. Fluid. Nimble. Gazelle-like. And above all, speedy.

Geez. That is what I don't look like when I'm running, I thought, trying to imagine what it would be like to be graceful and fast and not a Weeble-esque, hockey player of a marathoner.

"Nicely done, Coach," I said as Mr. Speedy Pants finished his quarters.

Mr. Speedy Pants walked about the track for several seconds, catching his breath.

"I went out too fast on the first one," he said as I tossed him his water bottle.

"Coach! What do I always tell you?"

He rolled his eyes. "And what do I always tell you? 'Do as I say, not as I do.'"

"Uh-huh. Lame."

He threw his bag over his shoulder and took another swig of water. "Ready?"

"Yep."

"Then stop dilly-dallying. Let's go."

As usual, it was National Landscapers Day and we ran our entire cool-down uphill. We discussed the Workout of Death, the necessity for a redemptive Workout of Death II in the near future, and the return of Mr. Speedy Pants to speediness.

"Well, somebody's gotta carry Team Rodrigo," he said as we made our way back to our cars and prepared to leave.

"Uh-huh."

Mr. Speedy Pants smiled. "Don't worry. You'll have your revenge on the Workout of Death. For now, rest up for tomorrow's TMBG. Bright and early at Castlewood."

"Sounds good, Coach."

"See ya, kid."

"Looks like it'll just be you and me today—for the run, anyway," Mr. Speedy Pants said as I pulled my trail shoes from the trunk of my car. "Big J's gonna catch up with us at Uncle Bill's."

"What happened to him?" I asked.

"He hurt his foot running hill repeats yesterday."

"Did he twist it or something?"

"I don't think so. He said he felt a pain in the top of his foot during one of the intervals, and the pain never went away. Apparently it's pretty swollen this morning."

"Yikes."

A heavy rain had fallen throughout the night, transforming Castlewood into a reservoir for mud, water, sand, and every combination of the three. In fact, the magical forests of Castlewood had had a rough go of it over the last two months. A wet spring coupled with successive summer thunderstorms had caused widespread flooding throughout the park, and the river's insatiable appetite swallowed the trails with sweeping intemperance. Giant trees lay prostrate across the trail, their long branches grasping at the hills beyond the reach of the angry river. Deposits of sand and sediment littered the path in incongruous piles, as did several token relics, the rusted residuum of a recent flood. An old washing machine. A car tire. Sporadic slivers of mystery steel strewn within the weeds and buried in the sludge. Some sections of the trail were washed away altogether. The river had been there, and it hadn't been kind.

It was the muddiest twelve miles I had ever run. Our shoes and legs had long since disappeared beneath a coating of viscous brown. Our shorts were barely recognizable. Even my face was speckled with bits and streaks of mud. (A result of the flying clumps being flung into the air by Mr. Speedy Pants's shoes.)

"Hey, kid," Mr. Speedy Pants said as our run came to a close, "wanna run through the creek to clean off?"

"Sure."

We broke away from the trail and ran down a grassy embankment toward a clear stream. The water was ankle-deep for the most part, but in several different sections it pooled to three or four feet. It rushed over my shoes as I followed Mr. Speedy Pants into the creek. And that's when I learned that you should never follow Mr. Speedy Pants into a creek.

I was about halfway across when he stopped, turned around, and sent a tidal wave of water into my face.

"Agh—agh!" I gagged. I made the mistake of screaming as I watched the wall of water come at me. I had swallowed a mouthful of water. And I was soaked. Completely soaked.

"Oh, my gosh! I can't believe you did that!" I said as I wiped the water from my face and tugged on my shirt and shorts, now plastered to my skin.

"Haha . . ." Mr. Speedy Pants laughed. "I can't believe you actually followed me into the creek. Did you really not know I was going to splash you? That's the oldest trick in the book!"

"No! I thought we were just gonna run through and get the mud off our shoes. Geez . . ."

I could only imagine how bedraggled I looked, dripping wet, hair tangled and shorts mud-stained. Mr. Speedy Pants just stood there, shaking his head and smiling. I couldn't help but laugh.

"You're a piece of work, kid," he said.

"Yeah, yeah. Whatever."

I made my way across the creek, washing the final remnants of mud from my shoes and wringing some of the water from my shirt.

"Huh. Wonder what's going on up there," Mr. Speedy Pants said as we sloshed and squished our way down the main road toward the parking lot. "Looks like they're filming something."

They were, in fact, filming something. A local news station was reporting live from the haunts of the TMBG.

"Hey," Mr. Speedy Pants greeted the well-dressed news reporter as we entered the parking lot.

The cameraman turned to look at us. The well-dressed reporter—who bore an uncanny resemblance to Guy Smiley—also looked at us, though he finished adjusting his tie before doing so.

"Good morning!" said Guy Smiley. He surveyed our appearances, a slight quizzical look coming over his face when he looked at me. He recovered himself, however, and any questions he may have had regarding why or how I looked the way I did remained unexpressed.

"We're reporting on the recent flooding in the local parks," he continued, "and assessing their current conditions. You've been out on the trails, I take it?" he asked, tipping his head toward Mr. Speedy Pants.

"Yep. We were just finishing up a run," Mr. Speedy Pants replied.

"Do you run here often?"

"Eh, pretty often. Goes in spurts. Haven't been able to run out here much lately, though, because of the flooding."

"Would you be interested in answering a few questions about the park's conditions? I'd like to get the opinion of a regular visitor."

"Sure."

The cameraman spun around, aiming the giant camera at Mr. Speedy Pants. Guy Smiley, for his part, counted down from three, turned to Mr. Speedy Pants, and, plastering his face with genuine concern at the count of one, began the interview. He asked Mr. Speedy Pants about the flooding. He asked Mr. Speedy Pants about the current state of the trails. He asked Mr. Speedy Pants how disappointed he was about the flooding and how happy he was that he could finally run the trails again. Throughout the interview, he referred to Mr. Speedy Pants as "a gentleman who often frequents Castlewood State Park."

Meanwhile, I stood there, completely ignored by Guy Smiley but standing close enough to Mr. Speedy Pants that I couldn't tell if I was in the camera shot or not. Thus, I smiled and nodded at everything Mr. Speedy Pants said.

Finally, Guy Smiley finished interrogating Mr. Speedy Pants. He thanked us for our time, which action jogged his memory regarding my existence. He turned to me awkwardly, as if responding to an after-thought, and asked if I had anything to add. I said something in con-currence with what Mr. Speedy Pants had said. Guy Smiley thanked me and turned away, having determined one question would suffice.

"So, the reporter talked to me for a full five minutes—maybe more—and he didn't even look at the kid," Mr. Speedy Pants laughed as we sat in our regular booth at Uncle Bill's. He had recounted to Big J the morn-ing's adventures, including the sorry state of the trails, and how I had fallen for "the oldest trick in the book" by following him through the creek.

"Ha. He probably didn't want to interview you because you were all wet," Big J said. He added a packet of creamer to his coffee and took a sip. "You would have looked funny on television."

"Well, she looks funny anyway," Mr. Speedy Pants rejoined. "That's a given."

I made a face at him and continued eating my oatmeal.

"Now, despite the fact that you looked like a drowned rat—"

"You still kinda do, actually," Big J said, pointing to my wet hair, which I had—unsuccessfully—tried to disguise beneath a baseball cap.

"Anyway," Mr. Speedy Pants continued, "despite the fact that you looked like a drowned rat, I think he didn't ask you any questions be-cause my answers were so awesome."

"Oh, brother. Maybe he didn't ask me any questions because your big head filled up the entire screen," I countered.

"Good point," Big J agreed.

"Hmm. Could be." Mr. Speedy Pants took a sip of his coffee and leaned back against the booth. "Well, I am kind of a celebrity now."

I laughed. "Sure you are. People everywhere are going to run up to you and say, 'Hey! Are you the guy from that news segment about flooding in local parks?'"

"And I'll say, 'Why, yes. Yes, I am.'"

"Man! I missed all the excitement!" Big J said shaking his head. "Stupid hill repeats."

We began discussing Big J's minor injury, which led to discussion about hill repeats, which led to discussion about the most grueling workouts of Mr. Speedy Pants's and Big J's college days, which led to several suspense-filled stories involving Mr. Speedy Pants and his old buddy Tim. We lingered in the booth and allowed the waitress to refill our coffee mugs. None of the TMBG was in any hurry to leave, and the time passed quickly. Mr. Speedy Pants eventually looked as his watch.

"Whoa . . ." he exclaimed, shocked by how late it was. He raised his hands in victory. "Longest TMBG breakfast in history!"

This discovery led to one more story involving Mr. Speedy Pants's old buddy Tim and the explosion of several packets of ranch dressing in a Jack in the Box parking lot.

"Thanks for the mud run, Coach!" I called as we left Uncle Bill's.

"Yep. And, kid, maybe one day you won't look so goofy and you'll make it on a news report."

"Maybe one day I'll shove you into a creek."

Mr. Speedy Pants laughed. "Fair enough."

Chapter Sixteen

The weeks following the Workout of Death brought redemption in several forms, the most direct of which was the Workout of Death II. This I completed with success seven days after the original. Further absolution came in the guise of the Wonder Run-der 5K, the track club 3K (aka the dreaded roller derby), and the long-anticipated Funky Monkey 5K.

The Wonder Run-der 5K was my first race since the You Run, Eye Run 5K. And like its predecessor, it carried with it several important installments for my racing portfolio. It was, first of all, another solo 5K journey. Mr. Speedy Pants had to fulfill his duties as Kronos; while he would be present at the race, his presence would be limited to the race-timing bus and the area immediately surrounding the start and finish lines. Second, it was a small race, a race small enough that anyone in the Zensah-fast category (including me) had a chance of winning.

"Okay, kid," Mr. Speedy Pants said as I hung around the race-timing bus, waiting for the call to the start line, "there's a good chance you'll be one of the top females going into the final mile. Don't be afraid to make a race of it. Don't do anything dumb, but if you think you've got a chance to catch the girl in front of you, go for it. If you're the lead female and there's a guy within striking distance, chase him down. The key is to find a target and start picking people off. Got it?"

I tightened the laces of my racing flats and stood up from the giant black plastic box on which I had been sitting. I had no idea what was in the box. Probably something electronic. I nodded at Mr. Speedy Pants.

"Yeah."

"And remember: Don't. Slow. Down. Not in the last mile, anyway.

You've gotta just grind your teeth and gut it out. It's okay if it hurts. Accept it. Once you accept the pain, it will free you to run faster."

I nodded, but I wasn't convinced.

Mr. Speedy Pants looked at his watch. "Better go warm up. Almost start time."

My stomach was in knots. My head felt—funny. Full. Heavy, almost. It was dread. I was dreading the race. I was dreading the discomfort and pain of racing.

"See you at the finish line, kid!" Mr. Speedy Pants called as I stepped out of the bus and began my warm-up.

The race followed the same progression as the You Run, Eye Run 5K. The sights and sounds of the first mile were drowned out by the adrenaline rushing through my body and the panicked beating of my heart. I looked at my watch as it beeped at the one-mile marker. Somehow I was right on pace. During the second mile, panic gave way to the nagging fear I was either running too fast or inadvertently slowing down. My watch beeped a second time. I had sliced thirteen seconds off my second mile.

Okay. Just relax, I told myself as my breath began to feel strained and my quads felt heavy with a reluctance to go forward. *It's just a little discomfort. It's okay. It's normal. Pain is normal. You're okay.* I was hurting and wanted to stop. *You can hold on. Don't slow down. Keep going.*

"First female! First female!" called a voice from somewhere along the course.

I looked up, noticing the spectators for the first time. There weren't many of them—a handful at best. But there was one man in particular, yelling, clapping, and waving.

"First female!" he called again.

And suddenly I realized he was talking about me. I was in the lead.

I surged forward, as if the man's words had uncovered a hidden reserve of energy and I was now being propelled by the force. There was half a mile to go. I could feel my body pressing forward, pressing the pace, pressing against the pain and the discomfort and the desire to stop running. I looked up at the next runner, a man in a blue shirt. He couldn't have been more than five seconds in front of me. I surged again, scared by how fatigued I was becoming.

The blue shirt came nearer. It was next to me. It was behind me. I could see the finish line. A volunteer waved us around a final turn as we looped back toward the parking lot where the race had started.

"First female!"

"Finish strong!"

"Lookin' good! Keep going! First female! First female!"

The voices grew louder as I ran. I was sprinting now. Gasping. Miserable. Praying the stupid race would end. It was horrible. It was unendurable.

It was glorious.

Mr. Speedy Pants was waiting for me at the finish line.

"Atta way, kid!" he said as I slowed to a stop and clasped my hands behind my head. I threw my head back, stretching my face to the sky (because, of course, that's where all the air is).

"Nicely done, kid. First female," Mr. Speedy Pants said, throwing his arm around my shoulders. "Not too shabby."

I was still gasping for air, but I managed a muffled, "Thanks."

"Your first time winning a race, eh? Congratulations."

"Thanks."

"How'd you feel?"

"Umm . . ." I panted. "Okay, I think. I kinda panicked during the second mile, but I kept telling myself that I was okay. The third mile, I was hurting. But . . ." I looked at Mr. Speedy Pants and smiled, "I didn't slow down."

"Atta girl."

I grabbed a bottled water from a folding table piled high with bananas, bagels, and donuts.

"All right, well, I've got to start posting results," Mr. Speedy Pants said. "You going to run a cool-down?"

"A really short one. I have to head straight to work after this. Actually . . ." I looked at my watch, ". . . yikes. Yeah, I gotta go."

"So, does this mean you want me to pick up your award for you?"

I smiled with affected sweetness.

Mr. Speedy Pants rolled his eyes. "Sheesh. Do I have to do everything for you? Oh . . . fine. I guess so. But I'm going to charge you extra for awards pickup service."

"Deal. Put it on my tab."

"You realize you're starting to build quite the hefty tab, don't you?"

"Whatever. What about all those invisible checks?"

"Uh-huh. Better go get your cool-down in, kid."

"Yeah, yeah . . ."

"And good job today. You toughed it out. I'm proud of you."

"Thanks, Coach."

It was a singular feeling, knowing I had finished as the top overall female. No, it wasn't the Olympics. And sure, there were only a handful of runners in the race. But the Wonder Run-der 5K had been special. It had been a mile marker, of sorts, in my relationship with pain. I still hated it, but I had finally accepted its existence. I finally had the mid-race wherewithal to tell myself the pain was okay. That I was okay. To not freak out. And yes, my moment of victory had been just that—a moment. Wherewithal soon gave way to panic. But I will never forget feeling fear and resisting it. In that moment, I didn't just tell myself I could keep going; I discovered I really could. By accepting a new level of pain, I met a new level of strength, one with which I was wholly unacquainted.

Maybe Mr. Speedy Pants was right. Perhaps I hadn't been giving myself enough credit. Perhaps I had been selling myself short. Strength ran deeper than I had thought. What if it ran even deeper still?

It was an extraordinary realization, both exciting and frightening in its potential. Because it was, in its own way, a responsibility. And it was terrifying. And it was empowering. And it was beautiful.

I rode the coattails of victory in the Wonder Run-der 5K as long as I could before the magic carpet dumped me, unceremoniously, at a waterfall start line. The dreaded roller derby 3K had arrived, courtesy of the local track club.

The Wonder Run-der 5K had been a success, other than the slight oversight on the part of the race committee in the construction of the overall winners' trophies—the male runner and female runner figurines that topped the trophies had been transposed— and I hoped the good karma from the race would carry over to the Brentwood track and the ensuing 3K.

"Here you go, kid. Congratulations," Mr. Speedy Pants said, handing me a brass trophy as we stood in the parking lot overlooking a flurry of runners stretching and warming up on the football field below. Several people were pinning on their race numbers—small, rectangular pull-tag sheets. Very old school. The track club thrived on the old school.

"Aww . . . Thanks, Coach," I said, accepting the award. A figure of a runner topped a glitter-and-gold plastic column mounted to a block of marble. FIRST PLACE OVERALL FEMALE, declared a tiny plaque glued to the base.

"Yeah, well, when I picked up your trophy, I realized the runner"— he pointed to the figurine—"was actually a male runner. But, because I'm awesome, I got it switched out for you."

"Haha . . . Thanks."

We embarked on a warm-up through the streets of Brentwood, which included an unscheduled bathroom break at a conveniently located grocery store. By the time we returned to the track, Big J had arrived.

"You ready, girl?" he asked, poking my shoulder.

I grimaced. That was my answer.

"Eh, don't worry. You'll be fine. It's fun."

"Not when it hurts."

"That's 'cause you fight it. Just let it hurt."

"I've never raced on a track."

"So? Just go out there and run. It's all in your head."

"What did I tell you?" Mr. Speedy Pants said, joining a conversation that was quickly morphing into a debate. "You actually have a good shot at winning this thing. You'll at least finish in the top three."

I took a deep breath and nodded. We began making our way down to the track.

"Now, if you find yourself in front with no one to pace yourself against," he continued, "you'll just have to use your watch and run your own race. Keep your pace steady. Try to kick when you get close to the end."

I nodded again. We had crossed the football field. A group of girls— no more than twenty—milled about the makeshift start line. Because of the distance, the race would begin at the two-hundred meter-line, a diagonal shot from the finish.

"Okay, now," Mr. Speedy Pants said, "don't start out at world-record pace like you did in your mile time trial. There may be some jostling for position at first, but, eh, it won't be anything aggressive. Everyone's just out here for fun. Find your rhythm and hang on."

I took another deep breath. I nodded, though by this time the movement was an automated response. Mr. Speedy Pants said something; I wagged my head, oblivious to the motion. I walked up to the start area where I was directed to the inside lane. The rest of the girls were directed in a similar fashion until we slashed across the width of the track.

"Go get 'em, kid," Mr. Speedy Pants called from the football field.

I looked ahead. The track looked blurry. The trees looked blurry. If they were trees. They may have been people.

There are no trees on football fields, I thought.

And then the starter's gun went off.

Don't start out too fast. Don't start out too fast, I chanted to myself. I was numb. Trapped in some kind of physiological phenomenon, I couldn't feel my own body, much less determine what pace I was running. I spent the entire first lap trying to run something between "too slow" and "too fast." I figured if I could do that, the first lap would be a success.

I found myself in the lead going into the second turn. As nervous as I was, I was grateful to at least have some breathing room. The roller derby images still loomed in the back of my mind. Four hundred meters down, I hit the lap button on my watch. I was right on pace—to the second. Incredibly enough.

Huh. That's a surprise. Cool, I thought as lap two began. I was kind of impressed.

"Nicely done, kid. Good job! Good job!" Mr. Speedy Pants called. He, too, had a stopwatch and was keeping track of my time.

I glanced over and gave a quick nod of my head, acknowledging the encouragement. I knew it would be the last time I saluted the outside world—at least during the race. Races had a way of turning into death marches for me. I flipped my wrist to catch a glimpse of my watch as the second lap came to a close.

Wha . . . ? After finishing the first lap, instead of hitting the LAP button on my watch, I had inadvertently hit the STOP button. Lap number two had been run at a mystery pace. I could hear Mr. Speedy Pants and Big J cheering me on as I fumbled with the buttons. Finally, the familiar beep of my watch signaled timekeeping duties had been resumed, and I continued running.

Around the far corner we ran. My lead was growing. *Don't slow down. Don't slow down. Push. Push.* It was a different mantra than the one I chanted at the beginning of the race. My body was still numb from nerves, and I had no idea how fast I was running. I assumed I was slowing down. Again my eyes wandered to my watch.

Wha . . . ? Not again! I can't believe this!

In my haste to restart my watch, I had hit the LAP button instead of START. I was heading into the fourth lap, and the numbers on the large screen strapped to my wrist hadn't moved in half a mile. I looked up. I could see Mr. Speedy Pants's face was calm, but slightly quizzical.

"You're a little slow!" he called as I ran by. "Pick it up, kid, pick it up!"

"I stopped my watch!" I yelled over my shoulder.

I couldn't see Mr. Speedy Pants's reaction to that enlightening piece of information, but I could imagine.

Rats, I thought. *I can't believe it. C'mon. Pick it up. Pick it up.* It seemed like such a waste. I was too slow—and for no other reason than I didn't want to run too fast. I double-checked my watch to make sure I hadn't hit the wrong button for the third time.

Finally, I thought. *Back on track.*

I was approaching the one-mile mark. The race was halfway over now. I zoomed past the stands where a few spectators sat on metal bleachers and eager runners stretched in preparation for their own upcoming races.

Halfway done, I told myself by way of encouragement. *Ugh. Only halfway done?*

Yeah, that didn't work. Instead of being inspired, I was overwhelmed by the thought that I still had just as much distance to cover as I had already completed. Suddenly I became aware of how uncomfortably fast the pace felt. I was beginning to grow tired. Ahead, Mr. Speedy Pants and Big J were watching me from their spot at the two-hundred-meter mark. Big J was crouching down on the grass.

"All day, girl. All day," he called as I ran by. It was not so much a cheer as a statement.

All day. All day. A wave of calm washed over me. *All day. All day,* I repeated. A strange phrase to bring comfort. But it did. "All day" was Big J's way of showing his confidence in me and my ability. "All day" was his way of telling me that this pace was easy for me, to just relax. "All day" was his way of telling me that I could just sit back and enjoy the scenery because, by golly, I could hold this pace all day. "All day" meant worry was pointless. "All day" meant I had this race in the bag.

It didn't matter if it was true or not. I believed it. It took my head out of the game. It freed me from overthinking. It freed me to just run.

"Back on pace, kid!" Mr. Speedy Pants shouted as I started the fifth lap. "Good job!"

All day, I repeated to myself. *All day.*

By some bizarre phenomenon, I was still the lead runner. The fifth lap passed by. Then the sixth. The burning in my lungs evolved from unpleasant to unbearable, my quads from heavy to immovable, my thoughts from *I'm tired* to *Somebody please kill me!* In short, I was miserable. Or, as Big J would have put it, I was racing.

Finally—mercifully—I threw the last two hundred meters behind me. I was done. I slowed to a jog. Then a walk. Then some kind of standing fetal position.

"Nicely done, kid," Mr. Speedy Pants said, throwing his arm around my shoulders. He and Big J had made the trek across the football field and greeted me with congratulations and a bottle of water. "That wasn't so bad, huh?"

I raised my eyebrows and shot him a wry smile. I figured my frenetic gasping for air was answer enough.

"Eh, that's racing. And look at you! You've got a nice little winning streak going on."

I laughed. How bizarre.

"Yeah, well, no one can bat a thousand for long."

Big J gave me a big hug. "Told you. You've just gotta stop thinking so much and run."

"Yeah. Thanks, Big J."

We lingered on the football field a bit longer and watched the rest of the 3K heats. Mr. Speedy Pants, being the eminent mythological ancient Greek god of race timing that he was, socialized with several members of the local running community. And other than a brief, unpleasant span during which I felt the urge to vomit (it must have been a delayed reaction to the nerves and exertion), the rest of the post-race festivities were quite enjoyable. I had just survived the roller derby 3K. In first place, no less. Huh.

"Hey, kid," Mr. Speedy Pants said as we finished our cool-down through the streets of Brentwood, "you ready for the Funky Monkey 5K?"

I took a deep breath.

There are more experienced runners, good runners, true runners, who enter races with eager, daring anticipation, who know their bodies are fit and prepared, down to the smallest tendon and tiniest ligament. Mr. Speedy Pants was one of those runners. I was not. I still dreaded 5Ks. I still feared the pain.

Ever since I could remember, I had been infatuated with the romanticism of triumph and defeat in sports. Dramatic overtime victories. Heart-wrenching, final-second losses. Slow-motion cameras. It's like soap operas for sports fans. Cheesy. Predictable. Clichéd. Indulgent.

Running, of course, lends itself well to the mélange of melodrama. Perhaps it is the elemental nature of the sport itself, a Hellenistic purity preserved throughout the ages, that makes it especially apropos for drama. Each race, each violent blur of man against time, is a microcosm of humanity's volatile relationship with mortality and the finite. It is the fundamental triumvirate of sport. Distance. Time. Man.

There is no better theater for Aeschylean athletics than a race, the ultimate test of human will over human endurance. Reeling from pain, grimacing in agony, staggering, surging, fainting from the effort but ultimately conquering the distance with upraised arms and a body depleted of every ounce of energy—that is how I envisioned the end of my races. Bring in the slow-motion cameras. Cue the music. I cross the finish line with one last swell of determination before collapsing in a pile of glory. That is the runner I was in my head.

Enter reality. As much as I dreamed of an effort worthy of a three-minute documentary narrated by Bob Costas, the truth was, I had never collapsed at the end of a race. I had never even thrown up at the end of a race. In fact, I think throwing up is gross.

So there you have it. My confession. Despite the dramatic scenes and Herculean performances I pictured in my head, I was really quite the anti-drama queen. I ran hard. I crossed the finish line. I grabbed a bagel. And I went home. End of story. Not exactly *Chariots of Fire* material.

To be fair, I was tired after my races. And during the race itself, I felt like I was running as hard as I could. As the Wonder Run-der 5K and the track club 3K had demonstrated, I had pushed myself to the point of panic. Yet sometimes I wonder if it was not the panic of someone in the throes of death, but merely the panic of someone who suddenly realized that what they were doing had ceased to be fun. Not quite as impressive. If only I had thrown up, perhaps I wouldn't have felt so guilty.

Alas, it seemed Bob Costas would never narrate a moving account of one of my races. (Perhaps such a loss comes with the territory of the Anti-Vomit Pacing Group.) Either I didn't have what it takes to run to the point of system failure or I had too great an awareness of the world outside of running to push my body to that point. Yes, I ran. But I also played hockey. And shopped. And ate cookies. And went to baseball games.

If the ultimate threshold of human endurance were a ten-gallon jug,

I would be the equivalent of a Dixie cup. Is it practical? Or wimpy? Looking at the ten-gallon jug in all its commodious glory, the Dixie cup can only dream of what it must be like to hold that much—whatever. Yet, conversely, a three-ounce drink can pack quite a punch in its own right—if it's filled with the right stuff. It really all depends on what's in the cup.

I stood in awe of those who can push themselves to the breaking point. I respected them. I cheered them on. I wondered what it would be like to run a race with such ferocity that I fall to the ground in sheer exhaustion. I wondered if, one day, I would ever have that chance. I wondered, if I did, if I would take it.

Running is such a weird sport. It marries torment and elation in an extraordinary union to entice unsuspecting victims. It confuses with a love–hate relationship. It thrills. It hurts. It gives mortals the ability to fly. Like a color scale morphing from the brightest white to the darkest black and back again, so my affection for the sport traveled across the broadest spectrum of emotions before finally returning to its rightful shade: a deep, constant, sometimes obscured but never departed, indelible, incurable love.

Yes, the Funky Monkey 5K scared me. Yes, the whole love–hate thing still composed the primary elements of my running universe. But for the first time, I was ready to move forward, to learn, to push myself—in minuscule bits—more than I had in the past.

"Yeah, Coach. I'm ready."

Chapter Seventeen

Goal races have an uncanny way of sneaking up on you. One minute your big race sits aloof at a comfortable distance; the next, it's sidling up next to you and calling you "buddy." Races are fickle that way.

I had been justifiably distracted over the past few weeks. Both Mr. Speedy Pants and Big J were injury-free and running once more, and we celebrated the health of the TMBG with a commemorative lap of Forest Park and a lengthy breakfast at Courtesy Diner. Mr. Speedy Pants's old buddy Tim resurfaced in the form of numerous stories—such as one particularly intriguing tale involving a fellow track team member named "Hemo," a theme park, an exaggerated gash on Hemo's leg, a wheelchair, and the sudden advent of unlimited rides minus the inconvenience of waiting in line. Big J, for his part, reminisced about the SEC and the persistent temptation to up and move to the Pacific Coast. Then, of course, there were the speed workouts. Yeah.

In the end, however, the suffering paid off, and I found myself with a trace of respectable foot speed and a reasonable chance of setting a PR in the Funky Monkey 5K. Which, as one may infer, was now breathing down my neck and asking me to pass the popcorn.

"So, tell me again how you managed to hit the wrong button on your watch. Twice," Mr. Speedy Pants asked, referring to the debacle during my 3K.

We were warming up for the Funky Monkey 5K, which was to begin in less than thirty minutes. I say "we" because the race had fallen on one of the rare Saturday mornings on which Mr. Speedy Pants did not have race-timing duties, though we would be running our cool-down with a can of spray chalk in order to mark a course for a race the next day. But frequent stopping to draw arrows on the pavement was a small price to pay for the pacing services of Mr. Speedy Pants.

"I don't know!" I answered. "I just accidentally hit the STOP button. And then the LAP button. And then I had no idea how fast I was running." I shook my head. "I can't believe it. I know I could have had a better race. I didn't even know I was running slow."

"Yeah, I figured something was up when you came by six seconds slow on the third lap."

"Ugh."

"That's why you need to learn to pace yourself off perceived effort. But, eh, it takes time."

"Attention, runners! Please make your way to the start line. The Funky Monkey 5K will begin in five minutes!"

"All right, kid," Mr. Speedy Pants said as we threaded our way toward the start line, "you ready to PR?"

I took a deep breath and nodded.

"Good. Just stay right with me. We're gonna run even splits. Then, that last half mile, I want you to give me everything you've got. You gotta just gut it out."

"Runners! On your mark . . ."

The shrill blast of an air horn announced the beginning of the race. And just like that, all my training—all those sweltering summer miles and crippling workouts—was put to the test.

There are very few things I remember about racing the Funky Monkey 5K, but what I do remember is sharp and fragmented. Like mental splinters. So to speak.

The first mile was a blur. I remember the pace feeling unreasonably quick, as though I were shot out of a cannon. I remember thinking that Mr. Speedy Pants's watch was broken and that he was running way too fast.

The second mile was also a blur, though I have the vague impression that it was the best of the three miles. By the time Mr. Speedy Pants announced our first mile split, I had tucked myself behind him and settled into position. The pace still felt impossibly fast, but the initial shock of being launched from a cannon had faded to a lingering reverberation. We pulled smoothly ahead of pace and cruised into the third mile.

The third mile remains the most vivid. The wheels threatened to come off during this mile. They didn't, but they threatened to.

"C'mon, kid," Mr. Speedy Pants called after looking back and discovering I was lagging behind. "Stay up with me. C'mon."

I was tired. We were running PR pace. And I felt it.

"Second female!" came a cry from the spectators as Mr. Speedy Pants and I ran by. The first-place girl was perhaps a full minute in front of me. I knew I had no chance of catching her. Mr. Speedy Pants had said she was "a stud runner." I was perfectly content with second place.

My lungs burned. My legs burned. I wanted to stop. I dropped a few more yards behind Mr. Speedy Pants.

"Second female! Second female!" a man in the crowd yelled. And then, less than three seconds later, disaster struck.

"Third female! Third female!" the same man yelled.

Ah! Oh, my gosh! The third-place girl is right behind me! I started to panic. I was being chased. I hate being chased. It paralyzes me.

"Second female!"—a pause—"Third female! C'mon! You can catch her!"

Ah! She can catch me! I thought. They were cheering the third-place girl, urging her on, telling her she could overtake me. Sheer terror propelled my legs forward. At any moment she—whoever she was—would pass me. I was freaking out.

Mr. Speedy Pants glanced over his shoulder—first to check on me and second to check the position of the third-place girl.

"C'mon, kid. Keep going. Push. C'mon."

He was perfectly calm. He didn't say anything about the third-place girl. He didn't say, "Kid! She's right behind you! She's breathing down your neck and if you don't pull yourself together you're gonna lose!" That's what I would have said. That's what I was thinking.

And so I ran. Out of fear. Plain and simple. Somehow, miraculously, I pulled even with Mr. Speedy Pants. I couldn't breathe. I felt like I was going to die, which at the time seemed like a pleasant alternative to running. I wanted to look behind me and catch a glimpse of the third-place girl, but I didn't have the energy. Everything I had was focused on moving forward.

Three miles down. Mr. Speedy Pants picked up the pace even more. We were sprinting now. All-out sprinting. I looked up. I could see the finish line. I wanted to cry. I wanted to stop. I wanted to look behind me and see just where the heck the third-place girl was.

And then we crossed the finish line. And it was over. And I was done. I forgot about being chased. I forgot about the third-place girl. I never even saw her cross the finish line. All I knew was I could finally stop running.

"Good job, kid," Mr. Speedy Pants said as I staggered my way through the finish chute.

I looked at my watch. *Huh . . .* I looked at my watch again, then at Mr. Speedy Pants. The time was slower than if should have been. No PR. My confusion must have been evident on my face, for he answered my expression by shaking his head.

"The course was long—by at least a tenth of a mile. Maybe two-tenths."

I sighed. "Yeah."

"That was a PR, kid, even if the numbers don't show it."

I'm not sure why I wasn't more disappointed than I was at that particular moment. Perhaps I was still reveling in the relief of being done with the whole ordeal. But for some reason, I was strangely positive.

"It's okay, Coach. I know it was a PR. You know it was a PR. I've never raced that hard in my life."

Mr. Speedy Pants looked at his watch, still shaking his head as he clicked through our splits.

"So," he said after reading the splits to me and factoring in the extra distance, "that's what you would have run had the course been accurate. It's a shame—it would have been a pretty big PR for you."

I shrugged. "Yeah, that stinks. But it was an impressive showing for Team Rodrigo."

"I'm proud of you," he said, giving me a quick hug. "Good race."

"You, too, Coach."

We grabbed some water from our cars and exchanged our racing flats for trainers before embarking on a cool-down, cans of spray chalk in hand. Every so often, Mr. Speedy Pants stopped to draw arrows on the ground. And considering the race followed a looping, hilly jackknife of a path—in both a 5K and a 10K distance, no less—it demanded quite the quiverful of chalk arrows.

Before the Funky Monkey 5K episode came to a close, however, I did make a pleasant discovery. As the second-place overall female, I had won an award, which I made my way to the zoo's information center to retrieve. The award was, fittingly enough, a monkey. An electric blue monkey. Which meant that my award for the Funky Monkey 5K was a funky monkey. (How awesome is that?)

I set the little guy on the dashboard as I drove home, a quirky reminder of the dreaded race that had come and gone, leaving both satisfaction and disappointment in its wake. I had PR'ed on a technicality. Not exactly ideal, but still legit. It was the best effort I had ever put forth in a race, that I knew. The third-place girl never did pass me. (I was especially grateful for that.) And I had landed a blue monkey in recognition of my second-place finish.

It wasn't a bad day at all, really, I thought.

The monkey agreed. And I drove home.

No, it hadn't been a bad day. And, taking the course's inaccuracy in stride, I handled the post-race disappointment very well. Impressively, even. I was positive. The numbers didn't show it, but I had raced a PR. I knew it. Mr. Speedy Pants knew it. And that was enough. I was satisfied.

That lasted, like, a day.

Whatever positive vibe I had upon crossing the finish line at the Funky Monkey 5K soon gave way to consuming dissatisfaction. I wanted that PR for real. And I wanted it bad. So, it seemed, did Mr. Speedy Pants.

"So, what do you think of doing another goal 5K—this time on a certified course?" Mr. Speedy Pants asked as we ran the roads across the river valley. The torture sessions often referred to as tempo runs had given me a new appreciation for flat terrain, and I had grown fond of the pancake monotony of the river valley.

"I was thinking the Old Town Moonlight Run," he continued. "It's flat and, of course"—he rolled his eyes—"certified. No more long courses. Plus, it's an evening start, which is cool."

An evening race. I had never run one of those before.

"Hmm . . . That sounds good. When is it?"

"Four weeks. Now, it's a race I'm timing, so you won't have me to pace you, but you'll be fine. You just need to not freak out."

Ah, the magical caveat.

"Okay. Let's do that. The whole Funky Monkey thing is killing me."

"Yep. Well, we'll fix that. We really should have picked a certified course in the first place. You always take a chance with uncertified races, but I didn't think the course would be that long."

"Yeah."

"The good news is that racing is racing, and now you've got more experience running at that pace."

The next day, 5K training resumed. The Old Town Moonlight Run would redeem the Funky Monkey's indiscretions. Mr. Speedy Pants sketched an extension of my speed training, and I marched my reluctant self back to the track.

Why I always require two-part trials, I don't know. First there was the Super Secret Workout, I and II. Then there was the Workout of Death, I and II. Now I was staring down the throat of the Funky Monkey 5K, Part II, and I wasn't exactly thrilled about the whole thing.

Alas, I had to redo it just the same. Racing flats in hand, smeared with a generous application of NASA-approved sunscreen, stopwatch primed for action, sufficiently hydrated to survive several days in the Gobi Desert with nothing but a visor and a decent pair of socks, I began the first of four more weeks of 5K training.

Alas.

Chapter Eighteen

I was two weeks into my Funky Monkey II training when I began to feel tired. It was not merely the sensation of fatigue, but an overwhelming state-of-being caused by running. Long. Hard. Day after day after day.

A Spartan ideology undergirds marathoning. It is dogma in the Nation of Running. It mandates the physical exhaustion of its subjects, subjects who willingly surrender the freedom to sleep late, become slaves to weekly mileage, and accept the perpetual feeling of being hit by a semi-truck. Runners surrender to the sport's dictates. They do not question the logic of filling bathtubs with ice. Advil is a cultural delicacy. Rigidity of schedule is uncompromising. To fall short in any way is treason.

On the day in question, it was nine thirty-seven in the morning. I had yet to run. There was a cup of coffee perched next to my laptop. I was, in fact, still in my pajamas. The guilt was almost unbearable.

Yes, that morning, I was living in apostasy. I had succumbed to the fatigue. The weight of exhaustion was too heavy to bear, and despite my allegiance to the Nation of Running, despite my adherence to its code of conduct, its traditions, its values, and all that it holds dear, I, the wayward citizen, overslept. And missed my run.

To make matters worse, it wasn't just a daily run I missed. It was a track workout, the holy grail of a runner's week. Listening to my alarm blare the inspiring melody of Barry Manilow's "Copacabana," I couldn't find the strength to pull myself out of bed. I knew I needed to. My schedule depended on it. It demanded it. I needed to run my workout early in the week in order to have time to recover before my long run. Schedule realignment was impossible.

My alarm clock continued to blast Barry Manilow's voice. My mind reeled at the horror of the consequences of sleeping in.

You need to get up! I told myself. *You need to . . . You need . . . You . . .*

"*At the Copa, Copacabana, the hottest spot north of Havana . . .*"

I tried to open my eyes. Nothing happened. *Think about what you're doing!* I barked at myself. *Get up . . . speedwork . . . Copacabana . . .* I was fighting a losing battle. *It's time to get up. It's time to . . .*

"*At the Copa, Copacaban-aaaa! Music and passion were always the fashion at the Copa-aaaaaa . . .*"

Overcome by delirium, I silenced my alarm clock in all its Barry-blaring glory, rolled over on my side, and fell back asleep.

And thus I arrived at nine thirty-seven AM. Nothing accomplished. Behind schedule. No way to redeem the situation. The choice had been made. The damage had been done. Barry had been silenced.

The humid haze hovering over the pavement and hanging in the trees mocked my missed opportunity to run in the cool of the dawn. My fellow Nation of Running patriots had long since finished their runs, showered, enjoyed a hard-earned cup of coffee, and were now busy with their daily activities. I glanced at my cup of coffee, half empty, unearned.

I wished I had possessed the mental fortitude to wake up. It would have made things easier. The one redeeming aspect of the morning was that I had planned on running the workout alone anyway, due to Mr. Speedy Pants being otherwise occupied by race-timing duties.

Once, during marathon training, I had forgotten to set my alarm for the following morning's run with Mr. Speedy Pants. We had planned on running Forest Park, and he waited twenty-five minutes at the visitor center—in vain—before calling me to inquire into my whereabouts. My whereabouts being in bed, Mr. Speedy Pants offered to meet me for a shortened run halfway between Forest Park and my home in the boonies. This we did, which redeemed the morning somewhat, though I was duly punished for my negligence. I had stepped out of my car only to discover I was wearing my tights inside out.

At least I didn't stand him up . . . again, I consoled myself, taking another sip of coffee. Perhaps it wasn't such a disaster after all. I mean, there I was, sitting in a plush, overstuffed chair, holding a cup of coffee and eating a cookie. My body obviously needed sleep. Perhaps oversleeping had fended off an otherwise impending collapse. Perhaps I would feel refreshed from the rest. Perhaps I would be better for it. Perhaps it was just what the doctor ordered.

My delusion was short-lived. Though I tried to throw a positive spin on my exhaustion and consequent oversleeping, I was simply ignoring the signs. Something was bound to give way soon.

As it turned out, soon came five days later.

I could feel it happening. Slowly. It was clandestine in its approach, but I could sense it coming like enemy forces creeping across allied lines. I tried to ignore it. I tried to fight it. But in the middle of a run, in the middle of a track workout, I succumbed to its attacks. I officially burned out.

There had been signs that pointed to an impending breakdown. It was more than just oversleeping my alarm. It was a few seconds off pace here and a few seconds off pace there. It was daily runs that became progressively slower. It was the inability to maintain tempo or to recover after runs. It was the persistent, nagging oppression of being constantly worn out.

To make matters worse, my official burnout moment came not only on the track, not only in the presence of Mr. Speedy Pants, but also during the same workout at which Mr. Speedy Pants's old buddy Tim made a triumphant reappearance after six months on the DL. The cool kids were back, and I was running with them. And then I pooped out. In front of them. How not awesome is that?

I was supposed to run twenty quarters, Mr. Speedy Pants's favorite workout. It was the first time I had attempted that workout since the in-famous twenty quarters in the rain. My memories of it were positive and even a tad sentimental, and thus Mr. Speedy Pants used these san-guine feelings to bolster my confidence.

"Remember, kid," he said, giving me an encouraging pat on the back as we climbed down from the bleachers and made our way to the start line, "that was your moment of glory during marathon training. That will always be the definitive workout in your running career—to me anyway. That's when I knew you had what it takes."

I nodded. "Yeah." I still felt tired. I tried to picture what it felt like that day, in the rain, at the fourteenth lap, the fifteenth, the sixteenth. *You toughed it out then*, I told myself. *You can tough it out now.*

We were all running quarters that day, the cool kids and I. Mr. Speedy Pants needed to chalk off sixteen; Mr. Speedy Pants's old buddy Tim—whatever his leg let him do.

The first lap, I hit my time on the nose (a rarity for me).

"Too fast!" Mr. Speedy Pants and Mr. Speedy Pants's old buddy Tim yelled in unison as I lapped the first quarter.

I looked at my watch. Nope. Right on schedule. I informed my doubting companions of my punctuality as they took off for their next quarter. They were surprised. I smiled in my momentary victory.

And momentary it was. The next lap was harder. The lap after that, much harder. A few laps after that, too hard.

"Hey, Coach," I gasped during one of the rare times my rest inter-val aligned with that of Mr. Speedy Pants's, "I'm tired. Like, really, re-ally tired."

"What was the time on your last lap?"

I told him.

"And the two laps before that?"

Again I reported the bad news.

"Okay. Well, don't panic. Don't look at your watch this next lap. Run on feel. See what you do."

His rest was over. I still had twenty seconds left. *Run on feel. Feel*, I repeated to myself. Four hundred meters later, feel brought me in about five seconds too slow. I relayed my time to Mr. Speedy Pants.

"My legs feel like dead weight. And I can't breathe." I demonstrated this last fact by gasping for air.

"What lap was that?"

"Twelve."

Mr. Speedy Pants's old buddy Tim joined our discussion, and there was soon a symposium regarding my fatigue.

"Well, kid," Mr. Speedy Pants said after we had analyzed not only the past few laps, but also the past few days and failed runs, "looks like it's time to shut you down for a couple of weeks. You're officially burned out. Nothing you can do."

Burned out? Shut down?

"So, what does that mean?" I asked, biting my lip. I couldn't tell if I was upset or relieved.

"It means we've been running you too hard lately. Your body is worn out. You need to take a couple of weeks off. Rest up. Maybe do an easy three- or four-mile run every couple of days, but nothing long and nothing hard."

I looked at Mr. Speedy Pants, then at Mr. Speedy Pants's old buddy Tim, and then back at Mr. Speedy Pants. I took a deep breath. I dropped my gaze to stare at the track. It was porous, dusted with tiny specks of gravel. I looked at my racing flats, orange as ever, lightning bolts still slashed across the mesh. Well, then, that was that.

In that moment, I emerged from denial and accepted my fatigue as more than just a string of bad days. My body needed rest. Plain and simple.

There was some sorrow in surrender, but there was also a strange element of freedom in acceptance, for I could finally call my fatigue what it was and stop denying my body's persistent request for time off.

Mr. Speedy Pants finished up his quarters, as did Mr. Speedy Pants's old buddy Tim, who by that time was running only every other lap in order to stretch his leg and tend his injury in the interims. The workout ended by Mr. Speedy Pants informing us that he was the only one to earn an "A" for the day, since I had to quit and his old buddy Tim had to alternate rests.

Mr. Speedy Pants and I ran our cool-down as Team Rodrigo, Mr. Speedy Pants's old buddy Tim having to leave immediately after the workout. In addition to National Landscapers Day, we were treated to several extraordinary sights, including an apocalyptic abundance of mattress delivery trucks.

When I finally did return home, I tossed my duffel bag on the kitchen floor and announced audibly and in no uncertain terms (even though I was the only one home) that I was officially on break. Then I opened the refrigerator door and reached for some leftover Mexican food, which had infused my refrigerator with a remarkable odor.

As I sat there eating a chicken taco drowning in guacamole, I realized I felt a sense of authority in my declaration. I felt like a doctor giving orders to a patient. In fact, as I let the idea of going on break settle in, I even began to feel impressed with myself, as if the fact that I had to go on break implied I was some kind of serious runner. Like one of those runner-runners. I also realized a sizable chunk of my schedule had just opened up. No more long runs. No track workouts. No two-a-days. It was like being released from prison. Or at least paroled.

The change in my routine, however, was most noticeable in the mornings. Gone were the harsh alarms. Instead, I was gently awakened by warm sunrays streaming through my bedroom window. For the first time in months, I was able to get out of bed without the urge to hurl my alarm clock against the opposite wall. Instead of donning my running shoes in a groggy haze, I put on slippers in a groggy haze. (Running or not, I'm groggy in the morning.) I even found myself doing early-morning activities that running had precluded, such as watching the *Today* show.

The *Today* show was a whole new world to me. Who knew you could learn about the Middle East crisis, hair removal, pirate-themed parties, the national debt, and chocolate cream pie—all in the same show? What kind of hidden treasure was this?

I even began to analyze the quirks of the show's cast members. *Are they called cast members?* I wondered. *Maybe they're anchors. Or personalities. Or hosts.* I took another sip of coffee. *We'll go with crew. Crew is generic enough.* And then Matt Lauer attempted to roast an unidentifiable vegetable on a giant barbecue pit in the middle of Times Square. And I laughed. I was a normal person. Not a runner. But a normal person. I watched the *Today* show. In a matter of days, I had morphed into some kind of Al Roker groupie, cheering from the couch, "C'mon, Al! Tell me what the weather is like in my neck of the woods!" Because, of course, no one is more normal than an Al Roker groupie.

And yet, even though I enjoyed the respite from training, and both my body and mind felt rejuvenated from the rest, it wasn't long before I began to long for a run. A real run. I missed running with Mr. Speedy Pants and Big J. I missed the glorious feeling of having completed a tough workout. Yes, the break provided much-needed refreshment, but it also brought with it an opportunity to remember why I love running so much. Running is invigorating. Challenging. Satisfying. Empowering. Even purifying. The self-discipline mandated by a rigorous training schedule brings structure and consistency to life no matter how hectic things get. Knowing that you faced the fiends of fatigue and won, that you pushed your body to keep going when it most wanted to stop, creates a sense of accomplishment that sweeps over you in an all-consuming wave of post-run exhaustion. You are mentally cleansed. You are physically strong. You are a runner. And I craved that.

Watching Matt Lauer grill butternut squash on the streets of New York City is an excellent way to start your day. And somebody's gotta tell us how to make lobster bisque on a budget. But it's just not the same as the crisp morning air rushing through your lungs, the rhythmic beat of gravel crunching beneath your feet, and the exhilaration of floating across the surface of the planet with every liberating stride.

My break was lovely. Needed. Unavoidable. But I found myself suffering from runner's envy. My running shoes looked lonely, the roads looked lonely, and at the sight of other runners doing what runners do best—running—I felt lonely, as if I had lost a dear friend.

Only a few more days, I told myself, *and then you'll be back to early-morning alarms, tired legs, two-minute showers, and a schedule surrendered to the dictates of the miles.*

With this pleasant reminder, my faltering lasted only a moment. I was content with the luxury of being burned out. After all, there was always the *Today* show, and I couldn't watch Al Roker in all his cheery, weather-forecasting glory if I was up and running. Yes, I would miss old Al when my break ended. But, eh, I'd get over it.

Chapter Nineteen

There are certain things in life that seem so perfect, so fitting, it is unimaginable they will ever change. Their very existence becomes as expected and routine as coffee in the morning and the delivery of the mail. We take a child-like delight in them. They are the things that not only bring the simplest joy to our daily routines, but add stability and the subtle reassurance that everything is okay. We simultaneously appreciate them and take them for granted—partly because we recognize them for what they are and partly because we can't imagine it being any other way. Such was the trio of friends that formed the TMBG.

Over the course of a few weeks, I slowly recovered from my burnout and integrated running back into my life. The TMBG returned to Forest Park and Queeny Park, as well as to Courtesy Diner and Uncle Bill's. Our debates, discussions, and mutual derision continued. Debate made a particularly triumphant return via the topic of rabies and the contraction of such.

"Bats? Bats is your first thought?" Mr. Speedy Pants exclaimed, incredulous. "You think of rabies, and the first thing that comes to mind is bats?"

"Yes! Totally bats. I don't know why that's so strange to you," I responded.

"What about dogs? Haven't you seen *Old Yeller*? Who gets rabies from bats?"

"Who gets rabies from dogs?"

"More people than who get rabies from bats, I can tell you that."

"Nope. No way."

"Okay, fine. We'll look it up. You're wrong."

Big J, who had assumed his usual stance of neutrality, laughed and interjected with random quips, first supporting my bat theory and then supporting Mr. Speedy Pants's dog theory.

"Hello!" he called to a group of elderly ladies walking the path. Big J was especially cordial that morning, greeting our fellow early risers. Only half of our fellow early risers returned his greetings.

"You go, girl! Way to keep up with those boys!" called a pair of power-walking ladies.

I smiled and waved by way of thanks. Little did the ladies know "those boys" were doing all they could to slow down to my pace. But, that was a perk of running with Mr. Speedy Pants and Big J. They were runner-runners. They looked fast, and I looked fast just by being with them.

It was good to be running with Mr. Speedy Pants and Big J, again. Things were falling back into place. My body was back to normal. My schedule was back to normal. The TMBG was back to normal.

We were a triumvirate of friendship, so to speak, a friendship that grew with the miles we ran and the coffee we consumed. We trained together, we raced together, and we ate together—until we were no longer just running buddies, but family, and our little weekly run-and-dine jaunts were no longer just something we did, but part of who we were. Week in, week out, we met. And we never bothered to think that one day things might change. Until one day came, and Big J announced that he was moving. Soon. Halfway across the country.

"I wanted you to know before I told everyone else," he had said one evening over the phone. "I told Kronos, but that's it."

I bit my lip and nodded silently. Silence was answer enough.

It was as though Mr. Speedy Pants, Big J, and I were in the middle of a movie and the film cut out, ending the show before the story was finished. I should have known that it was bound to happen, that Big J's nomadic ways would eventually push him to the Pacific Coast. He had talked about moving there. About the trails there. About running there.

193

But he had talked about a lot of things. Yes, it was only logical that the Thursday Morning Breakfast Group would come to an end at some point. Most things do. But the inevitable always comes as a surprise, and even the anticipation of an impending conclusion doesn't completely dull the pain. Happy ending or sad ending, it is an ending nonetheless.

We made an extra effort to relish the last few weeks of the TMBG's existence. We laughed just as much as we always did—probably more so as we remembered all the goofy times we had shared. We even planned a grand finale at Uncle Bill's the morning of Big J's departure, making a TMBG run and breakfast literally the last thing Big J did before he, his pickup truck, and a U-Haul trailer headed across the country. Over giant plates of hash browns and grits, we relived stories of subzero training runs, heated trivia debates, puddle splashing, snow-plowing, name calling, Mario Lopez, LL Cool J, Mystical Land tours, cornfield bathroom breaks, blowups at mile twenty, my initiation into the world of trail running, and the use of sketchy bathroom facilities across the metro area. We drew out every minute of our breakfast. We took pictures. We laughed. We refilled cups of coffee, laughed some more, and refilled our coffee cups again. We let the bill sit on the table long after our plates were empty. Then, finally, reluctant to acknowledge breakfast was over, we left.

Standing outside our cars, awkward, not wanting the time to end but knowing there was nothing left to do, we said good-bye, and the two of us who were staying behind stood in the parking lot waving as Big J climbed into his truck and pulled away. Then he drove off. And he was gone. And, just like that, it was over.

It's funny how running works. It brings with it rising moments of elation and sinking moments of struggle. It makes us stronger and breaks us down. It gives us reason to be proud, and it humbles us with a single stroke. And in the midst of these ups and downs, we discover that each of these moments has its own pace, its own rhythm. We also realize that one can hold a pace only so long before something gives. Pace and the changing of pace is, after all, the nature of the sport.

But while the fast pace doesn't last forever, it sure is a lot of fun. And when life hands us disappointments and struggles to interrupt our stride, we can find strength in remembering what it was like when we were flying.

Things would definitely be different now that our trio had been reduced to two. But Mr. Speedy Pants and I—Team Rodrigo—would be just fine. We were runners, after all, and runners adjust to pace in the full knowledge that faster times are in the future. Always moving forward, but occasionally glancing back at where we've been, we are better and stronger and faster for the miles behind us.

I turned to look at Mr. Speedy Pants. He looked at me.

"It's okay, kid. You know Big J. Always going somewhere."

"Yeah," I said back.

And we parted ways.

Chapter Twenty

My first run after Big J's departure was at Queeny Park. I was alone. It was raining. And a sad, eerie haze hung over the trees and fields of wildflowers. I was affected by the gloomy ambience, and I very nearly cried.

The Old Town Moonlight Run was now off the radar. My burnout and brief dalliance with the *Today* show had cut into precious training time, and there was no way I could pull myself back into racing form in ten days. Plus, as Mr. Speedy Pants had reminded me, it was time to pick a fall marathon and begin training. We could always throw a 5K or two into the marathon training program. If I happened to pull out a PR, well, it'd be a bonus.

I ran by a field of yellow daisies, bright, vibrant in the rain, bobbing with the gentle prodding of the droplets. The park seemed different today. Reflective. Withdrawn. It was the rain. Not a familiar, friendly rain that visits on summer afternoons and cools the earth, but a colder rain, indifferent and unfamiliar. It came down in steady, even strokes, as though wiping clean a slate in order to begin a new story.

"So, what about the Bleeding Heart Marathon?" Mr. Speedy Pants had asked a week earlier, when we first discussed forgoing the Old Town Moonlight Run in favor of fall marathon training. "It's a flat course. Small race. Plus," he said, smiling, "I'm gonna race it, too. Mrs. Awesome and I are heading down there for the weekend to visit her family. We'll have a place to stay, good food to eat, and a whole cheering squad for the race. We can make it an official Team Rodrigo event. Our first out-of-town race."

"That'd be awesome! You guys wouldn't mind if I tagged along?"

"Nah. I'll check with Mrs. Awesome's family, but"—he paused—

"they're awesome, obviously."

I smiled. "I'll sit in the backseat and bother you guys during the car ride."

"I don't doubt that. You're always bothering us."

"Well," I said, "cool. A Team Rodrigo road trip."

"Yep. And I've thought about trying a new training program for you. It's higher mileage. More tempo work mixed in. We can always back down if you need to," he continued, "but you thrive on high mileage. Strong as an ox. That's where we need to get you."

"An ox?" I laughed. It wasn't the most flattering description, but I got his point.

"Yep. It's a great feeling, hitting that high mileage. Your body is fatigued, but it keeps going. You get to a point where you feel like you can run forever. Like an ox."

"Huh."

He continued. "When I was running my highest mileage, I felt terrible at the beginning of every run. Awful. Sluggish. But a couple of miles in, my body would start clicking. PR'ed in eight distances that year."

Strong as an ox, I told myself as I ran, one week removed from my commitment to run the Bleeding Heart Marathon. An ox was in stark contrast with the exquisite daisies tossing about in the rain at Queeny Park. Then again, the daisies were there nonetheless. Delicate. Lovely. They seemed to like the rain. They thrived on it. They danced in it. It made them stronger.

Strong as an ox, I repeated, and I left the daisies to finish my run.

H. G. Wells once said that when he saw an adult on a bicycle, he did not despair for the future of the human race. Evidently, he never saw me on a bike. If he had, he would have either taken back his statement or qualified it in some way.

Mr. Speedy Pants was healthy again and, in addition to coaching me, was training to race the Bleeding Heart Marathon himself. The same could not be said for his old buddy Tim, whose obstinate femur refused to heal. In fact, the last workout I ran with the cool kids was the last time Mr. Speedy Pants's old buddy Tim ran at all. He was back on the DL, and Mr. Speedy Pants was without an equal training partner.

Furthermore, Mr. Speedy Pants accompanied me on all my long runs, not only telling stories, but also carrying my water bottle and providing pacing service along the way. This meant he was running not one but two long runs each week—sometimes back-to-back. And the hardest run, his own, he had to complete solo. This, I determined, was a travesty. And that's where the bike came into play.

"How long is your run tomorrow?" I asked between sips of water as we stood outside our cars. We had just finished running Grant's Trail. My long run was done for the week.

"Twenty."

"Where are you gonna run it?"

"Eh, I was thinking Forest Park. I need to get an early start. I've got a nine o'clock meeting with a race director."

"Hey, I was thinking . . ."

"How'd that work out for you?"

"Whatever. I was thinking . . . How'd you like some company tomorrow? I need to pay you back with some bike time anyway. I mean, you did all those long runs on the bike this winter—in the cold, and the wind, and the rain. Time I paid my dues."

"Hmm . . ." he said, contemplating the proposal. "It was pretty miserable out there."

"So?"

"Sure, kid. Thanks."

"Not a problem, Coach."

The moon was still a vibrant white crescent when I pulled into the visitor center's parking lot the next morning. Mr. Speedy Pants was there waiting, stifling a yawn and holding a blue-and-silver mountain bike. He had already equipped the bike with two giant water bottles and a large, black pouch stuffed with energy gel, Advil, and car keys.

"You," he said, handing me a headlamp, "are going to wear this."

I strapped on the headlamp and took the bike. However, not yet being fully awake and apparently lacking some key coordination skills, I managed to fall over twice before realizing the height of the bike seat had been set for a rider one foot taller than I am. This minor setback was corrected by a quick seat adjustment, and I was soon able to wobble my way forward without tipping over.

I expected the ride to be slow and tedious. I was on a bike. Mr. Speedy Pants was running. Riding a bike twenty miles alongside someone on foot isn't exactly the Tour de France.

Yeah, well, they don't call him Mr. Speedy Pants for nothing. I actually had to pedal to keep up with him. I was actually getting tired.

I was amazed by how quickly we reeled in the scenery before us and left it behind in our wake. The air felt different. It felt stronger and louder. All other sounds deferred to the sound of the wind rushing past us. The trees, the lakes, the fountains, and other park visitors were swept together in a blur of color and obscure outlines. *So this is what it feels like to be fast*, I thought. It wasn't like running at all. It was more like flying.

"Lookin' good, Coach," I said as we made our way around the back side of the park, which was the hilly side. "Keep it up."

We didn't talk much. We didn't talk at all, really. Mr. Speedy Pants had built pacework into his long run, which meant there would be no stories and little conversation. We were both fine with silence. It wasn't about the words; it was about being there. Every now and then, I yelled a brief snippet of encouragement. Occasionally, I handed him water. Twice I gave him an energy gel packet. Other than that, I didn't do much. He ran. I biked. And I couldn't have been prouder.

Perhaps it was finally being able to help Mr. Speedy Pants during his long run, even if it was to a negligible degree. Perhaps it was the chance to be the water caddy for a change. Perhaps it was the rare opportunity to pay him back for the countless miles he had sacrificed to run with me and bike next to me and put up with all of my freakouts. Perhaps it was the sheer camaraderie of Team Rodrigo. Whatever the case, I felt just as proud, just as contented, as I would have had the twenty-mile run been my own. There I was, dressed in soccer shorts, a T-shirt, and a headlamp, pedaling frantically just to keep up with the runner next to me. But I felt cool. I felt fast. I felt like I was, in a manner of speaking, running with Mr. Speedy Pants.

Yes, the sport of running had revealed yet another of its lovely dimensions, a facet made visible only through the lens of friendship.

Running, as it turns out, is a team sport.

AUTUMN

Chapter Twenty-one

The scene: early morning. The sun is just starting to peek from the behind the blanketing horizon. I have finished my warm-up, and I line up with the other runners. A few people are chatting. Some are squeezing in a quick, last-minute stretch. Others are resolute, focused, eyes straight ahead. It is race day. It is time to get serious. Only I don't feel like racing. At all.

The local track club was hosting two races that morning—a four-mile and a ten-mile—and Mr. Speedy Pants and I had decided to tackle the races as Team Rodrigo. He would run the shorter distance, and I would run the longer. Not only was it a convenient way to incorporate social pacework into our Bleeding Heart training, but the course was flat. This I greatly appreciated.

However, as I stood in the little battalion of runners readying themselves for the fight, another conflict was taking place inside my head. Instead of rehearsing my race plan, I flouted mental discipline and thought about the most random topics.

Can contestants on The Price Is Right *cash out their prizes? What if you win a dinette set that doesn't match your dining room? People are always winning dinette sets.*

Let the race begin!

The starter's gun sounded. A rush of bib numbers. A rush of synthetic fabric. A rush of shuffling feet as the mob surged forward across the start line. I took the first few steps of a looming ten miles. The nomadic thoughts settled in.

I'm tired.

I had covered approximately seven feet.

I wish this race were over. I wonder if the Keebler elves hang out with the

Rice Krispies elves . . . ?

Fifty feet. Tops.

I bet if you cash out the dinette set you only get a fraction of what it's worth. That would totally stink. Unless you sold it on eBay. You could probably get more money for it on eBay. Geez. I'm tired.

Half a mile had gone by. It was going to be a long race.

My concentration floundered as opposing forces struggled to gain control, and my mind feebly attempted to focus. The Snowflake series course, while flat, was boring. It cut ninety-degree angles through fields with no crops. It was like running on a giant dirt grid, the highlight of which was the occasional right turn. The road before me seemed to stretch on with no purpose. I began to experience fatigue, both mental and physical. Somewhere ahead of me, Mr. Speedy Pants was racing. Probably racing well. My determination wavered. I looked at the other runners around me. They looked strong. They looked focused. They looked like they wanted to be there.

What's wrong with me? Why can't I focus? Why can't I get my act together? Oh, man. I smell French toast. How weird is that?

Needless to say, I wasn't having the best day. The procrastinating mile markers lumbered by—slowly, painfully—as I struggled to stay on pace. I failed. My pace per mile progressively declined. I was twenty seconds behind my goal time. Then thirty. Then a full minute. Yes, I was tired. Yes, it hurt. But the mental fatigue was what hurt the most. My mind hated where I was. Hated what I was doing. It wanted to stop. I was not having fun. And I was frustrated about not being able to cash in that ugly dinette set for its full value.

The race eventually came to an end, though I was certain the course was four or five miles longer than it should have been. I slowed to a walk and put my hands on my hips, stretching my face to the sky. I breathed a long sigh of relief. It felt good to be done.

Mr. Speedy Pants met me at the finish line. He had long since finished his race.

"How'd it go, kid?"

I gave him a performance report. The dinette set was a recurring theme.

"And you?"

We continued our discussion as we headed out for a cool-down. The sun had now fully risen, and a determined breeze blew across the streets, reminding us winter was approaching even in the warm autumn air. As it turned out, Mr. Speedy Pants had won his race. He had been quite the connoisseur of focus, for despite results suggesting otherwise, he hadn't had a great race, either. He, too, struggled from the beginning and felt the insidious forces of doubt and mental fatigue. However, not succumbing to the sinister distractions, he had readjusted his focus, concentrating his race into one-mile, half-mile, and quarter-mile increments. He assumed command over doubt and surrounded the mental insurgents with controlled, calculated reason. He said nothing about *The Price Is Right*.

"When I'm having a tough race or I'm just not feeling it that day," he explained as we ran, "my mind goes into survival mode. What will keep my legs moving? What do I need to keep pushing?" He brushed aside a few unruly strands of hair that had fallen across his eyes. "You gotta race on the bad days, too, kid. It'll make you tougher."

I nodded in agreement, though I knew Mr. Speedy Pants was unable to see my response, primarily because at that point I was running directly behind him. I likened his mind to a neatly organized tool chest. There was a place for every mental tool, and every mental tool was in its place. Focus. Confidence. Determination. Willpower. Ability. Purpose. Resolve. Each instrument was sharp and clean, ready and accessible for an urgent call to duty.

My mind, on the other hand, bore an eerie resemblance to a junk drawer. Yes, there may have been a tool or two, but there was also a pen, a paper clip, a half-eaten cookie, a rubber band, a marble, a battery, a feather, and a baggage claim ticket from the Baltimore-Washington International Airport.

My mind was a jumbled mess, and I found myself wasting energy during races, blindly searching for the right tools to get me through the miles. And often, just when I thought my fingers had wrapped around the focus I was searching for, I would jab myself with that stupid paper clip. Such is the plight of the junk drawer mentality.

"A dog in the hunt doesn't know he has fleas, kid," Mr. Speedy Pants said, concluding his speech with the unsanitary proverb.

"Haha . . . What?"

"It's what one of my old coaches used to say. Means when you're focused on racing, you don't notice anything else—not the pain, how tired you are, anyone else around you, anything. All you see is the finish line."

"Eh. Fleas are so gross."

"That's not the point."

"I know. But I hate fleas."

"Uh-huh. Obviously, you're distracted."

"By the fleas."

"Oh, my . . ."

Not all hope was lost, though. I was working on tidying the disorder. With every tough race, I removed some debris from my mind and filled its spot with focus. With every difficult training run, I threw out a useless knickknack and acquired resolve. With every daunting track workout, I removed the negative clutter and instead filled my head with neatly organized tools.

Thus, although phrases such as *mental toughness* and *mentally strong* made me grimace, I was improving in the headcase department. Yes, I pulled out the occasional rubber band when reaching for determination, but at least I knew determination was a part of the assortment.

And, no, my mind wasn't the meticulous tool collection of Mr. Speedy Pants, but at least the collection was growing.

Driving home from the race, disappointed but still too mentally tired to worry about it, I told myself that maybe one day I would have the ability to focus when I didn't feel like it. That one day I'd be mentally strong, able to grind my teeth and gut it out. Able to push through the pain. Able to do all those things the running clichés told me to do. But until then, I'd have to settle for the dinette set.

My reluctance to race spilled into the next few days. Not only did I not want to race, but I didn't want to run. My focus shifted from the pleasure of running to its demands, from the freedom of running to the constraints of a training schedule, and from the exhilaration of a steady rhythm to the drudgery of keeping pace. My little utopian world of running wasn't immune to erosion. And my running was suffering because of it.

The Tuesday after the race was particularly trying. A dreary, incessant rain and plummeting temperatures—coupled with my now fermented irritability—made me an absolute human crustacean, and I headed out the front door into a misty, dismal scene.

The rain wasn't heavy, but it penetrated everything it touched. My clothes, my skin, my crusty attitude. I ran down the gravel driveway, attempting to shake out the stiffness that had taken up residence in my muscles. I sloshed my way down the road. The skies weren't so much showering as they were melting. Every oozing drop that stung my eyes and splattered my skin felt cold and brittle. I shivered despite my exertion, and for a moment I considered turning around and skipping the run altogether. Coffee and a couch would be much better companions than a soggy visor and a pair of very, very wet socks.

Yet habit forced my legs forward, and I soon turned off my gravel driveway and onto the drooping country road that wilted around the hills and trees like a giant black ribbon draped across the landscape. I passed Mr. O. Stout's mailbox—valiant and white against a gray backdrop—and approached the buffalo farm. The buffalo looked like bearded specks dotting the hill. The donkey was also there, standing in the barn door, staring at me. He seemed to be standing farther back than usual. Even he didn't want to get wet.

As I ran closer to the buffalo farm, a wizened man in a flannel shirt and overalls came sauntering down a dirt path cutting across the field. He wore a stained, frayed trucker's cap over his white hair, and his hands were rough and black with dirt. I had never seen him before. I assumed he was the owner of the buffalo farm. He tipped his cap as a salutation, and I nodded back. Then he did something completely unexpected, completely out of accord with my own mood. He walked up to the wooden fence separating the buffalo from the road and stopped. Taking off his hat and holding it in his callused fingers, he began talking.

"Mighty rainy day we're having."

His tone was casual and familiar, as if we had been in the midst of conversation.

I slowed down, looking around to make sure the man had, indeed, addressed me. No one else being around, I stopped and answered back.

"Yeah, it is."

He looked at me. I looked at him. I was in a hurry to start running again. He was in no hurry at all. He introduced himself. His name was—incredibly—Bill. Buffalo Bill. He had been raising buffalo on his farm for the past fifty years. Did he take the buffalo to auction? Yes, he did. In fact, he was getting ready for auction in a few weeks. And were his buffalo sales going well? Well (and this he said very slowly and with a contemplative shake of his head), the buffalo market ain't what it used to be. He then directed my gaze to the fields.

"That one was born yesterday."

I looked at the baby buffalo, a miniature version of the rest of the herd. Its tangled beard looked out of place on so small a buffalo. The newborn tripped about the yard, throwing its head from side to side, always staying close to its mother. I laughed at its clumsiness. I never thought a buffalo could be cute. This one was.

I talked to Buffalo Bill a few minutes longer and then continued running, leaving him to tend to the baby buffalo. My shell had been cracked, and I could feel the hard exterior splitting apart. An ironic analogy, considering my next enlightening encounter involved a turtle.

I had entered the realm of Mystical Land by this time and was nearly at the lake when I saw a lumbering, bulbous figure sloughing across the pavement. It was a snapping turtle. Its jagged shell was at least ten inches in diameter, and its neck protruded menacingly as I ran by. The turtle—whom I have since dubbed Pete—didn't seem to mind the rain. In fact, I don't think he noticed it was raining at all. He was focused on crossing the road. A journey of approximately fifteen feet.

It's going to take him forever. And then, not giving the turtle any more thought, I ran on.

I circled the lake and began retracing my steps home. The route was actually very pretty, even in the dreary weather. The rain deepened the rich foliage surrounding the path and tapped the lake's surface with a million little drops. And then whom did I run into but my old friend, Pete the Turtle.

Pete was in the very act of completing his point-to-point course across the road. I was surprised to see him. Pete was one of the most plodding creatures I had ever encountered. Crossing the road was a high-risk undertaking for a turtle. And what was his reward? Nothing, that's what.

Yet Pete pressed forward. And I, for the second time during my run, stopped. I could have sworn Pete's black, beady eyes were focused on something much farther away than the other side of the road. I shielded my eyes from the rain and joined Pete in looking beyond the road, beyond the grassy field, beyond the splattering, splashing lake. For a turtle, that's a heck of a long way.

Finally, I turned my eyes from the gray, distant horizon and looked at Pete with admiration. I smiled. Pete reminded me of a poem I used to read as a child. It is a rather tragic poem about a man who is denied by his one true love. Overcome by despair, he decides to leave his life forever behind him, climbing upon the back of a giant turtle and asking that creature to take him out beyond the sea, never to return. Not exactly the tortoise and the hare.

It is a sad story, but there is something romantic about the idea of traveling beyond the sea, for therein lies the mystery of the unknown. Even though for Pete the unknown was simply beyond a lake, it was still unknown. Pete's journey was not in vain; it was merely a small adventure within a larger one. After all, no challenge is so insignificant that it adds not to the bigger story.

I left Pete to continue his journey, pushing a strand of wet hair from my face. Buffalo Bill and Pete the Turtle were wise. Buffalo Bill lived simply, unhurried. Instead of feeling entitled to time, he saw it as an opportunity not to be wasted. I wasn't just another stranger making my way down the road. I was a neighbor and a friend, someone he greeted and talked to and introduced to a baby buffalo.

Pete, for his part, was a model of perseverance. His destination was so far in the distance it could not be seen. He progress was so slow it could not be tracked. Like Buffalo Bill, he took his time. Yet he also kept moving forward. His focus was beyond his immediate surroundings. And what seemed painful and of no purpose to me was really a beautiful demonstration of resolve and conviction.

The miles, the workouts, the grueling schedule had made me tougher. But they had hardened me to the hidden treasures unique to a sport that provides the opportunity to push your body to the limit, yet also offers the chance to uncouple the weight of everyday stress and just

enjoy the moment. I had lost my focus. I had forgotten that running is
a privilege, not a chore. In my silly petulance, I had tossed aside the adventure of simply crossing the road.

I had always considered running a capricious sport. Moody. Unpre-
dictable. One moment it seduced with empowerment; the next, it dev-
astated with collapse. Yet I considered myself devoted. I forgave it,
returned to it, and was faithful. As Shakespeare said, "The course of true
love never did run smooth." The marathon must have been big in Eliz-
abethan England.

However, after my encounters with Buffalo Bill and Pete the Turtle,
I began to question my previous assumptions about the character of
running. I began to wonder if running is more constant than I had originally thought. What if instead of a temperamental love, running was
the constant friend, always quiet, always listening, imparting wisdom
without saying a word. What if maybe, just maybe, I was the fickle one
in the relationship?

It was raining harder now. The baby buffalo was still stumbling about
the fields, darting bravely into the stray breeze that ruffled the grass and
teased his twitching ears, though he never wandered far from his
mother's side. Buffalo Bill was nowhere to be seen. The donkey, however, was. He stared at me from his regal position on the threshold of the
barn door. Dripping, sopping, I stared back. We had a unique form of
communication, the donkey and I, and by some indefinable force of
nature, we had bonded. The donkey still believed in its own superiority. I didn't mind. No use complicating things by arguing with a donkey.

Past Mr. O. Stout's mailbox. Down the gravel driveway. Order had
been restored in my utopian world of running. I felt refreshed, silly for
having been so crabby, silly for having complicated things. Simple was
better. Simple is how running is supposed to be.

Chapter Twenty-two

Bleeding Heart Marathon training progressed rapidly. Mr. Speedy Pants implemented new track workouts and long run strategies in both of our schedules. We ran Forest Park, Grant's Trail, Queeny Park, Mystical Land, Webster Groves, Castlewood, the cornfields, the river valley, and even random routes in and around the city. And I was improving. Getting faster. Finally, I knew my efforts were not in vain. Finally, I could look at my training up to that point and realize, holy cow, it worked. It was epiphanic.

My peak mileage week finally arrived. After several weeks of hovering at comfortable high mileage, Mr. Speedy Pants moved the peg up a notch or two. He did the same for himself. It was a big week for Team Rodrigo.

We ended the week with a twenty-mile run at Forest Park. Mr. Speedy Pants had already run his own twenty-mile long run the day before and was going to recover by running twenty miles with me the very next day. (Back-to-back long runs was just another "feat of awesomeness," as he informed me.) He was particularly chatty as we looped our way around the park. With great attention to detail, he recounted his week of running, which included such highlights as finding a twenty-dollar bill on the side of the road and almost being obliterated by an oncoming freight train. He also expanded on the history of his former high school track teammate Hemo, whom he and his old buddy Tim once placed in a wheelchair for self-serving purposes at a theme park. A large portion of the Hemo chronicles was always dedicated to the peculiar naming system employed by Hemo's parents. Hemo's full name was Helaman Pericles. His brother and sister were given the equally imposing names Don Carlos Ulysses and Khorina, respectively. However, having splurged on the names of their first three children, Hemo's parents opted for a more economic nomenclature for the next three, finding the names Josh, Amanda, and Michael quite sufficient. This, Mr. Speedy Pants and I decided, was rather anti-climactic.

Per usual, our discussions covered a variety of topics. We talked about music. We talked about life. We talked about God. We talked about purpose and eternity and faith and college football. On many occasions, we disagreed. When the disagreement happened to be about college football, we made bets. Mr. Speedy Pants and I were fond of making bets, and we used Starbucks coffee as currency. It was very serious business.

This actually feels easy, I thought. A pang of fear shot through me. *I can't believe I just thought that. Oh, no . . .*

Easy is a four-letter word in running vernacular. To say something is easy is to sabotage your run. Before the word leaves your mouth, you hit the wall or twist an ankle or, as Mr. Speedy Pants nearly experienced, get hit by an oncoming freight train.

Don't think that. Just run. But it is easy. Agh!

Something was wrong. Terribly wrong. I didn't know what it was. But we were flying. And it was easy.

I commented on Mr. Speedy Pants's stories and tried to ignore how good I felt. I trash-talked the BCS and tried to ignore how good I felt. I placed a Venti Americano on the line and tried to ignore how good I felt. And then, at mile nineteen, close enough to the end of the run to feel a measure of safety, I said it.

"Okay, Coach, so this was, like, the best twenty miles I've ever run."

Mr. Speedy Pants looked at his watch. "Yeah, we've been going faster than usual. Feelin' good today, eh?"

"Yeah. I didn't want to say anything before. I was afraid of putting the whammy on it."

"You know, yesterday was my best twenty-mile, too. I felt really good, which is weird, because I should've been tired."

"Well," I said, matter-of-fact, "we are awesome."

Mr. Speedy Pants laughed. "Look at you, kid." He patted the top of my head. "I don't call you my protégée for nothing."

The Best Twenty-Mile Run of All Time was followed several weeks later by The Best Sixteen-Mile Run of All Time. This time progress visited Team Rodrigo at Creve Coeur Park.

Creve Coeur Park had become a regular haunt for Team Rodrigo. For one thing, it is flat (which I appreciated). For another thing, it features a six-mile(ish) loop and a four-mile(ish) loop, both of which wrap around a picturesque lake and two conveniently located bathrooms. Last, and perhaps best of all, the path crosses under a whopping monster of an overpass. It is quite thrilling.

I breathed in the crisp air as we clipped our way around the lake, leaving a trail of crushed brown leaves behind us. The rowers were also there, faithful to their nautical sport. Forward, pull. Forward, pull. The boats cut sharp military lines across the lake's surface. Each team was synchronized, precise, and fluid. Mr. Speedy Pants and I continued forward. Through open fields. Over wooden bridges. Beneath the shade of towering trees.

It was supposed to be a cut-down run, sixteen miles divided into an even first half and a progressively faster second half. Still riding the motivating high of the previous weeks, I ran oblivious of pace, letting Mr. Speedy Pants lead the way and simply falling in step.

"So," he said, glancing at his watch at the halfway point, "we actually started out too fast and never slowed down. How are you feelin'?"

"Good," I said, taking a sip from my water bottle. "Surprisingly enough."

"All right, well, time to start picking up the pace. Fifteen seconds a mile."

The sun was warmer now. We looped around the rowers. We flew across bridges. Each mile was faster than the last. Through the wooded havens. Faster still.

"Okay, kid. We don't have to pick it up any more than this. We can just hold this pace to finish it out. Up to you. What do you wanna do?"

My breathing was heavier now. I was tired. But I wasn't hurting. Not unbearably, anyway. I felt in control. I felt strong. I felt that maybe, just maybe, I could even go faster.

"It doesn't hurt to try."

"All right. Let's go then."

We quickened the pace. Three miles to go. Mr. Speedy Pants began to pull ahead. I pulled even. Two miles to go. I could feel it now. I was getting tired. But I could keep going. My mind was in complete control of my body, and I wasn't afraid. I knew I could keep running.

One mile to go.

We were at my 5K pace now. It felt like a sprint. But it wasn't torture. I was surprised. I wasn't freaking out. I was running fast. I was nailing the run. It was awesome.

"Nicely done, kid," Mr. Speedy Pants said, giving me a high five as mile sixteen fell beneath our feet and we slowed to a walk.

I laughed, thrilled with the run. "I can't believe it. I felt really good."

"I was actually surprised how easy it seemed for you," Mr. Speedy Pants said "I mean, not that I don't think you're fast, but . . ." He smiled.

"Yeah, yeah."

He put his arm around my shoulder. "Ah, I don't call you my star athlete for nothing. Stick with me, kid. I'll make you fast."

"Haha . . . Let me guess. Because you're awesome?"

Mr. Speedy Pants held up his hand for high five. "That's right."

"Oh, brother."

And I returned the high five.

Yes, when you love something, it's not work. It's fun. Running with

Mr. Speedy Pants was fun. Making progress was fun. And running for fun was fun.

The best place to run for fun was Castlewood. No pace. No goal. No plan. Abandoning the stern constitution of paved roads and intersections, Mr. Speedy Pants and I journeyed weekly to the liberated ramblings of trails. It was the grass roots of running.

In fact, it was the very grass and roots of Castlewood that spurred me to purchase my first pair of real trail shoes—bright, electric green trail shoes, no less. Yes, if I was going to join the nature-loving, tree-hugging, mud-flinging world of trail runners, I was going to look like a nature-loving, tree-hugging, mud-flinging trail runner. Somebody pass the granola.

So, kid, it's supposed to rain tonight, read Mr. Speedy Pants's text. *Castlewood tomorrow?*

I smiled. Over the course of marathon training, Mr. Speedy Pants and I had run Castlewood quite often. And because of the spring rains, Castlewood had been just as often a veritable mud pit. Our mud runs, as we called them, were highlights in my Spartan training schedule, the equivalent of the occasional hot fudge sundae in a strict diet of lima beans and wheatgrass. We became fond of our mud runs. And we became fond of rain, because rain meant the trails would be muddy.

You know it, I responded.

The next morning, the trails did not disappoint. The overnight deluge transformed the dirt paths into viscous rivers that threatened to suck the shoes off our feet. The mud had an insatiable desire to swallow our legs. The leaves were in league with the mud, for they had fallen from their respective branches and covered every rock and root along the path, creating a minefield of unseen obstacles. The trail itself had been transformed into a creek—a real, flowing, rushing, let's-go-fishing creek. We splashed our way up the switchback, avoiding the steeper route, known affectionately as "Cardiac Hill."

"This reminds me of a trail run my old buddy Tim and I did when we were in college," Mr. Speedy Pants said as we sloshed our way up the trail.

"Oh, yeah?"

"Yep. The middle of cross-country season. It had been one of the rainiest summers ever, and the river levels were off the charts. Anyway, at one point we had to cross a stream. The water was only knee-deep at first—"

"Ack! Wh-oaa!" I yelped. I pitched forward, barely catching myself before I crashed headfirst into the trail-creek.

"What are you doing back there?" Mr. Speedy Pants yelled, looking over his shoulder as he continued—smoothly—uphill.

"Oh, nothing. I almost died, but that's it."

"Oh, well, anyway," he continued, "the water was only knee-deep at first, but it kept getting deeper and deeper—until it was up to our chests. We literally had to swim to the other side."

"Haha . . . The ultimate adventure run."

"I know, but it gets better. One of the guys on the team ended up with an earthworm in his shorts."

"Oh, my gosh. That is so gross."

"Yeah, and it probably wasn't that pleasant for the earthworm, either."

We were drenched to the bone, covered in globs of mud. We tripped our way through the woods, weaving in and out among the trees and hurdling logs that had fallen across the path during the storms.

I struggled on the uphill climbs. Mr. Speedy Pants, for his part, did not feel the hills presented a significant challenge and would disappear in the distance as we ascended the bluffs overlooking the river. Try as I might, I could not keep up with him. I felt as though I were chasing Sasquatch through the forest, I always one step behind and he always just around the next bend.

However, Sasquatch waited for me at the top of each hill, and when

I finally did join him at the summit, we stood in silence and admired the view. Rolling hills melting into the horizon. Miles of treetops bounding across the sky and blanketing the landscape. The endless river, winding and weaving its way through the still, quiet valley below. Covered in mud, gasping for air, completely worn out yet utterly liberated, we stood.

This is why I run, I thought, struck by the beauty.

As we made our way back to the trailhead, Mr. Speedy Pants returned to his stories of cross-country running and the glory days. He told of the time he and his old buddy Tim got lost in a snowstorm in Wisconsin (again), prefacing the story, as he always did, with the inquiry, "Did I ever tell you about the time my old buddy Tim and I got lost in a snowstorm in Wisconsin?" I attempted to tell a story about losing four pairs of goggles, but Mr. Speedy Pants deemed my narration deficient, and once more assumed responsibility for mid-run entertainment.

Finally, we exited the wilderness of the trails, reluctant to return to the hard, black asphalt and constraints of civilized life. I threw my shoes in the trunk of my car and grabbed a towel. I looked at my legs.

It's gonna take a lot more than a towel, I thought, covering the driver's seat of my car with several plastic trash bags I had packed for that very reason. I happened to catch a glimpse of my ragged reflection in the rearview mirror. My cheeks were flushed from exertion in the cold, damp air, and there was mud smeared across my cheeks and forehead.

In any other circumstance, my initial reaction would have been to remove the dirt. But this time, for some reason, I didn't. I merely stared at my muddied visage with a sense of contentment. A flushed, dirty face framed by wild, unkempt hair and a knotted ponytail stared right back at me. And in that moment, I realized the transformation had taken place. I was a nature girl. I was earthy. I was a trail runner. Dude, pass the granola.

Chapter Twenty-three

The leaves were beginning to turn. Deep reds and brilliant yellows and glowing oranges poured from the casings of summer, spilling across the tops of trees and splashing across the hills. The sun dodged tired clouds as it climbed the horizon. The air was thick and dewy with the lingering breath of the night. It was a mild Saturday morning, ideal for running.

I took long, deep breaths as I ran the winding country roads. The length of my daily runs had increased since I began running with Mr. Speedy Pants, and, needing to fill the space with road, I had gotten into the habit of running the hilly route from my house to Mystical Land. Heading toward Mystical Land allowed endless variations on an out-and-back course—the lake, the cornfields, the river bluffs. It was convenient. Scenic. Challenging.

But my run that day was a recovery run, short and easy, not long enough to make it to Mystical Land and back. And I didn't need the hills. I decided to return to a flat, three-mile loop I had run nearly every day pre–Team Rodrigo, a loop that also happened to be the very first three miles I had ever run.

The road was lined with woods on both sides, except when the trees gave way to horse pastures and barns. One particular stretch cut through a string of equestrian farms with white fences lining the road as far as the eye could see. The stables, with their rows of shuttered windows, stood sharp and bright against the landscape. A tractor rested in the shade next to a faded red barn. A horse neighed in the distance. The crisp autumn breeze carried with it the smell of dirt and hay and, yes, horses. I had always loved the smell of horses. I closed my eyes and took a deep breath. I missed these roads. The roads I ran as a little girl. The same little girl I saw in my memory. The same little girl I saw so clearly it was as though she were standing right there before me. Right then. Right now.

She is looking up at her dad and smiling. Her long, brown ponytail swings back and forth as she bounces from one foot to the other, hands tucked up in the sleeves of her sweatshirt. Her dad looks down at her and rubs the top of her head. He, too, is dressed in sweats and well-worn running shoes.

"How far you wanna go?" he asks, challenging her with a raised eyebrow.

"I just want to see the horses!" she responds as she points down the meandering road ahead.

His eyes follow the direction of her finger.

"Hmm. We might have to go a couple of miles."

"I've never run that far before," she says. Her face is uncertain, and she scrunches her nose in a grimace.

Undeterred, her father smiles reassuringly. "C'mon! Let's go. You can do it!"

She looks tiny in comparison with her father, and her light frame flits down the road. She has to take two strides for every one of his, yet he never runs too quickly. He stays by her side, encouraging her at every step. A few times they stop to walk, but it is never long before they start running again. She carries the conversation easily, and they laugh often. She talks about friends, school, and what she wants to be when she grows up. And about horses. She would like a horse. He listens with affection and pride. As she talks, he sees his little girl. He sees her grow up, drive a car, get married, have children of her own. It happens quickly. He looks down the road. There is only a mile to go. He wishes it were a longer run. Much longer. So long that it would never end, and it would just be the two of them. Talking. Running. Father and daughter.

They reach the horses and pause to pet the furry noses poking over the fence. Her eyes sparkle, and her cheeks glow from the morning air and the exercise. They laugh as the horses blow into the young girl's outstretched hand and tickle her fingers.

After a few minutes, they start back up, again, homeward bound. The air is sharper now, the sun brighter. The dew that made the leaves sparkle and darkened the pavement has faded with the night, and morning gently gives way to day.

"How far did we go?" she asks, breathless, brushing away the loose strands of hair that have strayed from her neat ponytail and whimsically kiss her face.

"Just over two miles!"

It is her first real run. She has never run this far before. She grins widely, laughing a bit at the accomplishment.

"Cool!"

Her father puts his hand on her shoulder as they walk up the driveway to the house.

"Great job, honey! I knew you could do it! It won't be long before I won't be able to keep up with you!"

"Oh, Dad!" She thinks he is teasing her.

He smiles in response. He is not teasing. It is a thought that fills him with pride and the fleeting sweetness of today. Of this very morning. Of this very moment.

They sit down on the porch step. They are quiet now, soaking in the soft rays of sun poking through the trees. The sun's rays go up, up, up. Across the sky. Across the miles. So many miles that they travel across time itself, and it is no longer miles that are passing, but years. They pass quickly. Silently.

The sun is climbing the horizon, again. It shines on a country road, illuminating the drops of dew hanging from sleepy leaves. Its rays dodge the clouds and find their way to kiss the head of a not-so-young girl running a country road, breathing the sweet fragrant air, eyes closed, if only for a moment. Her long, brown ponytail swings back and forth.

She has run farther than two miles now. Much farther. She has run marathons and traveled the globe. She passes the horses that whinny their complaints, for she doesn't stop to pet their furry noses anymore. She smiles as they stomp their hooves and snort. She would still like a horse.

The trees cast shadows on the familiar road and her steady, powerful stride pushes the distance behind her. She thinks of when she first started and how she never would have imagined she could go so far. It feels as though eternity has passed since then. But perhaps it wasn't so very long ago. Perhaps it is today. Perhaps it is now.

The shadows of the little girl and her father began to fade as the familiar country road wound through the woods and fields. I tried to catch up to them. I called their names. I pleaded with them to wait for me. But they were running too quickly. They ran forward, forward. I tried to run faster, but they only pulled farther away. I realized they were not ahead of me, but behind. We were running in opposite directions. And I couldn't turn around.

I watched as the little girl and her father disappeared into the distance. They were content. Together. Always together. He smiled as he listened patiently to her endless stories about life and friends and dreams. So dramatic then, so trivial now. She talked and brushed aside the strands of hair that escaped her ponytail. She had never run that far before. But he knew she could do it. For he would be with her, running next to her, smiling, encouraging her, challenging her.

"How far you wanna go?"

Chapter Twenty-four

There have been all sorts of famous walls in history. The Berlin Wall. The Great Wall of China. Hadrian's Wall. The walls of Jericho. But then there is the wall I hit in the Wheatpatch Run for the Haystacks Half Marathon and Fun Run. In retrospect, I really should have signed up for the fun run.

The Bleeding Heart Marathon was three weeks out, and Team Rodrigo had decided a tune-up race would be a good idea. It would get our legs ready for race pace. It would keep us mentally sharp. It would be a helpful indicator of how the full marathon would go. The Wheatpatch Run for the Haystacks Half Marathon fell into our training schedule with perfect timing, and Mr. Speedy Pants and I had signed up.

"At the Copa . . . Copacabana . . . The hottest spot north of Havana . . ."

I reached for my alarm clock. It was four in the morning. In thirty minutes, I would be in a car with Mr. Speedy Pants, making the two-hour drive to the race. Even though I had PR'ed the distance during training for the GO! St. Louis Marathon, the Haystacks Half Marathon would be the first half marathon I had ever officially raced. It was time to PR in an actual race. And—since Mr. Speedy Pants would be running his own race—I would have to do it on my own. I was excited. I was nervous. I had my goal pace and no idea if I could hold it or not. I was still very much a novice.

"So, you know your game plan?" Mr. Speedy Pants asked as we made our way to the start line.

I nodded.

"Remember, don't get caught up in the numbers. Be smart, but trust your instincts. If you find yourself running next to someone in your pace range, hang with them for a while, even if it's a bit slower than your goal pace. It's easier to run with someone and pace yourself off them. You can always make your move later on."

"Runners . . . Take your marks!" the PA announcer called.

"Good luck, kid."

"You too, Coach."

It was a small race. Three hundred people, tops. A hush fell over the crowd in anticipation of the starting signal. I took a deep breath. This was it.

And then, out of the corner of my eye, I saw her. So-and-So. The experienced runner whom I admired. The same So-and-So whose very presence made me doubt my own ability. The same So-and-So whose speed and composure and mental strength made me feel inferior. As a runner. As an athlete. As a person.

"Go!"

The starter's gun rang through the air, and we were off.

So-and-So disappeared in the crowd as the surge of runners spilled down the pavement. Mr. Speedy Pants took off with the lead runners, an elite group that soon put a considerable distance between themselves and the plebeian masses. I followed, watching them pull away as I checked my pace periodically throughout the first half mile.

Find your stride. Fall into your stride, I told myself.

It was a lonely course, flat, sparse, and brown. Very brown. There were many monotonous straightaways. There were very few buildings. There was nothing of note. Just brown grass and gray pavement and, yes, the occasional haystack. There weren't even many of those. Nevertheless, I was running well. And at mile five, to my surprise, I found myself pulling even with So-and-So.

"Lookin' good," she said as I pulled up next to her.

"Thanks. You, too," I replied.

We were quiet for a while, evenly paced, striding in unison. Mr. Speedy Pants was right. It was easier to run with someone. I glanced at my watch. My pace had dropped a bit.

So-and-so must have slowed down since the first two miles, I thought. *Don't get caught up in the numbers. It's easier to run with someone*, I reminded myself. *But I feel good. And this is several seconds off pace . . .*

I debated with my better judgment for several minutes before making an executive decision. Better judgment, while sound, usually falls short in the world of mental semantics. I decided to push the pace and leave So-and-So behind me.

"You're looking strong!" she said as I began to pull away. "Good job!"

"You, too!" I called back. *That was really nice of her*, I thought. *She's really nice.*

Always beware of the really nice ones.

The next few miles were pleasant. By passing So-and-So, I had become the first-place female. I floated along at the fast end of my goal pace. The sun felt warm on my skin, offering a gentle preview of its forthcoming intensity. The brown grass and brown dirt and brown leaves even began to take on a golden hue. By now the race had spread out considerably. At times I could see no one in front of me or behind me. There were only one or two spectators per mile, and at two intersections I had to ask a random person walking down the street or sitting in a parked car which way I needed to turn to stay on the race course. "I think I saw a runner go that way" was the general response to my inquiries. And other than this minor inconvenience, the race was going quite well.

And then, unexpectedly, I blew up.

Until mile eight at the Wheatpatch Run for the Haystacks, I had never before hit the infamous "wall" that veteran runners know so well. I had been tired before. I had wanted to stop mid-race before. And during many a long run I had sworn off running as a whole and vowed to adopt a more practical hobby. Like stamp collecting. But for all the hard runs I had suffered through, I had never undergone a complete meltdown like I did in the Haystacks Half Marathon. At Haystacks, I learned that the difference between a hard run and hitting the wall is the difference between a leaky faucet and the implosion of the Hoover Dam. It is inconvenience versus catastrophe.

Oh, my gosh, I thought, despair sweeping over me. *This is not supposed to happen in a half marathon. Not at mile eight.*

My legs felt like they weighed a thousand pounds. I couldn't catch my breath. I could tell my body was pushing hard. I was tired. Too tired. I was extremely uncomfortable. I felt exhausted. It hurt to run. The hurt scared the heck out of me. I was freaked out that I wouldn't be able to finish.

Okay. Don't freak out. Keep going. You'll get your second wind.

I was lying. Even as I said the words, I knew there was no second wind on the horizon. My strength was gone. I was drained. I waited for determination to kick in, for some kind of unflappable tenacity, some kind of doggedness to keep me going. But no such luck. Everything I had was flappable. Nothing was dogged. I had no desire to finish the race. I didn't care. The thought of taking another step was unbearable. And, to top it all off, I was overcome with an overpowering desire to cry. And not just a few teardrops. I'm talking unabashed weeping.

Hitting the wall is more than just being tired. It is like getting beaten to the ground with a mailbox and then finding out that your dog just died.

The course wound through several blocks of cobblestone streets before jackknifing back up a long, sloping hill. The hill probably wasn't that steep. I felt like I was scaling Mount Everest.

One foot in front of the other. Like eating an elephant. An elephant. I feel like an elephant. I tried to apply the wisdom Mr. Speedy Pants had given me, but I was growing delirious, and I'm fairly certain I had no idea what I was saying. *Don't be a dumb elephant. I wanna cry.*

I looked up. The top of the hill was marked by a gas station. *Almost at the top*, I told myself. And then I blinked. I blinked again. There was a man standing at the top of the hill, just in front of the gas station. He looked like he was waiting for me. He looked like Mr. Speedy Pants. *Oh, my gosh. I'm seeing things. I'm dying. I'm going to die in Wheatpatch.*

But I wasn't seeing things. It really was Mr. Speedy Pants. And he really was waiting for me.

"What are you doing, Coach?" I gasped as he jumped into stride with me. "What happened?"

"Yeah, my race isn't gonna happen today."

He detailed his mid-race journey into four Porta-Johns, none of which had toilet paper. Finally, he was forced to run into a nearby gas station—and relinquish a possible top three finish.

"So, I was still in second place after the third Porta-John attempt, but after the fourth, I was just like, 'Forget it.' I ran into the gas station and figured I'd run the rest of the race with you. And speaking of you," he glanced over at me, "how are you feeling? You're breathing a little heavy there, kid."

From the corner of my eye I caught a glimpse of his concerned face looking at me. I had no doubt I looked horrible. I felt worse.

How do I feel? Awful. Maybe it will go away. I tried to make sense of my thoughts before I responded. *It's not going away. I shouldn't be this tired already. Oh, my gosh. I still have five miles to go. I can't keep this up for five miles. I don't want to be out here anymore. Why am I so tired? I wanna go home.*

I believe *I wanna go home* was the last thought that crossed my mind before I replied to Mr. Speedy Pants. My attempt to make sense of my thoughts hadn't been as successful as I had hoped.

"Uh . . . I'm actually really, really tired," I gasped.

"Okay."

"Yeah, I don't know what happened. But I think I'm going to die."

Mr. Speedy Pants listened to my speech. His response was calm and practical, like always.

"Well, don't panic. Just try to get your legs back under you and catch your breath. You just gotta grind your teeth and push through it. You'll get your second wind."

I nodded. I was just trying not to die.

The course was desolate at this point, the Wheatpatch Run for the Haystacks not having quite as many participants as one could hope. And because the course wound its way through naked cornfields and followed the cracked, broken asphalt of a neglected bike path, the number of spectators hovered between zero and, well, zero. Usually, I would have missed the spectators and their shouts of encouragement. This time, I was glad there was no one around. Things were going to get ugly.

"Uh, Coach?"

"Yeah, kid?"

"I . . . I think I'm getting all emotional."

Calm. Practical. "Okay. So . . . what does that mean?"

"I . . . I think it means I'm . . . gonna . . . cry . . ."

Mr. Speedy Pants looked at me. Though he tried to remain stoic, I could see the dread creeping over his face.

"Oh, no. No, no. No. Don't cry. C'mon, kid," he pleaded with me. "You know crying makes me uncomfortable."

"I'm . . . [sniff] . . . I'm . . . trying . . . [sniff] . . . not to . . ."

"C'mon, kid," Mr. Speedy Pants comforted me, "hang in there. Just a couple more miles. Just keep picking up your feet. One step at a time."

I couldn't respond. Misery had come upon me in a form hitherto unknown. It enveloped me. It overwhelmed me.

My pace was slowing considerably now. Every so often, Mr. Speedy Pants glanced behind us. I knew what he was doing. He was watching for the second-place female. She would be catching up to us soon. I had built a solid lead in the middle of the race, but it wasn't that big. And it was shrinking with every second.

"C'mon, kid. Hang in there. Keep pushing. You can do this. Think of all the hard workouts you've nailed. You've trained your body for this. Remember your twenty quarters in the rain? You were all guts that day."

My throat burned. My eyes burned. My lungs burned. My quads burned. I felt as though I were about to spontaneously combust and then extinguish myself with my own tears.

Mr. Speedy Pants glanced back. "You've got about twenty seconds on the next girl. Try to hold her off."

It was So-and-So. She was gaining on me. *Don't let her catch you*, I told myself, trying to find motivation in the fear of being passed. But it didn't work. In my misery, I didn't care if she caught me. All I cared about was being done.

And then, at mile eleven, So-and-So flew by me. She looked strong and her stride was effortless as she picked up the pace.

"Keep going!" she encouraged me as she left me in the dust of her fancy red racing flats. "You're running a good race—looking strong!"

It was very nice of her. She was really nice. Always beware of the really nice ones.

Mr. Speedy Pants, for his part, was experiencing another form of misery, the awkward misery of feeling just fine and running next to someone who does not. Yet he stayed by my side. He urged me on with his own stories of overcoming tough runs. He praised me for every mile we chalked off. He rallied me by announcing the nearness of the finish line.

At mile twelve, the third-place girl passed me.

"Almost there, kid. C'mon, kid, let's go. You've got it."

Shuffling, sniffling, plodding, I crept toward the finish line, each step a pathetic, spluttering breath. A half mile to go. A quarter mile. And, finally, the finish line. The end of my race was ugly. But I had finished. And there is something to be said for that.

As we crossed the finish line, Mr. Speedy Pants put his arm around my shoulders. I was quiet. I wanted to cry. I would have let myself cry, but I couldn't. My tears, like my body, were spent. We walked through the finishers' area in silence, grabbing some bottled water as we made our way back to the car. Finding a nearby curb, we sat down, stretching our tired legs and soaking up the morning sun now shining in full glory. Mr. Speedy Pants finally broke the quiet.

"I'm proud of you, kid. You know that?"

"I don't know what happened, Coach. I was too aggressive. I should have stayed with So-and-So. I totally blew it. I totally blew up."

"Eh, it happens. It's part of racing. But I'm proud of you. You hit a mental wall—it wasn't so much the physical wall as it was mental—but you gutted it out, and you finished. Racing isn't always about running a PR. It's about learning from your experience. As long as you learn from it, I don't care what happens out there."

"Thanks, Coach."

"Now, don't get me wrong," he continued, his mouth slowly curling into a grin, "I would much rather you run a great race—a smart race—and hit your time. But if you're gonna blow up, as long as you learn from it, it's cool." He threw his arm around my shoulders and gave me a quick hug. "You know you're still my star athlete?"

I smiled. "Yeah. Thanks, Coach."

We got up from the curb and climbed into the car.

"Man," Mr. Speedy Pants said as we drove away, dodging tired runners milling about the parking lot, medals around their necks, "I need some coffee."

"Hey, Coach?"

"What, kid?"

"Are you proud of me for not crying?"

"Dude! You know crying makes me uncomfortable!" He threw his hands in the air in exasperation.

"I know! That's why I tried so hard not to cry!"

AMY L. MARXKORS

"You almost did."

"But I didn't."

"But you almost did, which is almost just as bad."

"Whatever."

"I'm just sayin' . . ."

"Well," I conceded, "thank you for being almost uncomfortable when I almost cried, but didn't."

He smiled and looked over at me. "You're lucky I'm so awesome."

Yes, I had learned from my blowup. I learned that racing takes patience and faith and intelligence just as much as it takes endurance and speed. I learned that the mental can overcome the physical—for better or for worse. I learned that even when things don't go as planned, you can still walk away with a victory in hand. I learned that our defeats sometimes teach us more than our victories. And, most important, I learned to never, ever, ever run the Wheatpatch Run for the Haystacks Half Marathon. Ever.

Chapter Twenty-five

After the Haystacks saga, I had just enough time to regain my composure and pull together a few solid runs before the Bleeding Heart Marathon arrived. There is something so final about the last long run and the last workout before race day. The taper means you have run out of time. There is no point in cramming in another tough workout. You can't improve your fitness. You've done all you can do, and now you have to wait and see if it was enough. The taper is the great admission: "This is as good as I'm going to get before race day." Que sera sera.

It is a cheery fatalism, and with high expectations I checked off the final days of my Bleeding Heart Marathon training program. All things considered, training couldn't have gone better. That is, except for one minor issue that developed in the days following the Wheatpatch Run for the Haystacks. Mr. Speedy Pants's incorrigible Achilles flared up, and he was forced into an ill-timed training hiatus. After two weeks of no running, he made the official announcement: Racing the Bleeding Heart Marathon was out of the question.

There was, however, one redeeming circumstance in the whole ordeal. If Mr. Speedy Pants could get his Achilles in good enough shape to run even a little in the days leading up to the race, he would run the marathon with me, acting as coach, pacer, and provider of awesomeness. This is exactly what happened, and forty-eight hours before race day, a second official announcement was made: Team Rodrigo would be running the Bleeding Heart Marathon in tandem.

"So, kid," he said, "it's not a complete loss. I'm actually kind of glad I get to run with you. Granted, it would have been fun to race, but I do feel a sort of responsibility for you, you being my protégée and all."

"I really am sorry you're hurt, Coach." I bit my lip, trying to conceal a guilty, sideways grin. "But I guess if I had to pick an alternative to you actually running your race, this would be it."

"Uh-huh."

The guilty grin escaped.

"You look real sorry, kid."

"No! I promise! I am!" (I really was.)

"Uh-huh." He reached into his back pocket and pulled out an envelope. I knew what was in it. "Here you go. You know the rules."

I took the envelope. Scrawled across the front were the words FINAL RACE INSTRUCTIONS, VERSION 2.0. I did know the rules. I couldn't open the letter until the night before the race. It was Team Rodrigo tradition.

"Now, I know we'll be making the trip together, and I'll be running with you, and I'll be with you on race morning, so there's nothing in there that I couldn't tell you on race day. But, eh." He shrugged. "It's how I roll."

"Thanks, Coach."

"You ready?"

I nodded. "Yep. I think so. Hope so."

"You'll be just fine."

"Yeah."

Well, kid, here we go, again. You probably saw this coming, and if you didn't, well, then you haven't learned much in the last ten months or so. But, you know me. I like tradition and such, and I did set this precedent before St. Louis. So here are your final race instructions for Bleeding Heart.

Mr. Speedy Pants followed his introduction with a list of race day necessities, from socks and shoes to my racing singlet and throwaway gloves. Energy gels, watch, watch charger, post-race clothes, visor. The list was complete. I was going to be prepared.

In addition to the obvious perks of running with me—such as pacing services, storytelling, encouragement, harassment, and general awesomeness—you will also receive, as part of the Mr. Speedy Pants Pacing Package, running caddy service. I'll be running with a marathon pouch, so I can store your energy gels, my energy gels, and of course, Advil. Basically, I'll be a camel.

Now, as far as everything else goes . . . Well, you already know all of it. So on to the important part of this letter.

Am I the only one who is going into this race more nervous than I was for St. Louis? I have the feeling that you are, too. But, you should be more nervous. This is a whole new ball game. (Wait . . . This isn't comforting you? Oops.) Okay, okay. In all seriousness, kid, this race is a lot different than Round One in Go! St. Louis. First of all, we've chosen a much more aggressive goal for you. You'll need a perfect race to hit your time. In St. Louis, we were conservative. I would have been shocked if you didn't nail it. (You are one of those annoying overachievers, after all.) So, with no pressure, no real worries—you hit it out of the park. But this time is a bit different. Everything is going to have to fall into place. And I know you. If it doesn't, you're going to be disappointed.

But, that being said, I have every reason to believe you will meet success on Sunday. You are in great shape. The training is all there. If I didn't believe in you, trust me, we wouldn't be going into the race with the goal that we have. I told you before Haystacks that if the half marathon didn't go well, I would be adjusting your Bleeding Heart goal time. Well, Haystacks didn't go well, but I know it was a fluke. And guess what? Even with your blowup, you still rocked Haystacks. In fact, your "blowup time" projects a marathon time of your goal in Bleeding Heart. Crazy, huh? So, put a good race together, and it's in the bag.

I believe in you, kid. On Sunday, you just have to believe in me, believe in your training, and believe in yourself. Then, swing away.

233

We'll see what happens. I plan on running the first half relaxed, getting you in striking range of your goal. Then, be prepared to hammer the second half.

Now, because you now have a fear of "the wall," I'll address that. The bad news is, you've experienced the wall. And it's scary. The good news is, you've experienced the wall, and you know, deep down, it's not as scary as it seems. I can tell you from experience the first time you hit the wall is the worst. In fact, I've hit the wall four times in my marathon career. The first time was devastating. The next three times slowed me down, but I knew how to handle it. I kept going, and I did just fine. In New York, I hit the wall at mile twenty-three. I walked seven times in the last three miles—and I still ran a seven-minute PR. I knew I had hit the wall, and I knew my pace was going to drop. But I also knew that I could break the last three miles into walk/run segments and just get it done. You have to battle the distance. Battle yourself. Battle the wall. Sounds cheesy, kid, but it's true. So, while you should fear the wall and respect it, you need to realize that you can still conquer it, even if it knocks you down a few times. Got it? If you hit the wall, no need to freak out. We'll address it, change the game plan, and figure out the best way to finish it out. Keep in mind that just because you hit the wall early doesn't mean you won't catch a second wind and bounce back. It happens.

I can tell you this much: I know you are going to run well. While you might be disappointed in anything slower than your goal pace, I won't be. I always go into my marathons with an A-goal, B-goal, C-goal, and D-goal—with the D-goal being just to finish. You never know what the marathon is going to throw at you. You always have to respect the distance.

I will be proud of you if you achieve any of these goals. Obviously, if we're shooting for the D-goal, something has gone quite awry. But it won't matter. I will be extremely proud of you for finishing, because it can be very hard to have the desire to finish when you have such high aspirations for yourself and then realize it isn't going to happen that day. No matter what goal we are aiming for over those last few miles, I will be with you every step of the way, no matter what. Well, unless you start overachieving and I can't keep up. I'm kind of outta shape.

Now, in addressing this whole crying situation. I'm gonna be short: It isn't going to happen. Now, if it does happen, I guess I'll have to decide how to deal with it then. I'll probably beg you not to cry. We'll stop. You'll cry. I'll hug you, give you a minute, ask if you're done, and then tell you that now that you've got the girl out of your system, it's time to finish what we started. And then we'll finish the race. See how mean I am? I'd avoid crying if I were you.

But enough of the possibility of doom and gloom. I mentioned it because, well, it is a possibility, and I want you to know it isn't as doom and gloomy as it appears. I'm an old pro. Any doom and gloom we encounter, I'll know how to fix. I am awesome that way. The important thing to keep in mind is that this is just a stepping-stone to even bigger goals. This race will serve a purpose, no matter how it goes. What do I always say? As long as you finish and learn from each marathon, it is a success.

So, my final instruction, motivation, message, or whatever is this: You will be fine. (Deep, huh?) You really will be. I've learned a lot about you over the past year, and one of the things I've learned is that you are tough and can do anything you set your stubborn, goofy mind to do. I've also learned that you tend to underestimate yourself. So stop it. For my part, I will be proud of you no matter what. I can't imagine not being proud of you, kid. I know you too well and respect you too much. I am going to give you a big hug no matter what happens. I am going to continue coaching you no mat-

ter what happens. Unless you fire me, of course. And then I'll probably body-slam you. Basically, I'll coach you as long as you want me to coach you. Because coaching you brings me quite a bit of joy. Even if I have twelve kids, no time, and coaching means me sending you emails once a week. Sure, most of the fun is actually running with you and going on our goofy adventures, but I'm happy when you nail workouts and have great races and just enjoy running. I like watching you succeed. So, even if I just get the occasional email saying, "Hey, Coach, I just ran such-and-such time!" that will work.

Anyway, that's about it. That was entirely way too sappy. It's about time we got back to the name-calling days of old. So, to recap: Run well. Don't cry. Have fun. Don't be a dork.

Wow. I could have saved a lot of time just by typing that last sentence. Rats. Oh, well. Anyway, that's your mission, kid.

Good luck,
Coach

Chapter Twenty-six

The weather couldn't have been more perfect. The temperature hovered in the mid-thirties, but it was still dark. The sun would bring with it a few degrees of warmth. Mr. Speedy Pants and I made our way across the parking lot and into the community center where runners milled about, stretching, waiting in line to use the bathroom, and pinning bib numbers to their shirts. Bleeding Heart was a small marathon, and the atmosphere felt more like a local 5K than the culmination of four months of marathon training. Instead of requiring a three-hour excursion to a massive convention center flooded with vendors and mandating a GPS to navigate, packet pickup for the Bleeding Heart Marathon had been at a tiny running store nestled in a quaint city square. Many of the race participants knew one another and just as many spectators knew the race participants. The whole race had an aura of familiarity to it, as if Andy Griffith, Floyd the Barber, and the residents of Mayberry had up and decided to put on a marathon.

"How you feeling, kid?"

After using the bathroom one last time, we headed back to the parking lot to await the call to the start line.

I took a deep breath. Though I felt surprisingly calm, little knots in my stomach and a momentary flush of dizziness betrayed my inevitable pre-race jitters. My muscles felt tense. I attributed their stiffness to the cold rather than to the paralyzing anxiety flooding my body.

"Good."

"Good. I think it's time to toss the football around."

A week before the race, Mr. Speedy Pants decided I needed to establish a pre-race routine to calm my nerves and keep me from overthinking in the minutes before the marathon, something that would get my mind off racing and remind me that, in the end, the whole or-deal was actually meant to be fun. A game of parking lot football was only logical.

He reached into the backseat of the car and pulled out a football. Stretching briefly, he swung his arm in giant circles before calling out, "Go long, kid."

I laughed and ambled down the parking lot in a slow, lazy jog. Mr. Speedy Pants launched the ball. Whether it was because it was still dark or because I was still shaky with nerves, the ball bounced off my hands, onto the pavement, and against the side door of a red pickup truck.

"Oops . . ." I mumbled, retrieving the ball from under a minivan.

"Boo . . ." Mr. Speedy Pants shook his head in mock disapproval. "Nice catch, kid."

"Whatever. I wasn't ready."

"Uh-huh."

I am glad to report I didn't drop any passes after the first incomple-tion. However, we had time for only a few more pass attempts before the PA announcer directed all race participants to the start line.

"Time to rock it out," Mr. Speedy Pants said, patting me on the back as we trekked to the waving banners demarcating the marathon start.

I nodded.

"Remember: Just run. Have fun out there, kid."

"Runners on your mark . . ."

The starting gun's blast cut through the chilly air. The Bleeding Heart Marathon had begun.

The marathon is a paradox. It is both a culmination and a begin-ning. It is a fulfillment and a task at hand. It is the backdrop to a run-ner's moment of glory or scene of defeat. It is Waterloo, and each participant is destined to be either a Napoleon or a Wellington.

Suffice it to say my hand rested smugly in my waistcoat.

Miles one through nine were delightful. Effortless, almost. Within the first four miles I stripped off my long-sleeved shirt and throwaway gloves. I found my stride with surprising ease. Spectators waved and I waved back. Most of the cheers were on a first-name basis. We ran through picturesque neighborhoods, ethereal in the golden morning light and quiet except for the few people who had awakened early to cheer from their front yards, coffee in hand, some still wearing robes and slippers. A stiff breeze cut between the homes and assaulted the water stations, occasionally blowing the empty cups across the road. At mile eight, I glanced at my watch for the first time. We were ahead of pace—barely, but still ahead. I felt good. Strong. With each mile, I was that much closer to victory.

At mile ten, we entered the confines of an air force base, a highlight of the Bleeding Heart Marathon course. The base, as one would assume an air force base to be, was flat and exposed. It was also, for the most part, desolate. We wound our way through barren fields and across long, dreary runways. Every now and then, we passed a cluster of barracks and the spherical silhouette of an aircraft hangar. At one point we passed a retired fighter jet, permanently grounded and commemorated by a ring of daffodils and wooden benches. Mr. Speedy Pants paid homage to the aircraft by spreading his arms and giving his best fighter jet impression, which was basically a loud whooshing sound followed by a second, higher-pitched whooshing sound, which I assumed to be a missile launching.

The wind picked up at that point. What was a stiff breeze at the beginning of the race evolved into a Midwest gale storm, and it assailed us from every direction at thirty-five miles an hour. Conversation ceased, and I ran a good portion of the nine miles on the air force base with my head down, trying to shield it against the strong gusts. The headwinds blinded us, and the crosswinds caused us to stagger sideways across the path.

"Keep going, kid," Mr. Speedy Pants encouraged me. "Just gotta tough it out. It'll be better once we get off the base."

"Better" didn't happen until mile nineteen, and by that time, I was exhausted.

"Coach," I said, trying to catch my breath and throwing one leaden leg in front of the other, "I'm really tired."

"That's okay. That was a rough stretch there. Don't worry about your pace these next couple of miles. Just get your legs back. Find your rhythm again."

But it was too late. My rhythm was gone. My legs were gone. I was overwhelmed by my fatigue and overwhelmed that I still had seven miles to go.

Oh, my gosh . . . I thought. *I'm dead.* A wave of fear washed over me. It was a very distinct feeling. A familiar feeling. I had felt it once before. At Haystacks. It was the wall.

At mile twenty-one, my body balked at the idea of running. The love of running, the joy of running, the fun of running completely disappeared. It was as though the sport had forsaken me when I needed it most. I felt lonely. I felt small. I felt very, very tired.

It was only a matter of minutes before my mental strength surrendered to my physical fatigue, and I absolutely, completely, utterly blew up.

"I need to walk, Coach. Can . . . can we walk a minute?"

Mr. Speedy Pants looked at me, assessing my misery. "We'll slow down to a jog. Can you keep going just a bit longer? Try not to walk."

I was overcome by an irrepressible urge to cry. Weep, really. "I can't . . . I can't." My eyes burned. My throat tightened. A small but unmistakable sob escaped my lips.

Mr. Speedy Pants, sensing an impeding breakdown, did his best to forestall my collapse.

"Let's make it to the next water station, kid. Then we can walk a bit, okay?"

I nodded, my throat too tight to respond.

Just before we reached the water station at mile twenty-two, my legs refused to move forward, and I stopped. I gasped for air, partly from fatigue and partly from my efforts not to cry. And right there, four months of training and a thousand miles faded away. The race would not happen. We walked.

"It's okay, kid," Mr. Speedy Pants said, throwing his arm around me as we walked down the course. It was the first time I had ever walked during a marathon. Even at Haystacks I had managed to maintain a slow jog. But here, at Bleeding Heart, I was wholly defeated.

"The second-place woman is right behind you," a man at the water station informed us as I reached for a cup.

I hadn't realized I was in first place. I turned around. She was gaining on us. She looked strong. I knew it was only a matter of seconds before she passed us. It was Haystacks all over again. I had held first place in my hands, and I had let it slip away.

I looked up at Mr. Speedy Pants. My body was broken and my heart was breaking right along with it. All those months and months of training. Everything. To walk.

His arm was still around my shoulders. "It's okay, kid," he said again, a gentle smile on his face.

I nodded and closed my eyes as we began running once more. I was trying not to cry, trying to keep moving forward. I would have given anything to stop, to say, "I was wrong. I've changed my mind about this whole thing. I can't do it." But I kept moving. Because Mr. Speedy Pants was there with me. Because he was there for me. Because he wouldn't let me quit.

We ended up walking two more times in the last five miles. But finally, we finished. It was over. The race, my training—everything. I sat on the cobblestone path, just beyond the finish line, watching the other runners finish their races. A few raised their arms in victory. Many were greeted by waiting family members or by fellow runners, friends who had completed their own races and were now wrapped in Mylar blankets, cheering, celebrating. I sat cross-legged, body slumped forward, eyes closed. The wind blew my hair into my face and the sun, now warm with the late morning, made my skin tingle in the cool autumn air. I shivered. I wasn't cold.

"Here you go, kid."

I looked up. Mr. Speedy Pants handed me a cup of Gatorade.

"Thanks."

"Rough day for Team Rodrigo, huh?" he said, plopping down next to me.

I grimaced.

"It happens. We went out pretty aggressive. And that wind didn't help any. But that's what makes the marathon so challenging. You can do everything right for four months, but it all comes down to one day. One shot. Sometimes you have a good day. Sometime you have a bad day. It's a gamble, kid. Today just wasn't your day."

"Yeah. I know, Coach. Thanks." I wanted to cry, but I couldn't. I felt too tired. Too numb.

"You okay?" He looked concerned. He didn't want me to be disappointed, with the day or myself.

"Yeah. Just bummed."

He put his arm around my shoulder. "I know, kid. I know."

I assume it is natural to feel a sense of regret—mourning, almost—when something for which you have trained so hard and have anticipated with such expectations comes to an inglorious end. Yes, there was some sense of achievement in that I was able to finish a race after hitting the wall. And once more I had abstained from crying during the meltdown. But the whole ordeal was nothing less than painfully anti-climactic. It wasn't supposed to end that way.

The rest of the day, I couldn't shake my dissatisfaction. I knew I had a better race in me. If only I could have one more shot.

And that's when I was struck with an epiphany. Or insanity. Or a combination of both. I knew what I had to do.

"Hey, Coach," I ventured the next morning as Mr. Speedy Pants finished pouring himself a cup of coffee.

Mr. and Mrs. Speedy Pants and I, of course, were staying with the Awesome Family. And as one would assume from such a title, they were awesome. They had coffee and bagels—pure gold to a runner—ready every morning. Mr. Speedy Pants turned around and looked up.

I took a deep breath. "I want to do another marathon."

He raised his eyebrows. "Another marathon, huh?"

"Yep. What if we pretend Bleeding Heart was just another long run? There are a ton of fall marathons. There's gotta be one still open. One week, two weeks, three weeks out—doesn't matter. I know I recover well. I'll rest up, get my legs back, do a few short runs between now and the race—like a second taper. Then . . . go for it."

He looked at me as though appraising my physical, mental, and emotional health. There is, after all, a fine line separating determination and lunacy.

"Kid, you don't have to run another marathon. Sure, the race didn't go as you hoped it would, but it was still an accomplishment. You hit the wall and felt like giving up, but you didn't. You gutted it out and finished. And there's a lot to be said for that. Plus, you didn't cry"—he smiled—"which I am particularly glad about."

I smiled, but I wasn't going to budge.

"What do I always tell you, kid? I don't care what happens in a race as long as you learn from it."

"I know, Coach, and thank you. But I want to do this. I need to do this. I know I can."

He was silent for a minute, scratching his chin as if contemplating the idea. I stood there, silent, hoping I passed the test. He pulled out his phone, looking at the screen and tapping a few buttons before answering me.

"So, here's the deal. I'm going up to time the Capitol Marathon in a couple of weeks. Actually"—he slipped the phone into his back pocket and folded his arms—"I've been hired to assist the timing crew. I'll be the troubleshooter, so to speak. Anyway, because I know the race director—and because I'm awesome—I should be able to get you a late registration into the race. I won't be able to run with you, but I'll be there at least. Perhaps I'll even finish my race-timing duties in time to run the last mile or two with you."

"Oh, my gosh. Really?" It seemed too perfect to be true. "That settles it. It's meant to be!" I threw a victorious hand into the air. I would race the second marathon as if the first had never happened. It was a brilliant plan.

At least, I thought it was a brilliant plan—until Mr. Speedy Pants got off the phone with the race director, my registration official. In that one apocalyptic millisecond when Mr. Speedy Pants confirmed the details of the Capitol Marathon, the reality of what I had just done hit me in a cold tidal wave of panic. It was final. I would be running another marathon. In twelve days.

Over the next few days, I was a headcase—even more than normal. My desire for redemption was constantly besieged by self-doubt and fear. I began to question if I had the resolve or even the desire to give it another try. Sure, my first race hadn't gone as planned, but I had finished. That was good enough, wasn't it? I had the rest of my life to run marathons. Why not close this chapter of my training and move on? Why put myself through this torture? There really was no need to race another marathon just days after I had tried and failed.

But there was. It was a need that stemmed from the Super Secret Workout, Part II. And the Workout of Death, Part II. And the Funky Monkey 5K, Part II.

Over the course of several months and thousands of miles, in the difficulty of mastering fear and overcoming fatigue, in the pain of a body with nothing left to give and the power of a mind that believes otherwise, I had discovered unknown strength, unknown endurance. I had seen faith fulfilled, conviction confirmed, and perseverance rewarded. I had learned that fear and pride and even the joy of victory will go only so far. Eventually they fall by the wayside, and it is only love of the sport that drives us ever onward. These were the things I had learned and believed. These were the things that had changed me. The miles were my witnesses.

I had become a runner.

Chapter Twenty-seven

So, kid, this marathon wasn't planned and it's on short notice, but I'd hate to jinx your race by not following Team Rodrigo tradition. So, while I didn't have time to present your instructions in our traditional manner (I prefer the sealed envelope presentation), I decided an email would suffice. Plus, I wanted to let you know I'm charging you overtime for this.

The short turnaround makes these final instructions interesting. I mean, I could just tell you to read the Bleeding Heart instructions again (and, actually, you should), but we'll consider this a supplement to address the unique circumstances of this go-round.

Now for my thoughts on the Capitol Marathon. First, let me preface by saying this: I am just as okay with you not running Capitol as I am with you running it. I want it to be something you really want to do. Don't do it for me. I didn't want to say this before, because I didn't want you to be influenced by me, but . . . I'm glad you're racing it. The day after Bleeding Heart, when you first suggested racing a do-over marathon, you had the same fire in your eyes as you did when you just missed hitting your time in the Super Secret Workout, Part I. You decided you were gonna hit your time the very next week, even if it killed you. After Bleeding Heart, I could see in your eyes that you knew you had a better race in you. You just needed another shot. I want you to succeed, kid. To do well. But I also don't want you to be mentally tired of all this running and racing. So, I'm excited for you to run Capitol—but only if you really are up for it, you really want to do it, and it's really what you want.

You're gonna run well, kid. Sure, it's a bit unorthodox to crank out two marathons so close together. But you're an ox, kid. Your legs feel good, you're in tiptop shape, and we both know you still have a great race left in you. If I didn't think you had a good chance of doing well, I'd tell you. (I'm kind of protective of you.) I only wish I could run with you. As cheesy as it sounds, I'll be with you in spirit when you're out there running. And I'll be waiting for you at the finish. Probably with a big hug or something sappy like that.

I know you're gonna be shooting to score those Team Rodrigo bonus points—and I think you're gonna score a ton of 'em. But just deciding to attempt this earns you bonus points, kid. I couldn't be any prouder of you for this crazy idea. Part of me thinks you're crazy, but it sounds like something I would do, which of course means I'm proud. And, while I know you'll be fine physically, it takes some mental fortitude to bounce back so soon. So, yep, I couldn't be prouder of my star athlete who won't settle for less than her best. Even if it requires two tries (which it often does).

After this race, no scheduled training for a month. Just run when you want, how far you want, and how fast you want. Just be sure to invite me for some of the runs. Especially the fun ones.

So, go get 'em, kid. I know you're gonna rock it out, because, well, that's what we do.

Sincerely,
Coach

The marathon never ceases to amaze me. It is both a grueling challenge and a fragile art form. You must confront complete physical depletion and exploit the threshold of human endurance—kicking and screaming if need be—and yet not upset the delicate balance linking distance and the race against time. Like a gladiator showered by the jeers of a bloodthirsty coliseum, so the distance runner battles the internal torment of self-inflicted pain, showered by the silent jeers of a body and mind ready to fall beneath the sword. The battlefield is distance. The army is but one. It is both calculated and frenetic. It is complex and it is elemental. It is brutal. It is elegant. It is the marathon.

Perhaps because the marathon has so many facets—because it demands excellence from every fiber of human existence—we are forever learning from and through the experience. We learn about sport itself—about training and rest, about strategy and biorhythms, about the extent of mental stamina and physical endurance. We learn that pain is relative, that we can tolerate much more than we give ourselves credit for, that often when we think we have reached the breaking point, we are simply just afraid of doing so. We learn what motivates us. What discourages us. What brings us joy. What makes us tremble. We question why we run. We construct theories. We are proven wrong. We are humbled. We are edified. We are students in the hands of a silent instructor. We are taught covertly, without our knowledge, as we complete the workbook of miles. Our exams are lined with cones and barricades and spectators and aid stations. Each test begins with a pistol shot and ends with the breaking of a ribbon. There is but one question on the test.

I looked up. A large, canvas banner cut through the air, snapping and popping in the wind. It loomed above the runners waiting restlessly for the final minutes to pass. I stood at the start line, hopping anxiously from one foot to the other, surrounded by thousands of people and towering skyscrapers, blowing into my hands to warm my fingers. Masses of rosy cheeks and puffs of breath clouded the chilly morning air. I scanned the top of the crowd with its sea of bouncing heads and splashes of gloved hands, doused in shadows by the tall buildings around us. This was a new city for me, a new landscape. The glass from the skyscrapers shined a brilliant gold, reflecting the glory of a rising sun. The crisp, blue sky stretched beyond the city limits, an ethereal blanket thrown across a fleeing horizon. The pavement was black and clean. The PA announcer began the final instructions. It was a matter of seconds now. The crowd shifted forward impatiently. The masses behind me pressed against my back. I felt small. Alone. I tried to rehearse my game plan, but my mind was fuzzy, clouded with nerves and the fear of the unknown. My resolve of the days before was gone. Optimism gave way to reality. Familiar panic swept over me, and I wanted to scream, "What the heck am I doing?"

In that moment, I would have given anything to be anywhere but on the start line of another marathon.

As we awaited the starter's signal in charged silence, my heart sank and I felt sick. It wasn't nervousness. It wasn't even the notorious Excitement and Dread that inevitably accompanied every race or workout I'd ever done. It was something different. Something deeper.

Fear.

Time stopped in the two seconds before the pistol shot announcing the start of the Capitol Marathon rang through the air. I knew I was ready to race. I knew I had built the foundation to cover the distance. The Twenty Quarters in the Rain, the Super Secret Workout, the Workout of Death, the Funky Monkey 5K, the Haystacks Half Marathon, and the Bleeding Heart blowup had taught me to trust my training. They had taught me that in order to succeed, I'd first have to fail a few times. They had taught me to run with perseverance and patience, in faith and confidence. They had taught me to stand on the boldness gained by running hard and smart, that how I run the first part of my race will affect the second. They had also taught me that fatigue happens, to accept it and get over it, to move on and keep moving. For in running, as in life, you must be both self-assured and daring, content with where you are yet always striving for something better. You must have a destination in sight but not forget to enjoy the scenery along the way.

All this I had learned, yet the fear remained. I realized that my challenge was not to hit a time goal. It was not to redeem Haystacks and Bleeding Heart. It was not to have the race of my life or discover the fine line separating an aggressive racing approach from self-imposed sabotage. The purpose was not to fight the wall once more or rise again after being knocked down by it. Standing on the start line of the Capitol Marathon, a distinct adversary threatened to rob me of everything I had worked for over the past year.

It was strange to think I had been battling that assailant for years and yet never truly saw it for what it was. Mistaking the symptoms for the cause, I had not been conquering my foe, but merely giving it a slap on the wrist. It wasn't until I toed the start line of the Capitol Marathon—Haystacks, Part III, if you will—that I finally recognized my true opponent in the ring. My what-the-heck-am-I-doing panic was born not of two marathons in as many weeks, but of the overflow of deep-rooted fear. For in that moment, when I had decided to conquer Haystacks and run the Capitol Marathon, I became painfully aware of my weakness and deeply conscious of dissatisfaction with what I had accomplished. I wanted to run better, but I feared blowing up in the attempt. I wanted to run faster, but I feared being unable to hold the pace. I wanted to push myself more, but I knew my own inadequacy and dreaded the overwhelming desire to quit. I was living in the self-inflicted torture of perpetually wanting more yet fearing I would only be capable of less. And I was terrified.

So what?

I was surprised by the question. I glanced around, half expecting to see Mr. Speedy Pants standing there, eyebrows raised, cavalier as always.

So what if you don't hit your time? So what if you fail? Who determines what "failure" is anyway? Who are you trying to impress?

It was my voice. I hadn't recognized it at first because it sounded different. It sounded wiser. More confident. More experienced.

Are you gonna let fear bully you like this? Sheesh. This is a race, for cryin' out loud. A race. As in running. You love to run. Why the heck would you let fear—and fear of what, might I ask?—why the heck would you let fear rob you of your joy?

I had a long way to go, yet in the grand scheme of things, not very far at all. One moment I would face an intimidating distance; the next, I would be looking back at the road behind me. It was a race. As in running. And I loved to run. Fear? Whatever. It would be over before I knew it. Why not run hard and see what happened?

The whole Haystacks–Bleeding Heart Saga had been a watershed in my running career, and the Capitol Marathon was simply an arrow at the turning point. It had nothing to do with a number on a clock. It had everything to do with a year of running, a year of friendships, and a year of adventures. A year that would change me forever.

Marathon training is a microcosm of life. In a very tangible way, it presents us with the challenges and the joys, the monotony and the adventure, the loneliness and the camaraderie, the failure and the triumph, of life. We love the sport. And we hate it. It breaks us down and lifts us up. It prompts us to respond to a never-ending succession of circumstances and trials. It is humanity concentrated into mere hours, simultaneously revealing our character and growing it. In exposing our weaknesses, it increases our strength. We are not the same for having run. We cannot be.

For a split second, the goofy grin that had so often plastered itself across my face reappeared. Who would have guessed? It was just a simple request for some training advice.

And with that, the signal sounded, and we were off.

Epilogue

I had promised to pace her to a Boston qualifying time. I knew she could do it. She had the fitness. She had the ability. The only thing holding her back was her head.

"Listen to me," I said. "You've got this. It's okay if it hurts. Let it hurt. But keep going. Just keep taking steps."

She nodded. Her body was bent forward with fatigue. Small gasps escaped her lips, the muffled cries of endured pain and a tired body. But she kept moving forward.

C'mon, c'mon. Keep going. I know you can do it. Just a bit longer . . .

"You've just gotta grind your teeth and push through this, okay? You've got it. It's all about gutting it out now."

She didn't answer. She didn't have to. Each step forward was declaration enough.

Finally, we saw it, waiting in the distance, glorious, constant, welcoming, steadfast.

"Look!" I yelled. "There's the finish! You made it! You . . ."

Holding hands, arms raised in victory, ecstatic with joy and weak from exhaustion, we crossed the finish line. We embraced as the tears slid down our faces.

"Did I make it?" she gasped, her voice raw with emotion and the exhaustion of having run twenty-six miles. "Did we make it?"

I laughed through my tears. "Yes! You're going to Boston!"

"Oh, my gosh! I don't believe it!"

"Ahhhhhh!" we screamed in unison, hugging once more.

We made our way through the crowd and plopped down on the white concrete sidewalk that traced a shapeless silhouette along the pavement of the finish chute. The sun baked the dried sweat on our faces, leaving a powdery dusting of salt, inside-out shadows along our foreheads and cheekbones. Immediately behind us lay just over twenty-six miles of asphalt and agony. Farther still lay many more miles. Hundreds of miles. Thousands of miles. They stretched beyond the weeks and months and, seemingly, into eternity.

I brushed the remnants of dirt from my shorts and looked across the crowded finish chute, across the hordes of sweaty faces and Mylar blankets and bouncing finishers' medals and plastic water bottles. The uniform bib numbers and plastic timing chips were deceiving. They gave the impression of homogeneity. One race. One course. But I knew better. For there, straggling through the finish chute, some stumbling on the brink of the collapse and others appearing no worse for the wear, were a thousand unknown stories. Individual. Unique. And yet, not unlike my own.

"So, how did it feel to be me?" Mr. Speedy Pants asked later that day, half in jest and half in earnest.

I laughed. Even over the phone I could see his smug little grin.

"Eh, it wasn't so hard," I replied.

"Yeah, yeah. Well, you did good, kid. Good job."

I paused.

"Hey, Coach?"

"What, kid?"

"Thanks."

"For what?"

I had changed over the past year. I was a different runner now. Confident. Capable. Strong. And, yes, even experienced. I smiled in remembering my timidity that cold morning, when I first made my simple request for training advice. It seemed as distant as the first miles themselves. I tried to imagine my life without the experiences of the past months, without the year that almost never happened. I could not. The miles had shaped my character, made me wiser, made me better.

And Mr. Speedy Pants, whether he knew it or not, was part of that change. Every crazy story, every word of encouragement, every nod that said, "Good work, kid. Keep it up." These were the moments that embodied my experience; this was the experience that morphed into wisdom; this was the wisdom that turned a goofy, timid girl into an experienced runner. This was the divine alchemy.

Moments, like miles, last only a second in the grand scheme of life, but they live forever in us. We carry them in our beings, reflect them in our actions, and share them with our words. It is the pollination of character spread from person to person, until what lasted but an instant in reality is perpetuated throughout the whole of mankind.

There are no ordinary moments. Our actions, for better or worse, live forever. That is the nature of eternal creatures. That is the consequence of running with immortals.

I smiled.

"Oh, nothing, Coach. Just thanks."

SOULSCAPES PHOTOGRAPHY

ABOUT THE AUTHOR

Amy L. Marxkors grew up in the rural outskirts of St. Louis, Missouri, a precocious youngster who spent her days climbing trees, building forts in the woods, and reading Nancy Drew books. She dreamed of one day being a cowgirl, a detective, an NFL quarterback, a Harvard professor, and a member of the U.S. Women's Olympic Ice Hockey team. Reality, however, did not always comply with Amy's dreams, probably because some of her aspirations weren't entirely practical. Undeterred and always the optimist, Amy had no doubt she would one day discover a hidden talent that would land her in the Olympics or the encyclopedia.

Melding her passion for sports with her love for literature, Amy began writing for local sports publications. Soon, she was also writing for publications that didn't have anything to do with sports, and her articles were no longer just local. In 2007, Amy began working for Fleet Feet Sports, a specialty running store. It was during her tenure at Fleet Feet that Amy fell headfirst into the world of competitive distance running. She has since logged thousands of miles and committed herself to one day running a sub-three-hour marathon. Amy has also since realized the irony of her teenage vow to never run a road race.

Amy would still like to go to the Olympics. And the encyclopedia wouldn't be so bad either.